This book is due for return on or before the last date shown above,
but it may be renewed by personal application, post or telephone,
quoting this date and the book number.

'Racial Matching' in Fostering

The challenge to social work practice

PENNY J. RHODES
Research Fellow
Social Policy Research Unit
University of York

Avebury

Aldershot · Brookfield USA · Hong Kong · Singapore · Sydney

Published by
Avebury
Ashgate Publishing Limited
Gower House
Croft Road
Aldershot
Hants   GU11 3HR
England

Ashgate Publishing Company
Old Post Road
Brookfield
Vermont 05036
USA

A CIP catalogue record for this book is available from the British Library and the US Library of Congress.

ISBN 1 85628 264 3

Printed and Bound in Great Britain by
Athenaeum Press Ltd., Newcastle upon Tyne.

Contents

List of tables and figures

Tables

Figures

Terminological note

The danger in a study like this, which employs sociologically defined terms which are also used and 'understood' by actors, is that of attempting to squeeze actors' constructs into the researcher's more tightly defined sociological constructs. These may be in common usage but have different meanings from the sociological definitions and different meanings for different people. Often they are used in a vague and ill–defined way but, nevertheless, have sufficient of a common core of meaning for people to 'understand' each other.

The term, *black,* was employed both in the professional journals and by the workers in the Fostering Team. Its usage can be teased out into three components: a political sense implying 'solidarity against racism' (BSA, 1990), as 'a generic term describing those of Afro/Caribbean and Asian descent who were being linked effectively as political subjects' through local government policy (Ben–Tovim *et al.* 1986), and as a synonym for ethnicity (Lawrence, 1982). It was in this latter sense that most of the workers in the Fostering Team seemed to use it. The 'black' foster parents and applicants who were interviewed for the present study, however, were less united about its use. Some objected to the use of a term which denoted skin colour and preferred to refer to themselves in regional or national terms or simply as 'working class'. All those interviewed were of Afro/Caribbean descent. As Naomi Connelly has recently remarked,

Like all other words and phrases we have available, the phrase is one of a number of possible ways of referring to a diverse and complex reality. Like them, it has advantages and limitations, and is accepted by some people and not others... (Connelly, 1989:5).

The term, *racial*, is used in its popular sense which refers to a combination of physical characteristics and cultural origin as in the phrase, 'race relations' or 'same race placement'. It is not used to designate 'races' in the biological sense (c.f. Ely & Denney, 1987).

Culture tended, in Lawrence's words,

(to be) seen as an autonomous realm... The effect of this is to produce a static and idealised vision of... cultures which cannot really take account of class, caste or regional differences and which cannot help us to understand how or why those 'cultures' have changed over time (Lawrence, 1982:113).

When they referred to 'culture', workers in the Team usually meant West Indian culture, which they seemed to conceive as a brittle and fragile anachronism rather than a plastic resource which could be adapted to changing conditions.

Integration refers to 'a process whereby a group with a distinctive culture (including religion) both adapts to and is accepted by a larger group without being forced to change its culture and associated practices in favour of those of the majority' (Cashmore, 1988:146-7). At the time of the field research, the concept of *assimilation*, as a uni-dimensional, one-way process by which outsiders relinquish their own culture in favour of the dominant society (Abercrombie *et al.* 1988:14), was rejected by many minority groups. The word had become unfashionable and had been replaced by the term, *integration*. The change in terminology, however, did not necessarily denote a change in the underlying concept and members of the Fostering Team seemed to use the two interchangeably.

Acknowledgements

I would like to thank all those who took part in the study, with special thanks to the foster parents and applicants and to the social workers in the Fostering Team. I would also like to thank David Divine, Ben Brown, Tony Hall and Vernon Harris for helpful comments and discussions in the early days of the project and the many people who gave me support and encouragement throughout, especially Professor David Smith and Drs. Jane Aldgate, Marta Bonn and Margaret Grieco. I would also like to thank my two examiners, Dr.Margaret Pearson and Dr.John Solomos. Finally, I would like to thank the two interviewers, Pauline Jacobs and Juliet Atkins, the Social Policy Research Unit of the University of York, especially Jenny Bowes and Sally Pulleyn, for help with the layout and typing, and the Economic and Social Research Council for financial support.

1 Introduction: The emergence of a new policy

The concern of this book is the emergence of a new policy, 'racial matching' in foster care, the matching of foster child and family on the basis of culture and 'race'. At the time of the fieldwork, the issue was not only at the forefront of arguments about child care practice within social work but had spilled into the arena of public debate. 'Racial matching' challenges fundamental notions about the nature of society and what it ought to be and about the objectives of social work and how social workers ought to address them.

Although the new ideas about appropriate placement for black children sparked off changes in policy and practice in a number of social service departments, the changes provoked widespread controversy. Social workers were divided: first, between the 'radicals' who espoused the new approach, the 'conservatives' who opposed it, and those who had not yet made up their minds or taken up a position; second, between those who wished to extend the debate on to the political agenda and those who wished to confine it to technical arguments about practice (Smith, 1985b).

The political and ideological arguments overlay what was essentially a 'market' situation. Black children began to be fostered and adopted in significant numbers when the supply of white foster and adoptive candidates exceeded the supply of healthy white babies (Gill and Jackson, 1983). The new policy of 'black homes for black children' drew black people, who had previously been excluded, into the fostering and adoption 'market', thus reducing the supply of children available to prospective white foster and

1

ptive parents and setting up competition with black candidates for a limited supply of children. In the case of fostering, where boarding-out payments are available, such competition can also be interpreted in terms of competition for fostering 'jobs'.

At the time of writing, the supply of children was disproportionately from the black community and the supply of substitute parents disproportionately from the white[1]. The alternatives were for the surplus of black children to remain in residential care until suitable black placements were found or for them to be placed transracially with white families. 'White' hostility to the new policy of 'racial' matching, although expressed in terms of 'the needs of individual children' and ideological resistance to 'racial' separatism, was, thus, reinforced by a potent self-interest.

The issue raises fundamental questions about the nature of personal identity and psychological health (Small, 1984a; Maximé, 1986) and about the role of professionals in prescribing how a child ought or ought not to identify. Previously, when a black child identified more with white people than with black, this was taken as evidence of assimilation and psychological well-being. More recently, it has come to be interpreted as a pathological misidentification (Small, 1984a; Maximé, 1986).

> Bonding without a sense of racial identity is pathological bonding and is against the best interest of the black child. (ABSWAP, 1983b:9)

The main question is, perhaps, not so much the extent to which professional judgement may be overshadowed by political goals as the extent to which the two can or ought to be separated.

This relationship between racial politics and placement practice exposes starkly social workers' role as social engineers. The political problem is outlined by Pryce (1974:384):

> We will have to face the more theoretical issue of reconciling the demands of the minorities for cultural pluralism with the goals of integration. The questions we need to ask are: should black foster parents be allowed to take white children, or should they only be allowed to take children from their own ethnic group? As well as recruiting more black foster parents, should there be a policy of deliberately placing black children in black-settled areas only, for ethnic identification purposes, or should there be a deliberate 'dispersal' strategy with a view to ensuring racial integration?

---

[1] Accurate child care statistics broken down by 'race' and ethnic origin were not available (Rowe, 1990).

2

The move towards 'same race' placement inevitably entailed changes in the ways in which substitute families were recruited. In order to attract applicants from groups previously under–represented in the foster carer pool, social workers were forced to review their ethno–centric notions of family life and the resources necessary to sustain it. Past failure to recruit black foster parents was construed in terms of failure to take into account cultural factors and the solution sought in the provision of a more 'ethnically sensitive service'. Economic considerations were conveniently side–stepped and the politically more contentious issue of 'race' elided with 'culture'.

The recruitment of black carers also undermined conventional ideas about fostering as a charitable vocation. Those local authorities with the largest numbers of black children needing placement tended to be those with the smallest pools of potential foster families with the characteristics of the 'typical foster family' identified by Bebbington and Miles (1990). The traditional and still widespread view is that a genuine motivation to foster is unaffected by payment (*op cit.*). Increasing boarding out payments should, therefore, have little impact on supply (Rowe, 1983; Shaw and Lebens, 1977; Smith, 1988). But, although fostering payments are ostensibly no more than maintenance payments, some of the poorest authorities, reacting to the unfavourable dynamics of supply and demand, are among those paying the highest rates. Applicants are likely to be less well–off than those from more affluent areas and, for many, financial motives may be important. With the change in placement policy, black applicants, more than others, are offering a scarce and valued resource. This, together with the high rate of black women's participation in the formal labour market, may have stimulated recruitment agencies into a review of boarding out payments.

These changes are part of a more general trend towards the 'professionalisation' of foster care. This has potentially revolutionary implications for the nature of fostering and of the fostering task and its designation as essentially 'women's work' – an unskilled and unpaid vocation rather than a skilled and demanding 'professional' role for which people should be trained and financially rewarded as in any other 'job of work'. These are some of the themes which will be explored in the chapters to follow.

The aims of the study

The aims of the research upon which this book is based were to examine the introduction of the new policy of 'racial matching' and to review its implications for the recruitment of black carers. The proceeding chapters describe, first, how the issue arose on the social work agenda and, second, how

3

it was approached within one London borough. Although it draws on general material, its main focus is the case study of a single borough fostering team. The account can be read on a number of levels: as a case study of the introduction of new policy into a climate of ideological contest –although the introduction of new policy is often controversial, rarely has it excited such a heated and emotional response; as an analysis of black foster carer recruitment practice; as a study of social work decision–making; and as a study of 'racial' politics, both on the macro level and the micro, inter–personal level of face-to–face interactions between workers and clients.

It is essentially an historical account describing the process of change in one London borough based on documentary records over a ten year period and fieldwork conducted in 1984 and 1985. The study captures a brief period in a context of continuing change and is, therefore, more of a snapshot than a template for the future. It was not chosen as a typical case and makes no claims to be representative of changes which were occurring in other boroughs. What it does describe is the process of interaction between different participants and the interplay of ideas and practical demands. The study deals with change – how change was negotiated and accomplished, first, between practitioners and, second, at the level of face–to–face interactions with applicants. It is both a descriptive account and an analytical attempt to examine the process from the perspectives of the different interest groups or actors in the light of the various constraints and opportunities of the context, in particular, the structural relations of relative power. By outlining these interconnections and constraints on individual action, it should be possible to draw conclusions which have relevance beyond the single case.

The intention was to shift the focus away from the objects of the placement process (the children) to the subjects (the placement agencies and their workers) and to look at process as opposed to outcome. The starting point is the first stage in the process of placement, the initial recruitment of families. This is a stage neglected in earlier British studies. The concern is with fostering as opposed to adoption placement. First, previous concern with adopted children ignored the fact that many foster placements are long term. Second, the assumption that foster children are less likely to suffer identity confusion is, itself, questionable. Short term placements and frequent moves between placement and between natural family and foster home may result in more acute identity confusion and conflict than for adopted children whose placements are usually more stable. Whereas previous research has been almost exclusively restricted to the evaluation of transracial placements, the present account describes one borough's attempts to achieve 'racially matched' placements. It is descriptive and explanatory rather than evaluative. While not trying to make prescriptions, its aim is to sensitise local authorities to the forms of debate and discussion which are likely to occur inside the

4

organisation and to generate conflict. Finally, there has been little research from the consumer point of view, especially of applicants' opinions and experience of the application and assessment process.

These processes are examined in the following chapters from the development of policy through to its implementation in practice at each stage of the recruitment process. Chapter Two is a discussion of methodological and ethical issues. Chapter Three describes how the new ideas gained prominence in social work thinking. Chapter Four presents a overview of developments London–wide as reported in a postal survey of Principal Fostering Officers. These provide the back drop for the case study of a single London borough which is introduced in Chapter Five. The fifth and sixth chapters examine the evolution of policy within the borough Fostering Team based on interviews with workers (Chapter Five) and an analysis of team meeting minutes (Chapter Six). Chapter Seven describes the recruitment campaign which is the focus of the study. Chapter Eight examines changing ideas about applicants' 'suitability' within a model of cultural diversity and, Chapter Nine, issues relating to professionalism and the acquisition of intercultural skills. Chapter Ten looks at different interpretations of 'public' and 'private' and Chapters Eleven, Twelve and Thirteen describe two innovative approaches to assessment: the introduction of group training and assessment and joint assessment visits with a black foster parent co–worker. The final chapter is an attempt to locate these findings within the broader context of socio–political change.

Social work, ethnicity and 'race': some dominant perspectives

The study's main theme is the negotiation of change between different interest groups within a context of unequal but changing relationships of power. It examines the strategies adopted at different levels, from the Association of Black Social Workers and Allied Professions' (ABSWAP) campaign of 'consciousness raising' in the black population and its confrontational stance with the 'white' social work profession to the strategies of consensus management and conflict avoidance pursued in the Fostering Team which was the focus of the case study.

Throughout, the role of language is central – from the different 'cultural' styles adopted by the protagonists, to the fashions in social work 'professional speak' which allowed workers to employ the terminology of cultural diversity and, so, to give the appearance of change without true ideological or practical commitment. Lack of clarity and ambiguity in their conceptions of 'culture' and 'the cultural' enabled them to communicate at the level of discourse and even to believe in the illusion of change, whilst preserving intact an ideological commitment to the conventional social work values of racial integration and impartiality in service provision. Ambiguity masked a fundamental ambivalence about the nature and direction of change. It enabled the more or less uneasy co-existence of opposing values as workers moved between different frames of reference or perspectives.

Ely and Denney (1987; Denney, 1983) have identified a number of 'dominant perspectives' in social work thinking within which the needs of minority ethnic groups and appropriate social service response have been variously interpreted. Although each follows on from the other in roughly chronological order, they do not constitute clearly defined stages but rather grade into each other and may exist concurrently. They represent more or less coherent, more or less fashionable paradigms upon which workers can draw.

Cultural deficit

Although largely superseded, elements of this approach persist in social work thinking (Atkin and Rollings, 1991) and remain part of the 'commonsense' stock of knowledge of the ideological right (e.g. Honeyford, 1984). According to the deficit perspective, black people's life styles, family patterns and child-rearing practices are deemed inappropriate to life in a modern, advanced, western society. West Indian family patterns, for example, are characterised by over-dominant mothers and weak or absent fathers and child-rearing practices condemned for being old-fashioned and repressive. Socio-economic disadvantage is blamed on black families' inherent inadequacy and inability to adapt. Racism and prejudice are seen as a 'natural' reaction to cultural difference which will decline as black people become assimilated. Responsibility for change is, therefore, that of the minorities, themselves. Social workers' role is to preserve the integrity of British cultural values and to facilitate assimilation.

A seminal work was Katherine FitzHerbert's study of *West Indian Children in London* (FitzHerbert, 1967) in which she tried to counteract the prevailing readiness with which social workers received black children into care by advising them to resist parents' propensity to use the child care services as a substitute for their extended families. FitzHerbert recognised some of the harmful effects of being brought up in care and her work was a timely antidote to the tendency of white social workers to assess black families according to the standards of white, middle class family life. She criticized workers for focusing on the children's immediate parents and for overlooking the potential roles of other relatives. Her concern, however, was not simply with the welfare of black children but with the misuse of services by their families and their failure to conform to British expectations. She advises that

6

it may be in the best interests of the child concerned to force parents to make their own arrangements for child care. If this is authoritarianism, its aim is simply to preserve individual responsibility (FitzHerbert, 1967:110).

Her aim was to promote assimilation through methods of social control. Although influential at the time, her work has subsequently been criticised for over–emphasising cultural arguments and for ignoring other social and economic difficulties which might have put black children at greater risk of reception into care (Stubbs, 1987; Holman, 1968).

Liberal pluralism

The liberal pluralist approach is grounded in Fabian ideas about the reduction of social inequality and recognises multiple levels of deprivation, from the poverty shared with the rest of the working class and associated with living in 'zones of transition', deprived inner city areas whose largely transitory populations were 'on their way to something better', to problems associated with the strains of immigration and adjustment, competition for scarce resources with poor whites and discrimination based on skin colour (Ely and Denney, 1987).

One of its main exponents was Juliet Cheetham (1972). Her work suggests a role for social workers as a bridge between immigrants and natives and, in situations of inter–generational conflict, between parents and children. The aim is to foster intercultural understanding and 'mutual tolerance' and to facilitate adjustment to life in Britain by helping black families to make better use of services. The main focus, however, is still on the problems of contact between the black family and social service agency rather than on agency policies (Ely and Denney, 1987) and the emphasis is on deprivation and intercultural misunderstanding rather than racism or structural analyses of relative inter–group power. White racism is not highlighted as a primary issue. Instead, the emphasis is on the phenomenon of racism and the victims of racism rather than its perpetrators (Ohri *et al.*, 1982; Chakrabarti, 1991). Social workers' own racism and the institutional racism of social services departments is not an issue (Ely and Denney, 1987).

Cultural pluralism

The main concern of the cultural pluralists was to counteract the liberal pluralists' emphasis on 'deprivation' and the deficit view that minority cultures are pathological and maladaptive by pointing up their strengths and ability to act as a buffer against the injustices of a racially inequitable society (Ely and

7

Denney, 1987). 'However derivative, degenerate or problematic such cultural systems may seem to others', wrote Catherine Ballard, 'they are best understood as vigorous, vital and inherently autonomous phenomena' (C.Ballard, 1979). Exponents advocated a shift in location of the 'problem' away from the minority culture to the ethnocentricism and ignorance of other cultures of agency staff and, second, the provision of 'ethnically sensitive services' grounded in a sense of 'cultural relativity' which recognised the strengths and autonomy of other cultures (R.Ballard, 1979:151). As Ely and Denney note, both FitzHerbert and the culturalists agree that the operation of social services across community boundaries embodies a cultural threat but differ as to whether the threat is to the white culture or from it (1987:96).

Pluralist approaches have been criticised for concentrating on cultural differences and ethnicity to the exclusion of other factors such as 'race' and class and for failing to produce an adequate analysis of wider power relations within society (Atkin and Rollings, 1991; Ahmad, 1988). The dangers of the approach have been pointed out by Bandana Ahmad (1988) who argues that the process of educating social workers to appreciate cultural differences may actually reinforce their prejudices and narrow their perspectives with cultural stereotypes (cf. Atkin and Rollings, 1991; Jervis, 1990; Chakrabarti, 1991). According to Atkin and Rollings, cultural packages aimed to inform social workers about the culture of their black clients, by 'providing over–generalised mechanical summaries of key cultural characteristics', present 'a dual danger both of assuming that this knowledge somehow solves the "problem" and of perpetuating and reinforcing cultural stereotypes and myths' (1991:46).

Other observers have noted that, although social workers pay lip service to cultural pluralism, they find it difficult to put into practice (Ely and Denney, 1987). An assimilationist/integrationist perspective still predominates in most social services departments (Chakrabarti, 1991; Roys, 1988). Although the pluralist approach attempts to give equal respect to different cultural practices, it fails to recognise that competing values do not easily co–exist and different cultural groups do not meet on equal terms; nor does it give any guidance as to how potential conflicts may be resolved. As Mona Chakrabarti observes,

> This emphasis on cultural diversity raises the question of what forms of diversity should be tolerated and even encouraged, and those where uniformity should be insisted on (1991:103).

Evers *et al.* (1988) identify three stereotypes or myths which characterise the practice of service providers: the view that black people are to blame for their own needs because of deviant or unsatisfactory life styles; that they are ignorant about what is on offer and require educating; or are not in need of help because of their family and community support networks. Each can be seen as a crude product of one of the three perspectives outlined above.

At the time of the fieldwork for the current study, social workers in many departments were moving away from colour blind or deficit approaches towards a model of cultural diversity. Radical black workers, however, had begun to reject a cultural pluralist approach in favour of what Ely and Denney have termed 'structuralist' and 'black professional' perspectives.

The structuralist position

The structuralist perspective derives from Marxist analysis and focuses on the socio-economic circumstances of working class and minority ethnic groups, racist attitudes and practices within social work agencies and the dominant ideologies of the state (Ely and Denney, 1987). In Dominelli's view,

> It is the lack of resources in education, housing and employment which initially creates the need for social work intervention at the individual level in a majority of social work 'cases' involving ethnic minorities (1979: 29).

Structuralists identify conflicting elements in the social worker's role: on one hand, job loyalty as a state employee, conservation of the *status quo* and reinforcement of dominant societal ideologies; on the other, a 'liberal' helping tradition. Much of what passes for 'social work values' and 'social work knowledge', they argue, are expressions of the ideologies of the white, middle class (Dominelli, 1979,1988).

The structuralist position directs attention away from the individualization of problems towards the structural determinants of the social worker/ client relationship and the institutional attitudes and practices which result. The aim is for a transfer of power and resources to the black communities, the employment of black workers, greater involvement of black community groups in service provision and a review of departmental practices and procedures.

In directing attention away from cultural towards structural and economic considerations, however, the situation of minority ethnic groups risks being regarded as simply an instance of the general working class condition. Black radicals who insist on the primacy of race over culture and class in determining black people's socio-economic position have been criticised for diverting attention from cultural factors (Modood, 1991) and from the broader class struggle.

9

The black professional perspective

The Association of Black Social Workers and Allied Professions (ABSWAP) has taken this analysis a step further and suggested that, rather than simply failing to provide adequate services to black people, social service agencies have actively disserviced them (Divine, 11 Mar.1983, 1984) and have simply operated as an agency of social control in black communities. This is exemplified by the 'unnecessary' removal of black children from their natural families and placement outside the black community (ABSWAP, 1983a)[2].

The 'black professional' perspective advocates the establishment of a power base for black people within social work agencies rather than a radical re-orientation and re-structuring of service provision. ABSWAP promotes a black 'professional' view of the 'best interests' of black children and black families rather than simply advocating the meeting of expressed needs within black communities (Ely and Denney, 1987:92). Although advocating greater consultation with community groups, primary reliance is on the black social worker's 'professional' judgement and sense of responsibility to the black community (Divine, 1 Apr.1983). The adequacy of such 'professional' representation of community interests, however, is not really questioned and the danger that this will simply replicate in the black communities tensions already existing in the white between social service agencies and their client communities is not fully addressed.

The present study was carried out during a period of ideological uncertainty and conflict. In those departments which had begun to embrace notions of differing service needs, the cultural pluralist perspective was the dominant paradigm, at least at the discussion level. In practice, most retained a strong integrationist thrust and ideological commitment to the liberal, colour blind values of impartiality in service provision. At the same time, a powerful critique of the individualised, problem–oriented casework approach was beginning to draw attention to the underlying socio–economic and political causes of social problems and to shift the locus of the problem from individual or family pathology to the wider socio–economic structure. A third strand was the emergence of a radical black critique which asserted the primacy of institutional racism within national and local authority structures. It was on this platform that the ABSWAP was founded. 'Culture', 'class' and 'race' became the crude, artificially competing symbols of an intense ideological debate.

---

[2] ABSWAP (1983) submitted evidence to the Social Services Committee (HCP 360–1 1984), which, however, did not print this evidence in its minutes, nor ask ABSWAP to give oral evidence. ABSWAP had conducted a survey of the views of black community groups and found that, in the latter's view, social services were 'enforcement agencies', which wittingly and unwittingly broke up black families and aimed to take black children away from home (Ely and Denney, 1987).

These issues were, perhaps, nowhere so heatedly contested as in the debate about 'same race' placement for black children in care. 'Racial matching' challenged the liberal notions of assimilation to which many social workers and families who had fostered or adopted transracially were so committed. Second, it challenged implicit assumptions of white cultural supremacy. The need to recruit black substitute families put to the test social workers' theoretical commitment to cultural pluralism and forced them to question the white, middle class mores and standards of bourgeois affluence which underpinned their notions of 'family life'. Third, it forced them to confront racism as a pervasive social force rather than the aberrant behaviour of a pathological few.

A critique of previous research

The debate about transracial placement has generated a number of studies which have attempted to measure placement 'success'. The most notable British examples have been the series of studies of 'coloured' children who were adopted into white families in the late sixties (Raynor, 1970; Tizard, 1977; Gill and Jackson, 1983). Although the authors concluded that the placements had been 'successful' according to the terms of the research, they were forced to add a note of caution and to warn that the situation may change in the future. The usual reason, given by both researchers and critics, was that the children were not old enough for the tests to have been conclusive. The studies assumed that the children would grow up in a stable social and political climate in which racialisation and ethnicity would become increasingly unimportant, assumptions which subsequent developments have thrown into doubt. Only recently have the methods and results been questioned and serious doubts about the wisdom of transracial placements been expressed.

The use of conventional measures of adoption 'success' has been criticised for bias towards the white, middle class perspective of the researchers and funding bodies (Divine, 4 Mar.1983). None of the studies incorporated adequate control groups of black children brought up in black families into their research designs[3], although the latest study (Gill and Jackson, 1983[4]) did

---

[3] Chimezie (2 Feb.1977) gives an outline of what he considers to be an adequate research design incorporating four subject groups:
1. black children living with white parents in a white community,
2. black children with white parents in a black/mixed community,
3. black children with black parents in a black/mixed community,
4. black children with black parents in a white community,

(continued...)

11

include a comparison group of eight black families who had adopted black children. Tizard and Phoenix (1989) have argued that, although comparable studies of children from the same backgrounds living with their families of origin have not been carried out with adolescents, where they have been completed with young children, there are many points of similarity with the findings about transracially adopted children. The danger of generalising from the small numbers involved, however, has been a general criticism of the British studies[5].

A recurring criticism has been the failure to include 'ethnic identification' as a critical measure of successful placement (Chimezie, 1977; Divine, 18 Mar.1983). Measures of 'ethnic identification', however, may be interpreted differently depending on whether 'success' is defined from an assimilationist or pluralist perspective. The criticism is, therefore, inspired as much by political considerations as by issues of child care. Some of the problems of interpreting studies of ethnic and 'racial' identification are discussed by Tizard and Phoenix (1989), Brummer (1988) and Foster Carter (1986).

The latest study (Gill and Jackson, 1983), like its predecessors, found that the children showed 'little evidence of a positive sense of racial identity' and, 'although not denying their racial background,... perceived themselves to be 'white' in all but skin colour' (p81). These findings were not considered to be a serious cause for concern. Divine has blamed 'the low priority given to the significance of ethnic identification' on 'the lack of involvement of any conscious black workers' and, thus, highlights a common problem in all the studies. 'White "experts" on blacks carry out the research on the grounds that, since the youngsters are white in all but skin colour, (they) will relate to them better' (Divine, 18 Mar.1983). None of the studies found evidence of identity

---

[3](...continued)
and both black and white researchers from opposing sides in the transracial adoption debate. In order to evaluate the children's social skills and ability to cope with discrimination and prejudice when they leave their adoptive homes, a further dimension needs to be added to Chimezie's design which would involve following these groups of children into later life and drawing further comparisons between those who chose to live in predominantly black areas and those who chose to live in predominantly white areas.

[4] *Adoption and Race* (1983) is a third follow-up study of the British Adoption Project (BAP) which was initiated in the mid-sixties to answer the question, `Can families be found for coloured children?'

[5] '(g)iven that upwards of 40 per cent of children in care in inner city areas are estimated to be black, it is fair to assume that a significant number of adoptions each year involve black children. However, in spite of this almost total lack of existing information, and concentration on so few children, the researchers at no point urge their readers to be wary of generalizing from the findings' (Divine, 4 March 1983).

confusion or conflict serious enough to give the authors cause for present or future concern.

A more recent study, conducted by a black researcher, however, has reported some disturbing findings (Maximé, 1986, 1987c) which seem to vindicate Divine's contention that '(b)lack workers would have radically altered the criteria for assessing 'success' of the placements' (Divine, 4 Mar.1983). At a conference organised by the National Association for Young People in Care many participants also spoke of problems of identity confusion (Black and in Care, 1986; Divine, 19 Sept.1983). For others, such confusion may not be encountered until later in life[6]. Other commentators, however, have criticised the concept of a 'positive black identity' for an over–simplistic association between racial identity and self–esteem and suggest that social identities are often more complex than the pigeonholes to which they are ascribed (Tizard and Pheonix, 1989; cf. Gilroy, 1987a).

Criticisms against transracial placements can be divided into those based on the anticipated experiences of the black child in the white family and those based on discrimination against the black community (Gill and Jackson, 1983). The research studies have concentrated almost exclusively on the former. Even in the, 1983 study, discussion of discrimination against the black community is left to the last chapter where it is dealt with 'almost as an afterthought' (Divine, 18 Mar.1983). Placement policy has been examined

---

[6] This is revealed in the testimonies of three black people interviewed by Jeremy Laurance (1983a): Mary, married to a white husband and living in a `white' area, says, `Black friends say I'm too white', whereas Susie, whose husband is black and living in a black area, says `Before all my friends were white. Now, since Frankie (her husband), they are all black. I don't know why but I'm beginning to feel black.' A third respondent, Martin, was brought up in Sidcup and then moved to London. `In Sidcup there were a few black guys. We used to mix with whites. Colour wasn't highlighted. In New Cross the atmosphere really changed. Whites still mixed with blacks – but they were trying to be black.' A second factor was `the trouble I get from the police. It made me think about my colour'. Although Martin, himself, claims to have `no identity problem', his brother, he says, had a much harder time. `He tried to force himself into being black. It wasn't coming natural. He's always trying to carry a swing – he's got a stereotyped image – that blacks have so many women, treat them like this, never do the washing up, smoke a lot of ganja.' For all three, colour became more significant as they moved away from the communities where they were brought up. In this context, the fact that Gill and Jackson found little indication of the 'failure of intimacy', 'diffusion of time perspective', 'diffusion of industry' and 'negative identity' which has been associated with 'identity diffusion' (Erikson, 1968: 168–9, quoted in Gill and Jackson, 1983: 90), may not be as reassuring as they claim.

independently of the political context and reduced to the experiences of individual children[7].

As a consequence of the studies' almost exclusive concern with the experiences of the black child in a white family, the adoptive families have been treated as islands or fortresses existing in isolation from the society of which they form a part and able to protect their adopted offspring from the harsh realities of the world outside. But, as John Small points out, the children 'cannot always live in the protective arms of the family' (1986a:82). There has been little examination from a structural perspective or analysis of the families' life–styles, attitudes and behaviours as they are influenced by the historical and contemporary social context. The significance of the disparity in social origin between the children and their adoptive families – black and working class compared with white and middle class – has been ignored except for the occasional reference to the children's upward mobility.

The parents in the British Adoption Project adopted their children at a time when 'racial' differences were deliberately played down. They believed (and, as Gill and Jackson's study reveals, still believed in 1983) that their actions were helping to promote a 'racially' harmonious society (cf. Harmony, 1983 No.41). Their conception was of a one–way process whereby black people are absorbed into white society. Despite their denial of any political motivation, both placement agencies and adopters were consciously engaged in an exercise in social engineering. The following comments from transracial adopters were typical:

> the sooner we can get everyone to see that physical differences in themselves do not matter a tinker's cuss, and ought to carry no social meanings at all, the better (Letter to *The Guardian*, 1 Feb.1983).

> ... a multiracial family is the first step towards a multiracial society. (Letter to *The Guardian*, 31 Jan.1983)

In light of the changing course of 'racial' politics, these children have been 'lost to the black community' (Divine, 11 and 18 Mar.1983; Reid, 1983a). They do not identify with black people or accept themselves as black, deny their 'racial' and cultural background and may even hold negative stereotypes and internalise hostile reactions towards other black people (Gill and Jackson,

---

[7] Divine criticises Gill and Jackson for trying to dodge the issue by attempting 'to divide the arguments against transracial adoption into two `separate' camps' and dealing 'exclusively with the administratively more convenient `anticipated experiences of a black child in a white family', as if it could be examined in a vacuum' (Divine, 18 March 1983).

1983; John Small, speaking to a meeting of ABSWAP in Brixton, quoted in Laurance, 1983a).

The liberal conception of 'racial' assimilation is at odds with the 'Black' ideology espoused by many members of the black population (Banton, 1987; Cabral, 1973; Gilroy, 1987a; Ahmed, 1988). 'To be Black or black?' asks a correspondent to the *Caribbean Times* (13 May 1983). The width of the political gulf is revealed in a comment from a white adoptive mother of a black daughter:

> They say black children of white parents have no clear racial self-image. Oh dear. Because *we* are saying: 'Great. It's the best thing for a multi-racial society' (quoted in Laurance, 1983a:499)

In other words, 'success' is defined from diametrically opposed standpoints. It is this political dimension which is ignored in the studies of placement 'success'.

By the early 1980s, the term, 'black', had become, for many black people, a political statement about where one stands in society and with whom one identifies. 'How do we develop a sense of worth centred around our blackness in Britain today?' asks David Divine.

> Perhaps, the first step is to be aware that one is black ... We have been 'made by devious devices to view ethnic identification as a self-defeating stance, prohibiting our acceptance into the mainstream. Black people are now developing an honest perception of this society – the myths of our assimilation and our inferiority stand bare under glaring light. We now proclaim our truth... and value ourselves without apology or compromise' (Divine, 18 February 1983).

Here, Divine is quoting directly from a National Association of Black Social Workers' statement made some ten years ago in the USA. 'Black people', wrote a correspondent to the *Caribbean Times*,

> need a unifying course ... to bring us all together ... There is a need for the generation of an ideology that will unite us, where success or failure for the individual becomes success or failure for the group (*Caribbean Times*, 99:14).

A 'black identity' was, thus, not simply an ascribed label or defensive reaction to racism but the positive, self-conscious construction of group esteem and a prescriptive strategy for the achievement of political power which transcends ethnic divisions. The opening speaker at the inaugural conference of the ABSWAP (London, November 1983) received a standing ovation lasting several minutes when he spoke on this theme.

The elevation of 'race' above culture or class as the prime determinant of a person's position in society and the promotion of 'race consciousness' as the most effective strategy for achieving power (cf. Vernon Harris' speech at ABSWAP Conference November 1983) sparked off one of the most heated debates of the contemporary political scene. It was a reaction against both traditional class politics and a naïve culturalism which equated culture with traditionalism. To the left, it was a form of 'false consciousness' which fragmented the working class and diverted energy away from the class struggle. To the right, the assertion of a distinctive 'racial' identity threatened the notion of nationhood based on cultural unity (Gilroy, 1987a).

These sentiments found expression in the transracial placement debate. Opposition to the political ideology which underpinned the campaign for 'racial matching' was inspired from both the left and the right but was expressed as a neutral technical debate about individual child psychology which revolved around questions of 'identity confusion' and 'coping strategies'.

On one hand, were those who believed that 'race' should be the single most important factor in any placement. In an article for *New Society*, Jeremy Laurance (1983b) describes the case of two half–Asian children who were taken into care when their white single mother was killed in a car accident. A black adoption officer recommended that, since Asian and mixed–race families are hard to find, the children should be placed with a West Indian family because 'the most important thing is to establish their racial identity'. According to a social worker who was present, 'The whole discussion focused on the racial issue (and) no other aspect of the suitability of the match was raised' (Laurance, 1983a:499).

Confusion over issues of 'racial' and 'cultural' identity, however, is revealed in a discussion of a similar case at a meeting held at London University in January 1983 attended by the author. A white social worker described her team's attempts to achieve '*cultural* matching' for 'a half–Malaysian, half–Pakistani baby'. After much effort, they managed to find a middle class Filipino couple living in a white rural area in the north of the country. Although speaking in terms of 'culture', these white social workers were clearly seeking a *physical* resemblance of the adoptive parents to the child. Colour, 'race' or racism, however, was not once mentioned in the discussion. Many of those present reacted against the political ideology which underpinned the notion of 'black identity' as a specifically 'racial' issue and seemed to find it more comfortable to talk about 'preserving the child's cultural heritage'. But, despite their reluctance to employ the language of 'race', workers continued to *think* in racial terms as the example cited above reveals.

16

The intimate and dynamic relationship between 'colour' and 'culture' emerges from Laurance's interviews with young adults who were transracially adopted as children. 'If Susie has not experienced an identity crisis she is experiencing a culture shock', he writes. 'When I first met Sue,' says her husband, 'it was a new thing to her – what I was doing, the way I enjoyed myself...' Another respondent, described his brother's inability 'to force himself into being black. It wasn't coming natural'. Both he and Susie when she says, 'I don't know why but I am beginning to *feel* black,' are referring to a style of living and outlook on life which transcends the ascriptive label.

To Kay FitzHerbert, a white researcher on child care and adoptive mother of a child of West Indian descent, the claim that black children need a black background to establish their sense of identity is 'a load of dogma'. 'Colour', she agues, 'is *one* element of your self–image... The opposers of transracial adoption elevate it out of all proportion'. According to FitzHerbert, 'lots of blacks want the same sort of life as the middle class – but they are just poor' (quoted in Laurance, 1983b:499–500). These are sentiments which Gill and Jackson also seem to hold. Economic advantage related to class is deemed more important than culture and colour (Divine, 18 March 1983), a view shared by many of the adoptive parents in the study who believed that the middle class advantages, both material and educational, which they were able to confer on their children would enable them to overcome any future difficulties they might experience on account of their colour.

For ABSWAP, the one–way traffic of black children into white families confirms the power of white people over black and has become 'a symbol of institutionalized racism' (Laurance, 1983a). It underlines the established social order: advantage is defined as being brought up in a white family (Divine, 18 and 25 Mar.1983). The assimilationist ideology which informed both placement workers and adopters and foster parents encapsulates a belief in the superiority of the 'white' way of life or, at least, a belief that a minority culture cannot subsist realistically alongside that of the majority and will eventually be subsumed by it.

Grow and Shapiro, writing about their American research (1974,1975a,b), found that 'a major difficulty' in answering their critics was

> the sense that answering them may be an exercise in futility. Those who have come to the conclusion that transracial adoption is wrong usually hold (such) strong convictions (that) one is hard put to imagine any feasible research project that would change this position (Grow and Shapiro, 1977:91).

This is because transracial adoption and fostering, whether seen in terms of the 'giving' of a black child to a white couple or in terms of a white couple 'giving' a home to a black child, is repugnant to many black people because it is reminiscent of colonial relationships (ABSWAP, 1983a). The issue is not simply a matter of objective measurement of placement 'success' but of politics and ideology.

In trying to separate 'issues affecting the black child in a white family' from 'issues affecting the black community', Gill and Jackson find themselves arguing that black families should be found for black children 'wherever possible', not because black children 'need' them[8], but because the black community needs to be given additional opportunities to preserve its 'dignity' and promote its 'self-determination'. To Divine (4 March 1983), the reasoning is 'defective, hypocritical and ultimately patronizing'.

> Having relegated ethnic identification to an irrelevance which is the effect of not including it as one of the 'crucial' ingredients to be noted in a 'successful' placement of a black child, one cannot turn around and argue, as an afterthought almost, about the 'dignity' and 'self-determination' of the black community and expect child care agencies and our communities to take it seriously.

Critics of matching policy, however, have refused to engage in political debate and have concentrated on the psychological arguments against mixed placements (e.g.Dale, 1987).

The debate has been criticised for being less about the needs of black children than about black politics (Brown and Reeves, quoted in Hodgkinson, 1985; Dale, 1987; FitzHerbert, 1984). Children and their substitute parents, it has been argued, are merely the pawns in a game of 'racial' politics (Ladner, 1977; Hadfield, 1989a)[9]. But, if 'racial' politics is a game, it is a game played by both sides. The practice of transracial placement is no less 'political'. Each placement is itself a political and ideological act, a manifestation of the assumptions of those involved about society and how it will or ought to develop (Silverman and Fiegelman, 1977).

---

[8] As Divine points out, using the measures of adoption success employed in the study, the children do not need them (4 March 1983: 4).

[9] These ideas have recently resurfaced in the controversy over the separate refusals of two London boroughs to allow the adoption of a black child by her white foster parent (eg Hadfield, 1989b; Fletcher, 1989; Mills, 1989; Birrell, 1990; Fenton, 1989; Ferriman, 1989).

A policy of 'black homes for black children'

Placement practice is intimately bound up with the changing politics of 'race relations'. Gill and Jackson add a note of caution to the analysis of their results. 'It must be remembered', they point out, 'that these parents adopted their children at a time when *not* highlighting their child's racial background was regarded as the appropriate approach' (1983:70). Today, adoption and fostering policies have radically changed in many areas and the 'melting pot' ideology to which Gill and Jackson refer appears to have been widely abandoned (Johnson, 1991; Radio Four, 1991). 'The position in this country', they wrote in 1983, 'now appears to be similar in many ways to that in the USA a decade ago (and) strong claims are being made that, wherever possible, black and mixed-race children should be placed with parents of their own racial background' (Gill and Jackson, 1983:3).

The resemblance to the United States is not coincidental, nor does it necessarily mark a parallel development either of racial politics or of child care policies: they were consciously imported. British discussions of the subject quote freely from the American literature; black Britons travelled to the United States with the specific aim of finding out what their 'black brothers and sisters' were doing; British representatives were sent to conferences organized by black organisations in the United States and representatives from these organisations were invited to speak at British gatherings[10]. When the Association of Black Social Workers and Allied Professions (ABSWAP) was launched in Britain in the spring of 1983, one of the founding members (David Divine) attended the fifteenth Annual Convention of the American National Association of Black Social Workers (NABSW). He reported back in a series of articles published in the *Caribbean Times*, one of which was entitled 'Forging links with black American Social Workers' (6 June 1984). 'Black Britain', he wrote, 'needs to learn from Black America and further develop studies of our social reality from a black perspective' (Divine, 1 July 1983).

---

[10] e.g. Leora Haskett Neal, Director of the New York Chapter Association of Black Social Workers Child Adoption and Referral Service, described in *The Caribbean Times* (2 August 1983) as `a pioneering black self-help child care agency' and Dr. Na'im Akbar from Florida State University `an internationally celebrated lecturer, author, scholar, theoretician and Islamic Minister ... (and) ... an acknowledged authority in the field of "Black Psychology"' were among the principal speakers at the first national conference of the Association of Black Social Workers and Allied Professions (ABSWAP) (`Black Children in Care' The First National Conference ABSWAP Friends Meeting House, Euston Road, London (15 November 1983).

According to Simon and Alstein (1977), the practice of transracial placement in the United States

> began in the late 1940s... gained momentum in the mid 1950s... diminished during the early 1960s, rose again in the mid 1960s, and waned in the early 1970s.

Its significance for 'race relations' politics is clear. 'Most of the social forces that define white – non–white relationships' they write,

> are evident in the development of transracial adoption, from white paternalism, through the civil rights movement, and culminating in a militant awareness of non–white racial minorities of their social, economic and political influence.

By 1975, the numbers of transracially adopted American and Indian children by white parents was 'so small as to be insignificant'.

The reasons most usually cited for this sharp decline were twofold: first, the policy of transracial placement was consistently attacked from numerous quarters but primarily from black welfare groups; second, and largely in response to this, was the realisation that it was possible to recruit foster and adoptive parents for black children from within the black population. 'Vehement opposition' to the practice of transracial placement was expressed at the 1972 conference of the NABSW which condemned it, in highly emotive language, as a form of 'genocide' in which the black community's most precious resource – its children – was being taken from it to satisfy the needs of childless white couples. These sentiments were being echoed in Britain in the early eighties. Writing in the *Caribbean Times* about Gill and Jackson's study, David Divine claimed that

> The children in this study have been lost to our communities... No community can afford hundreds of such casualties each year. No community can be so profligate with its most precious resource – its children (Divine, 18 March 1983).

Similarly, the ABSWAP condemned

> local authority (and voluntary agencies) provision for black children in care... as posing one of the most serious threats to the survival of the black community (*Caribbean Times*, 2 August 1983).

Its report to the House of Commons Social Services Select Committee investigation into *Children in Care* (1983) referred to transracial placement as a form of 'internal colonialism' and 'a new form of slave trade, (although) this time only black children are used'.

The initiative of the American black groups was taken up by social scientists. The ability of white foster and adoptive parents to fully understand the experience of being black in a white society and to enable the child to develop a sense of black identity was questioned (e.g. Samuels, 1979; Chestang, 1972; Chimezie, 1976,1977). 'Can white families assure black children an environment in which there is optimal opportunity for growth, development and identification? (Chestang, 1972) was the question on many people's lips. By, 1973, the Child Welfare League of America had changed its policy on transracial placement to include in its guidelines the statement that

> it is preferable to place children in families of their own racial background because children placed in adoptive families with similar racial characteristics can become more integrated into the average family group and community (cited in Gill and Jackson, 1983:2)

According to Billingsley and Giovannoni (1972), same race placements had at one time been the norm in the USA because white couples refused to take black children. As the supply of white babies declined, transracial placements became fashionable. With the rise of the Civil Rights and Black Power movements in the seventies, the political climate changed and placement agencies reverted to their previous practice of matching child and family by 'race' and ethnicity. In Britain, by contrast, there was no formal tradition of same race placement for black children who remained overwhelmingly in residential care (Rowe and Lambert, 1973; Johnson, 1991).

Placement practice in Britain

It is difficult to gauge the extent of transracial placements in Britain, although Gill and Jackson suggest that they become numerically significant later than in the United States (1983:2). The number of transracial placements increased from the mid–sixties and further during the early seventies as the number of healthy white babies available for adoption declined. The primary objective of placement agencies, according to Gill and Jackson, was to provide childless white couples with babies and the needs of the children, themselves, were regarded as secondary. This may have been true in a general sense but it was clearly not true of the British Adoption Project (BAP) (Raynor, 1970) whose main objective was to find homes for black children who would otherwise

21

have spent the rest of their childhoods in care. In the early seventies, 'coloured' children were still considered 'hard to place' and fell into the category of 'children who wait' for substitute families (Rowe and Lambert, 1973).

Formal adoption and, to a lesser extent, fostering have long been a middle class preserve (Holman, 1978) involving what some have regarded as a one-way traffic of working class children into middle-class homes. When the BAP project was instigated, the channels for recruiting working-class parents did not exist and those involved looked to the middle classes for a pool of potential adopters. Gill and Jackson note that, compared with the United States, Britain had a proportionately smaller black population and did not have an established black middle class (1983:3). Black families, who were, on the whole, working-class, were not considered (personal communication from a worker involved in the BAP). The guidelines for adoption were biased towards white, middle class nuclear families (Ahmed, 1980) within an ideological framework shaped by assimilationist aspirations and notions of 'rescue'. It is significant that groups specifically set up to promote racial integration were established at this time (e.g. Harmony). It was assumed that time was all that was needed for black or 'coloured' people to become fully assimilated into British society and adapted to the 'British way of life'.

To those involved in the BAP, the needs of the children were a paramount consideration but their needs as *black* children were neither recognized nor accepted. Those who took part describe their feelings of elation when the first black children were placed together with their blissful ignorance of later developments which many now accept to have been dangerously naïve. The emergence of a conscious movement amongst the black population to 'forge and proclaim a political unity' as 'Black' people (Ahmed, 1988:9), the emergence of colour and ethnicity as platforms from which to agitate for political power, the links with Black movements in the USA and, above all, the persistence of racism – none of this was foreseen by the BAP workers, heady with the naïve and optimistic liberalism of the sixties.

As the birth rate fell and the supply of healthy white babies declined, black and mixed-parentage children were increasingly placed for fostering and adoption, although there was virtually no corresponding effort to recruit substitute parents from the black population. Black families were considered 'unsuitable' as substitute carers and the black population in general apathetic and lacking in interest. Informal care arrangements, however, have always operated independently of formal agency services within black communities both in the Caribbean (BASW, 1982) and in Britain (Ahmed, 1980).

By the early eighties, however, the situation in the UK had come to resemble that existing in the USA a decade earlier. Same race placement was widely advocated among black social workers (Fitzgerald, 1981; James, 1981;

22

Lambeth Social Services Good Practice Guide, 1981; ABSWAB, 1983a,b), although consensus within the profession as a whole was by no means universal (FitzHerbert, 1984; Dale, 1987; Kerridge, 1985). Despite obvious confusion and conflict, the slogan, 'black families for black children' gained increasing acceptance during the 1980s.

Policy and practice or even beliefs and practice, however, do not always mesh, as Jenkins and Morrison's study of service delivery in a sample of U.S. child care agencies illustrates[11]. According to Gill and Jackson, the majority of workers in their British sample 'appeared to accept the desirability of finding black homes for black children' (1983:3) but the extent to which these views have become fully accepted and reflected in practice remains an open question (Kaniuk, 1991). Gill and Jackson contacted thirty adoption workers involved in the placement of black children in seventeen agencies and found that 'although some successes (were) being achieved in finding black homes for black children, the most likely placement... (was) still with white families' (p.3). Even in Lambeth, where the commitment to same race placements was, perhaps, strongest, transracial placements were common (Bhatia, 1983). Most of the workers contacted reported difficulty in finding 'suitable' black families for their waiting children. Three questions immediately spring to mind: How appropriate were respondents' definitions of a 'suitable' family? What was the extent of their individual or their agencies' efforts to recruit black families? How appropriate were these efforts?

Apathy or an unstated commitment to transracial placement as a means of promoting 'racial' assimilation may lead workers to hide behind an apparent shortage of 'suitable' black homes. Unless an agency commits itself to a specific policy of recruiting black families and is prepared to provide the necessary resources, the pressures of the casework load may prohibit individual initiative.

---

[11] The commitment to delivering services which take account of the cultural and special needs of minority groups in ethnic agencies and in a national sample of child welfare organizations was gauged by examining views about the content and delivery of services along three dimensions – `mixing or matching', `cultural content' and `power and decision–making' in terms of three ideological positions – `equality', `cultural pluralism' and `ethnic identity'. The results indicated that, ideologically, field workers took a rather conservative position between `equal rights' and `cultural pluralism'. A selection of responses about service delivery also `illustrate a moderate and mixed response not usually reflected in American literature on the welfare of children' (Jenkins and Morrison, 1977, cited in Cheetham, 1981b: 60).

Individual effort is also hindered by the concept of 'permanence'[12], whereby the child is 'freed' for adoption and placed as rapidly as possible in order to prevent drift in care and to achieve stability. 'Permanence' in placement practice also has significant implications for the rights of the child's natural parents which are usually severed on placement. Gill and Jackson found that, although same race placement might be considered the first choice for a particular child, workers reported that 'delay in finding a suitable placement was often a key factor in the decision to place with a white family' (1983:3). Financial limitations on the ability to launch campaigns to recruit black families were also cited among the reasons for continuing to make transracial placements. Some respondents considered such ventures unjustified in view of the fact that there were numerous white couples waiting to adopt or foster similar children.

The relationship between social workers and prospective adopters and foster parents is different from that between social workers and their other clients, not least because they are from a different class (Rees, 1978). They provide the child care service with an essential resource, since most social workers believe that family life is preferable to a childhood spent in residential care (Stubbs, 1987). As the pool of applicants began to outstrip the supply of healthy white babies, the balance of power between agency staff and prospective carers tipped in favour of the former. The model of the 'suitable' family came to be more and more narrowly defined, effectively excluding many potential black applicants. The new policy of 'black families for black children' and relative shortage of black carers have helped to redress the balance and sets black applicants apart from the childless white couples who queue to adopt a dwindling supply of healthy white babies. This is a significant departure from the usual black client – white social worker relationship (Dominelli, 1988). The admission of black people into the formerly white, middle class preserve of formal adoptions and, to a lesser extent, fostering must have significance for the position of black people in British society in general.

This situation, however, is not without its dangers. People may apply to adopt or foster for a variety of reasons (Small, 1986a,b) not all of which may be in 'the best interests of the child'. In a situation of shortage, there is the danger that less stringent assessments will be made of black applicants than of white and, as a result, some black children may be placed in less than satisfactory homes. This is especially likely where white workers are unfamiliar with the cultural contexts of applicants' lives.

---

[12] For a discussion of the permanency principle in child care, see Hart, 1986; Hillman, 1986; Jordan, 1985; Morris, 1984; Parton, 1986; Stubbs, 1987; Thoburn et al., 1987; Vernon, 1985.

Rachel Jenkins (1963), reporting in the 1960s when there was a shortage of people who were willing to adopt or foster 'coloured' children and those who came forward were nearly all white, found differences in child care officers' assessments of families who had fostered 'coloured' children compared with those who had fostered white. The CCOs tended to rate the same home more highly for a 'coloured' child than for a white child. Jenkins explained these findings in terms of a pre-disposition to looking favourably on offers of a home for hard-to-place children and noted that, although nearly all the applicants in the study were asked whether they would take 'coloured' children, most refused. She also found significant differences in the motivations of the couples who applied to foster 'coloured' children compared with those of the other applicants.

Within the black communities, attempts to recruit black carers have met with an initially guarded response. The relationship between state social work and its client communities is built on a history of class antagonism and tensions between its 'caring' and 'controlling' functions (Jones, 1983; Corrigan and Leonard, 1981). In its relationship with black communities, these are interwoven with 'racial' inequalities which cannot be reduced to a simple matter of cultural difference. Through placement practice, the concerns of the child care services and of 'race relations' politics have coincided and been mutually reinforcing.

The tension between social work's 'care' and 'control' functions is, arguably, nowhere so acute as in the provision of child care services. In the name of child protection, poor, working class children are removed from their natural families and placed in middle class homes where, it is assumed, they will lead a better life. Through social work, state intervention in family life has been legitimised on the grounds of 'family pathology', a 'culture of poverty' or 'cycle of deprivation'. 'Child protection' becomes the 'policing' of families and removal of children and the containment of 'difficult' and disruptive children.

The conceptual apparatus constructed around the issue of 'problem families' in poor, working class communities was, thus, already in place for an interpretation of black family patterns and life styles in terms of family pathology and cultural inadequacy. Black children, adrift 'between two cultures', were considered to pose a threat to the social order and their families neither capable of bringing up their own children properly nor of providing substitute care for others. Black cultures became marginalised and equated with social pathology, a handicap to their members and a threat to the general social unity. An assimilationist rationale guided social work intervention and resulted in a disproportionate flow of black, working class children, first, into white institutions and, second, into white, middle class families. The placement of black children in white families was regarded as an act of 'rescue' from the poverty and culturally inadequate environment of their natural families and a first step on the road to cultural assimilation. That the black community, itself, could provide a resource for these children in terms of substitute family care was considered neither feasible nor desirable.

It is, thus, a short step to analysis of the interventions of the child care services as the punitive and repressive actions of a white agency of social control in black communities and hardly surprising that the ambivalence with which the social services are regarded in white, working class communities turned to fear and hostility in many black communities. Only recently has location of 'the problem' of black family recruitment shifted from the black population to placement agencies, with their white, middle class bias (Adams, 1981; Ouseley et al., 1982; Ahmed, 1980; ABSWAP, 1983a) and intimidating barrage of interviews and form-filling (Ahmed, 1980; Arnold, 1982; Cheetham, 1981b). The new promotion of an 'ethnic sensitive service', however, has met with a guarded response. A history of experience of the Social Services as an essentially punitive organisation cannot be wiped clean overnight and many black people were inevitably sceptical of the sincerity of the commitment to change.

The 'success' of the campaign for 'racial matching' in child placement can largely be attributed to two critical developments. First, the new ideas were given an initial boost with the setting up of the New Black Families Unit in Lambeth. Although it had a difficult start[13], its success in recruiting black families provided an example which stimulated others into action. Second, the founding of the Association of Black Social Workers and Allied Professions and the adoption of 'Black Children in Care' as the theme for its inaugural conference not only gave the campaign additional momentum but provided it with an organisational base. Both developments were initiated by black social workers which gave their approach a credibility and legitimacy which white workers could not have commanded.

ABSWAP's conference manifesto set the agenda for subsequent debate. Three main changes were proposed: the provision of 'an ethnic sensitive service', the employment of more black social workers and consultation with black communities. These themes represent strands which run through the subsequent analysis and will be returned to in more detail in the final chapter.

---

[13] In the first year, no black children were referred to the Unit from Lambeth social services (personal communication).

2 Power and perspective: Key methodological issues

The main concerns of this chapter are with the case study approach and with strategies of data collection. These included a postal survey, document analysis, participant observation, qualitative interviews and elements of the action research approach. Chapters Three and Four, however, are concerned with the emergence of new policy and developments which were occurring London-wide in order to locate the case study within the general context of change. Particular attention is drawn to the ethics of research, especially questions of ideology and power.

The case study approach

This was chosen as the most appropriate strategy for the detailed examination of the way in which a general change of policy, which was beginning to occur nationwide, was accomplished and translated into practice in a single borough. Whereas statistical surveys provide snap-shot pictures of a particular point or points in time, case studies can reveal changes in process, the interaction of groups and individuals and their responses to events over a period of time (Nixon, 1983). Stoecker defines case studies as 'those research projects which attempt to explain wholistically the dynamics of a certain historical period of a particular social unit' (1991:98), a definition which, he claims, integrates a multi-methodological approach (Yin, 1984; Runyan, 1982) with theoretical emphasis (Mitchell, 1983) and adds a crucial historical component (1991:97–8). The particular importance of a case emerges when it is set against a knowledge of the background (Mitchell, 1983). This is provided in chapters three and four which present an overview of developments in London based on a review of the literature, conversations with social workers[1], Fostering Officers, foster parents, black councillors and activists, attendance at meetings and a postal survey of Principal Fostering Officers.

A frequent criticism of case studies concerns the extent to which it is possible to make generalisations. The mistake, in Stoecker's view, is to equate the case study with method:

> the case study is not a 'method' in the most typical sense but more a 'design feature' (Platt, 1984) or, even more broadly, a *frame* determining the boundaries of information–gathering (1991:98).

As Mitchell has pointed out, such criticisms arise out of the misguided assumption 'that the only valid basis of inference is that which has been developed in relation to statistical analysis' (1983: 197). Although statistical inferences based on correlations may indicate the existence of a relationship between variables, they reveal little about possible causal linkages. The validity of extrapolation from case studies, by contrast, 'depends not on the typicality or representativeness of the case(s) but upon the cogency of the theoretical reasoning' (Mitchell, 1983:198). The analyst's concern is with the 'specification of the dimensions of differentiation' rather than with questions about representativeness and generalisability (Platt, 1988,1986). It is sometimes argued that case studies are little more than a collection of anecdotes or a good narrative but, as Schuller (1986) rejoins, the approach is deliberate whereas anecdote is merely random and, second, has some degree of theoretical and explanatory power which goes beyond the story. Stoecker goes further and suggests that 'the charge that case studies are good for little more than description applies much more thoroughly to extensive research. Likewise, the assertion that extensive research better establishes causation is patently false' (1991:95).

---

[1] Interviews and discussions with workers from a number of organisations were conducted before the onset of the fieldwork for the case study (See Appendix Two).

28

The selection of the case

The borough selected[2] shared many of the characteristics of other inner London boroughs which were in the vanguard of policy change: inner city location and a significant black population. Second, the central organisation of the fostering services limited both the number of people and of organisational tiers through which the application to carry out the research had to pass before approval. Data collection was also much easier than in a borough where family recruitment was dispersed throughout area teams. Third, since the aim of the research was to study the process of change and not simply to catalogue reasons for failure to change, it was important to choose a borough which was actively changing its approach but which did not have a high public profile which might have generated defensiveness among workers. Time constraints precluded the study of additional cases.

Gaining access

Gaining permission to carry out the research was one of the most difficult and time–consuming stages of the project (cf. Dowling, 1989). In all, five boroughs were approached. There were no guidelines for correct procedure and the full weight of bureaucratic machinery was brought to bear both as a delaying tactic and a means of discouragement. Departments considered the research to be potentially threatening and were afraid of exposing themselves or their workers to criticism. The borough eventually 'selected' took little time to consider its decision and was initially the most enthusiastic[3]. Even here, however, senior management did not want the researcher to contact Council members or interest groups in the community for fear of the issue being exploited politically. Permission had been granted and the fieldwork was well underway when it was announced that the proposal had to be put before the Council for ratification. In the event, it was passed without opposition.

This experience reveals how easily those in power can defend themselves from the unwelcome attention of researchers and can set the conditions and terms of the research. Although the research was welcomed 'in principle', this was only so long as it was carried out 'in practice' on somebody else's doorstep. Where permission was refused, the relatively unassailable reasons

---

[2] The word, 'selected', is not strictly accurate. The borough was the fifth to be approached, two having refuses permission for the research to go ahead and the others still not having made a decision after months of negotiation.

[3] These factors clearly influenced my relationship with members of the Fostering Team.

of staff shortages and re-organisation were given, rather than criticisms of the project, itself, which could have been challenged or accommodated.

Strategies of data collection

Multiple strategies were adopted in order to examine the process of change from different perspectives, expand the data and analysis and so gain a deeper understanding (cf. Silverman, 1985). Denzin (1970) has advocated 'method triangulation" as a means of validation: each method is used as a façadek on the validity of the others rather than as an alternative approach which can generate an account with its own autonomous validity. Similarly, he treats data from different sources as different aspects of a single reality but, although a salutary reminder of the partiality of any single context of data collection, the strategy fails as a means to overcome this partiality (Silverman, 1985). In the present study it would have been inappropriate, for example, to try to façade social workers' accounts against those of applicants or *vice versa*, under the mistaken assumption that there is a single 'correct' version which informants are tempted to distort.

Postal survey

A postal survey of Principal Fostering Officers was conducted in 1986 in order to evaluate the impact of the changes in thinking London-wide. This is discussed more fully in Chapter Four. A copy of the questionnaire is contained in Appendix 1.

Document analysis

This included an examination of the minutes of Team Meetings over a twelve year period, various Working Party reports and policy guidance documents. The details of the analysis are discussed in Chapter Six.

Participant observation

This involves 'taking the viewpoint of those studied, understanding the situated character of interaction, viewing social processes over time, and can encourage attempts to develop formal theories from first-hand data' (Silverman, 1985:104 following Denzin, 1970:7-19). Unlike survey research, 'the participant observer is not bound by prejudgments about the nature of his problem, by rigid data-gathering devices, or by hypotheses' (Denzin, 1970:216).

As a research technique, however, it is not without problems. Many of the criticisms have been inspired by the interactionist objective of studying meanings that arise in natural settings and have concerned the question of bias and the impact of the researcher's participation and relationships with informants upon the data that are gathered. This perspective has been criticised on several counts (Hammersley & Atkinson, 1983; Silverman, 1985). First, observation is not a pure, 'uncontaminated' activity. The observer may influence the setting and/or miss the effects of temporal cycles. Second, the aim of observing 'things as they really are' is atheoretical and makes a misleading distinction between 'natural' and 'artificial' settings. Third, it limits research to 'cultural description'. Although members façadek claims and make causal assertions, the observer is prohibited from so doing and members' understandings are treated as if they were immune to assessment or explanation. Finally, the approach shares with positivism a desire to eliminate the effects of the observer upon the data.

A more productive approach is to treat the researcher as an integral part of the research setting (Agar, 1980) and to treat the research practices and interaction between researcher and researched as topics for investigation in their own right. This follows Schutz' recognition that commonsense is not simply the restricted property of the subjects of research but underlies the entire research enterprise (1954:266–7). As Turner puts it, 'the equipment that enables the 'ordinary' member of society to make his daily way through the world is the equipment available for those who would wish to do a science' of that world' (Turner, 1974:197 cited in Silverman, 1985). The task of the sociologist is, first, to recognise dependence on commonsense and, second, to render it 'problematic in a way that would never arise for members' (Silverman, 1985:168 following Turner, 1974:204).

Gold (1969) has distinguished four ideal typical field roles: the complete participant, the participant–as–observer, the observer–as–participant, and the complete observer. In practice, these roles are rarely clear-cut and several roles may be adopted during the course of an investigation (Patrick, 1973; Burgess, 1984). Which is/are adopted is/are rarely, if ever, the decision of the researcher alone but the product of negotiation between researcher and researched. In the current study, the investigator's role was modified with different actors and as the situation changed in different stages of the field work. I was provided with a desk in the 'Team Room' and so could observe the day–to–day activities and interactions of the Team members. As my presence became accepted, I began to take a more active part in interactions and discussions. I was invited to 'Information Meetings' for applicants, discussion groups, the meetings of the 'Black Action Group' and to Team meetings where I was invited to give preliminary reports of the research findings. Later, I participated on a training and assessment course for prospective foster parents.

The researcher's social role Burgess (1984:88) notes that little account is usually taken of the researcher's social role, the relevant dimensions of which he lists, somewhat sparsely, as experience, age, sex and ethnicity. Their relevance, however, cannot be taken for granted as unchanging dimensions of the field work but is actively negotiated and varies with the actors and the context. I was easily accepted into the predominantly white, middle class, all-female Fostering Team and my student status was, for many, a sufficient reason for wanting to do the research without looking for ulterior motivation. On the other hand, my previous experience as a social work assistant[4] was important in gaining credibility. A black researcher would probably have been less easily accepted and social workers may have been more wary of appearing to speak or act in a prejudiced fashion. Maureen Stone, for example, reported that

> ...although being West Indian had certain advantages in the community groups I visited, mainly in being permitted access in the first place (although this was not always the case and I was refused access to a number of projects), within the school system this could (and I think did) work the other way in terms of what was said to me and what was made available to me (Stone, 1981:90).

My lack of institutional affiliation (other than as a post-graduate student to the university) was important to both social workers and fostering applicants. With applicants, the high value placed on education meant that people were usually happy to 'help me with my studies' (cf. Cornwell, 1984). Colour and ethnicity were not treated as potential contaminants, as they would have been by both positivists and interactionists, but as additional dimensions which could influence the interaction and the quality of communication between interviewer and informant in varied and interesting ways.

Insider/outsider status The social distance and difference in roles between the actor categories (social worker and applicant) and the element of conflict engendered by the process of selection meant that too close an identification with one or other party risked alienating or losing the confidence of the other. The boundaries between insider and outsider status, however, were not clear-cut. My previous experience in a social work setting meant that I was

---

[4] I worked for eighteen months as a social work assistant in a North London borough in 1980 and 1981.

accepted, to some extent, as an insider within the Fostering Team but my role as researcher prevented the attainment of full insider status (cf. Cavendish, 1982; Burgess, 1984). Never wholly familiar with the culture of the Team because my presence within it was temporary, as a partial outsider, I had a certain 'stranger value' (Beattie, 1964). According to Merton, 'it is the stranger ...who finds what is familiar to the group significantly unfamiliar and so is prompted to raise questions for inquiry less apt to be raised by insiders' (1972:33). At least initially, I was ignorant of and, more importantly, not a party to the internal politics and personality differences which shaped relationships within the Team; my presence was temporary and I had no loyalties. As an 'outsider', I could be trusted with confidences, information and opinions which, workers confessed, they would not have revealed to each other.

Applicants, on the other hand, seemed to divide the world into social workers and non-social workers (cf. Liverpool, 1982) and, in this sense, related to me as one of themselves. On the other hand, as a double outsider, that is, not party to the assessment procedure either as a social worker or a fellow applicant, I was assumed to be more trustworthy and less judgemental than an insider would have been. As one person explained,

> I wouldn't discuss these things with my neighbours. People that live round here have a big mouth. You tell one and soon they all know. You got the whole lot know your business.

Applicants valued the opportunity to express their 'side of the story' and the opportunity to convey their views, through the research, to a wider audience was important to them. Both within the Team and in the discussions with applicants, my presumed ignorance as an outsider proved to be a valuable resource. Informants treated me to information and explanations which they would have assumed was the taken-for-granted knowledge of the insider. My outsider's ignorance as a white person was especially valuable in discussions with black applicants about racism and discrimination. As one person explained, so much less could be taken for granted. Within the Team, by contrast, my colour conferred status as an insider. I too was struggling with the issues and presumed to be a victim of racist conditioning since childhood.

Open and closed roles   The debate about the relative merits (Denzin, 1968) and demerits (Erikson, 1967,1968) of adopting an open or closed research role has a long history (Bulmer, 1982; Burgess, 1984) but, as Roth (1962) has pointed out, the distinction between the two approaches is not clear-cut. All research is, in some sense, 'secret': researchers rarely know everything they wish to investigate at the beginning of a study which makes informed consent difficult. They may not want to influence the behaviour of their subjects by indicating their particular area of interest and, even where precise details are provided, they may have different meanings for different individuals depending on their differing experiences and conceptions of the goals of the study (cf. Roth, 1962). Even where the research is nominally 'open', 'it is difficult to uphold the principle of informed consent' (Burgess, 1984:201). There a tendency to stress certain aspects to some actors and other aspects to others but, without actually telling a lie, the suppression of certain information and highlighting of other can produce the same effect. In the current study, the approach was as open as possible but, even so, some people had obviously not realised how difficult they would find some of the questions to answer, particularly those touching on racism, and some found that they opened up painful memories.

Action research

A variant of participant observation, where the researcher adopts the dual role of investigator and activist, is action research. The aim is to accomplish change, while that of conventional participant observation, at least within a strict interactionist perspective, is to disturb the field as little as possible. Otherwise, the same tensions exist between participation and observation, although usually described in terms of action and research. One of the main problems, as Ben–Tovim and his colleagues found (1986), is the division of responsibilities between those who research and those who act and the resultant failure to take into account the political context. Their suggested solution is to abandon the formal division of research and action and to fuse the roles of researcher and activist. This strategy challenges to the notion of apolitical, value–free research. First, the implications of research become an object of investigation in their own right; second, an analysis of the means by which they might be implemented or used becomes an integral part of the research process and contributes to the organisation's effectiveness in realising its objectives and, third, the direct reporting of the researcher's own experience is set against the indirect reporting of observations or other people's accounts.

Although the approach has much to commend it, there are advantages to be gained from the adoption of a less openly active role. As previously noted, where there are clear factions, the non–affiliated researcher occupies a neutral position and is, therefore, perceived to be a person in whom it is 'safe' to confide. The research may be regarded as a vehicle through which to pass on information to a wider audience in an anonymous and, therefore, 'safe' form. Not only might it be unethical to conceal the research role but, where the roles of researcher and activist are fused, it may be more difficult to determine the ways in which the activist's research capacity influences others' actions than where the division is more formally acknowledged. Finally, there is something to be said for allowing actors 'to make their own mistakes' and 'to find their own solutions' on the grounds that, first, the researcher may not always 'know best' and, second, careful documentation of the process may enable others to foresee the pitfalls and take appropriate steps to avoid them.

The present study was not designed as an action research programme, although it incorporates elements of this approach. Not only would it have been difficult to refuse social workers access to the findings until completion of the study, but there was an ethical dilemma in delaying the dissemination of findings which could benefit practice. Reflexivity was achieved through informal discussions with social workers and, more formally, through the presentation of the research findings at Team Meetings and at a special Study Day. As a consequence of this feedback, small changes were made in both policy and practice and these changes, in turn, became incorporated into the field data. The research, itself, was not so much an extraneous contaminating factor as an integral part of the process of change: the fact that permission for it was granted in the first place and the subsequent co-operation of members was indicative of the Team's commitment to change. The research did not effect major change nor alter direction but served as a catalyst which enhanced commitment and enthusiasm and stimulated the Team to introduce small modifications to a process already in motion. Changes directly influenced by the research findings included the decision to hold an open 'Information Meeting' for anyone wanting to find out more about fostering black children; a re-evaluation of the style, purpose and direction of questioning during assessment interviews; a decision to hold more frequent meetings and training sessions with smaller groups; to contact applicants before meetings; show more personal interest in them, and explain more fully what to expect from the assessment process.

Interviews

Interviews were conducted with management, social workers, foster parents and applicants and, where possible, were taped.

Social workers Informal interviews and discussions with social workers generally took place in the 'Team Room'. Longer interviews with the workers who were directly involved in the recruitment of black foster parents were usually arranged in workers' own homes where they felt more at ease, without the fear of being interrupted or overheard.

Applicants   The names and addresses of all those who had responded to the advertising campaign for black foster parents were recorded by the receptionist. After the campaign had been running for seven months, there had been 120 enquiries. From this list, every second name was selected. The sample ranged from those who had pursued their interest no further than an initial enquiry to those who had completed the full assessment and been either approved or rejected. Many had withdrawn at varying stages during this process. The initial approach was made by letter which briefly explained the purpose of the research and sought permission for an interview. Where possible, this was followed up by a telephone call. The letters were hand-written on unheaded paper and the wording was friendly and informal[5].

Of the sixty people contacted, forty nine were interviewed. When joint interviews with spouses or other family members are included, the total is increased to sixty three (Table 1). Only three people refused[6]. In addition to the widespread suspicion of 'officials' which was encountered in the black community, there was a risk of confusion with the social workers who were carrying out the assessments. For these reasons, the interviews were conducted after the assessment interviews had been completed but, often, before the result of the application was known. It was important to emphasise the independence of the research since some informants were afraid that information would be passed back to social workers. Informants did not seem to object to a white researcher, although such objections may have underlain some people's excuses for not co-operating. In addition to these sixty-three people, twelve of the sixteen who attended the training and assessment course at which the researcher was a participant observer were interviewed and a further eight from the 'black' course (Table 1). None of the problems described above were

---

[5] The letter explained that people's identities would not be revealed in the research and that all information would be treated 'in confidence'. Despite these precautions, some people may have been put off by the wording of the original letter and subsequent letters were consequently amended. As one person explained:

> When I saw that word, 'confidential', I thought `What is this about? What is this 'confidential'?' and I was a bit worried, I suppose. I think some people they just see the word, 'confidential', and they think it is going on a file on them or something. It's the word. They don't stop to think what it means.

[6] One person did not want anyone 'keeping a file' on her, the others were wary of questionnaires and interviews. I suspect that at least three others may have effectively chosen not to take part by being out when the interviewer called. It was difficult to keep appointments with people who were not on the telephone and most of those who were not interviewed did not have a telephone. One person was away on holiday, one had moved, another was in hospital and, for two, it proved too difficult to arrange a mutually convenient time, although this may have been a ploy to avoid being interviewed.

encountered because informants already knew the researcher from the course. The respondent group is broken down by age, gender and stage of the assessment process in Tables 2, 3, and 4.

The conduct of the interviews. The interviews were conducted in respondents' own homes and were tape-recorded. A semi-structured questionnaire was designed in consultation with social workers and existing black foster parents but this format was abandoned in favour of focused interviewing after a pilot where it was found to hinder rather than promote communication[7]. A more flexible, interactive interviewing procedure allows the researcher to find out how different issues hold different significance for different people (Stoecker, 1991:95). Denzin lists the advantages of focused interviewing as allowing respondents to use their 'unique ways of defining the world', assuming that no fixed sequence of questions is suitable to all respondents and allowing respondents to 'raise important issues not contained in the schedule' (1970:125). In addition, the approach promotes a more egalitarian relationship between interviewer and informant by giving the latter greater control over the direction of talk and is a more familiar form of communication since it conforms more closely with 'normal conversation'. In a structured approach, it is the language of the researcher which shapes the communication and its content: using a less formal, flexible approach, the language of the informant may be the dominant influence.

Several writers have shown how the survey method reflects the wider system of gender stratification (e.g. Smith & Noble-Spruell, 1986; Graham, 1983). It embodies 'the masculine imagery of detachment and control' (Graham, 1983:134) and conforms with the conventional distinction between the public domain of 'the male social universe' and the relatively hidden private lives of women. It is the presence of men, Shirley Ardener (1978) notes, which typically defines a space as 'public' and the province of sociology. In the context of the social significance of skin colour, it was also the presence of white people.

---

[7] Three informants actually refused to participate when a questionnaire was used and said that they preferred to 'just talk'. They seemed to find the formality of the approach intimidating. Some seemed to think that there was a right and a wrong answer to the questions and, where they could not guess what would be most acceptable to the interviewer, would decline from expressing an opinion altogether (c.f. Cornwell (1984) on the nature of public and private accounts). After it had been completed, informants would breath a sigh of relief and all that they had been unable or unwilling to say in response to the questionnaire would spill out.

37

Table 1
Fostering applicants who participated in the study

	Black	White
Individual assessments		
Number of people contacted	60	–
Of those contacted, number interviewed	49	–
Total number interviewed		
(including spouse and other family members)	63	–
Numbers interviewed by white interviewer	41	–
Number interviewed by black interviewer	22	–
Group assessments		
Number of people who attended 'mixed' course	11	6
Number interviewed	4	8
Number of people who attended 'black' course	11	1
Number interviewed	8	–

Table 2
Age range of people who were interviewed

<20	20–29	30–39	40–49	50–59	>60
0	18	16	14	19	11

Table 3
Gender of people who were interviewed

	Black			White			All		
	M	F	All	M	F	All	M	F	All
Individual assessment	18	45	63				18	45	63
Group assessments	4	8	12	2	6	8	6	14	20
	22	53	75	2	6	8	24	59	83

Table 4
Numbers completing different stages of the assessment process

	B	W	All
Total number of enquries	57	5	62
Total number of applications	48	5	53
Individual assessments			
Number dropped out before assessment	12	–	14
Number dropped out during assessment	8	–	8
Number completed assessment	17	–	15
Number approved as foster parents	10	–	10
Group training assessment			
Number failing to complete training and assessment	1	1	2
Number completing training and assessment	7	4	11
Number approved as foster parents	7	3	10

*   Numbers interviewed include spouse and other family members and, therefore, do not equal number of enquiries.

Hilary Graham distinguishes four properties of the survey method which make it particularly unsuitable to the present study. First, individuals are divorced from their social context and social phenomena such as gender and 'race' are treated as properties of individuals rather than dimensions of social structure. Second, surveys tend to treat individuals as equivalent units in order to provide a basis for measurement. Galtung points out that this 'presupposes verbal interaction that is friendly, or at least not hostile' and 'thus has ideological implications in distorting the total image of society' (1967:158–9, cited in Graham, 1983). Such cautionary comments assume a special significance in the context of gender (Graham, 1983) and colour stratification and conflict. Third, the method assumes that 'social phenomena have an existence separate from the social relations in which they are embedded' and that, through talk, they can assume a form which can be defined, labelled and measured (Graham, 1983:142–3). Jones (1980) and Spender (1980), however, argue that, while participating in the man–made language of the public domain, women communicate their personal experiences through an oral culture untapped by social scientists. Similar arguments have been raised to explain the dual competence in both the 'black' and 'white' social spheres of black people (Small, 1986b; Harris, 1987) who have available to them not only two different modes of expression (Kochman, 1981) but 'two mutually incompatible world views' (Harris, 1987), either of which may be tapped depending on the context. The language of surveys is not only that of men but that of white people and may doubly fail to capture the lives of black women. Finally, Graham recalls Smith's observation that the measurement systems of survey research contrive 'a forced set of categories into which women must stuff the awkward and resistant actualities of their lives' (Smith, 1979:141). The same comments could equally have been written about black people.

The practicalities of research interviewing have been discussed by Ann Oakley (1981). She notes a contradiction in the advice usually given to interviewers: generating the rapport necessary to gain the interviewee's co-operation is hindered by the requirement of objectivity and detachment, by the depersonalisation of both interviewer and interviewee and by the hierarchical relationship which exists between them (Oakley, 1981; Silverman, 1985). In order to achieve a balance, 'both interviewer and interviewee 'must be "socialised" into the correct interviewing behaviour' (Oakley, 1981:35)[8].

Interviewees, however, may find the interview protocol alien and restrictive and object to the subordinate and passive role which they are obliged to adopt. A number of writers have described how interviews can be dominated by sexual politics and class antagonism (e.g. Cornwell, 1984; McKee & O'Brien, 1983). The influence of the politics of race has been less widely commented upon in Britain. The constraints on free expression and the surrendering of power imposed by the conventional format may reinforce suspicions about the benevolence of the research objectives. Oakley advocates an alternative interactive approach and, although referring specifically to women, where interviewees are both female and black, her comments are doubly appropriate. 'The goal of finding out about people through interviewing', she suggests, 'is best achieved when the relationship of interviewer and interviewee is non-hierarchical and when the interviewer is prepared to invest his or her own personal identity in the relationship' (1981:41).

In the present study, an interactive approach was encouraged in a number of ways. The adoption of a pupil-teacher stance helped to break down the hierarchical relationship between interviewer and interviewee (cf. Agar, 1980). Second, as Oakley found in her study of pregnant women (Oakley, 1979), it was often more appropriate to try to answer informants' questions than to try to parry them. This not only enhanced rapport but was a small return for the investment of time and effort which informants made in agreeing to be

---

[8] The survey method not only masks relationships of power but actively reinforces them. There is an inbuilt hierarchy of control and authority between researcher and researched, interviewer and interviewee, which is inherent in the question-and-answer format of surveys (Silverman 1985; Oakley 1981) and which reinforces the wider social relationships of power between male interviewer and female respondent, white interviewer and black respondent, middle class interviewer and working class respondent.

interviewed[9]. Some people extended this to considerable hospitality: I was plied with numerous cups of tea, coffee or rum, invited to family meals and provided with escorts to bus stops and tube stations[10].

When asked directly about my own views, it was not always appropriate to maintain a neutral stance. In situations where there is controversy, the pretence of neutrality can be counterproductive. It made people suspicious that I was somehow concealing my 'real' views and, as a consequence, they responded with the least controversial or committal statements. The dilemma was most acute in respect of social workers. There was a danger of becoming too closely associated with the radical faction within the Team which was strongly in favour of 'racial matching'. Not only did I run the risk of alienating other members of the Team but of unwittingly being drafted into the radical group and 'used' to give authority to its views.

An attempt was made to involve informants as active participants in the research process. At the end of each interview, they were invited to comment on the content and style. These were modified in response to their comments and their reactions were also treated as part of the research data. The following example is a comment from a black applicant in response to the question: 'What do you think about the following statement made in a recent newspaper article: "People who look different from the normal white British stereotype do not in any sense share a common identity"?'

MrsB When you say 'normal white' that mean to say the others aren't normal. It don't sound right... Some people are black and everybody start to get annoyed about that. They don't want to answer any more questions, you know. What did you say about 'normal'? That implies that everybody else normal and they are not. And the white child is and the black child is not and that don't sound right.

PR And that would put people off you think?

MrsB Oh, yes it would.

PR ... from answering other questions?

MrsB Yes, they would feel very upset, right, straight away.[11]

---

[9] The questions asked usually concerned the current study and purpose of the research, my own background and reasons for interest in the subject and requests for information about fostering services and assessment procedures. When asked about my own opinions, I said I was generally in favour of 'racial matching' in foster care but not of a rigid policy.

[10] This was especially appreciated since many of the interviews took place at night in estates with an extremely 'rough' reputation.

[11] Such comments on other people's likely reactions may often have been a cover for informants' own opinions.

Public and private accounts   A distinction often made in qualitative research is that between public and private accounts. Cornwell (1984), for example, describes how 'using the "right" words and saying the "right" things' mattered to the working class respondents she was interviewing. She attributed this to the unfamiliarity and inequality of the interview situation. The activities of 'managing appearances' and 'controlling information' are inherent in all social interaction (Goffman, 1959) and, for Cornwell's respondents, were a way of 'putting on their best face'. Uncertain of their own positions in relation to the interviewer, they resorted to the 'culturally normative pattern' (Laslett and Rapoport, 1975:973) and the 'relative security offered by "public accounts"' (Cornwell, 1984:15). Cornwell describes public accounts as 'sets of meanings in common social currency that reproduce and legitimate the assumptions people take for granted about the nature of social reality... in sticking to the public account of whatever it is they are discussing... the person doing the talking can be sure that whatever they say will be acceptable to other people' (1984:15).   In other words, public accounts conform to 'least common denominator morality' (Douglas, 1971:242). The 'opposite of the public account', according to Cornwell, is the 'private account' which 'spring(s) directly from personal experience and from the thoughts and feelings accompanying it' (1984:16).

This simple distinction can be challenged on three counts: first, is the implicit assumption that private accounts are intrinsically 'better' and more closely reflect a person's 'real' or 'genuine' feelings and opinions than public accounts which are merely a gloss or façade; second, is the assumption that there is a single 'truth' which it is the purpose of research to reveal and, third, social life is compartmentalized too rigidly into public and private spheres (cf. Berk, 1980). If, as Goffman proposes, 'managing appearances' and 'controlling information' are continuous elements of all social interaction, all accounts are, in some sense, public. People may have available to them a number of levels of interpretation and are capable of holding a variety of opinions about a subject (Donovan, 1986), some of which may appear contradictory but which are, none-the-less, 'real' or 'honest' to the person expressing them and any of which may be tapped, depending on the context. Attitudes often serve a social and expressive rather than a rational function (Lalljee *et al.*, 1984) and, as such, are intricately tied to the contexts in which they are formed and expressed.   In a discussion about transracial fostering with a white husband and a black wife, for example, I was treated to a different style of response depending on whether or not the spouse was present. The 'significant other' seemed to be the interviewer when either partner was interviewed on his/her own but the spouse when they were interviewed together. I suspect that the topic had not been discussed between them previously because it potentially

42

threatened their relationship as a mixed couple which seemed to be based on the premise that 'colour does not matter'[12].

Cross-racial interviewing   The idea that one type of account is somehow more 'accurate' or 'genuine' than another underlies many of the criticisms of cross-racial interviewing and, since many of the interviews with black people in the present study were carried out by a white researcher, this needs some justification.   While recognising that, in a 'racially' conscious society, the colour of an interviewer's skin will probably influence the way in which a person responds, it is erroneous to assume that a qualitative difference necessarily means that one type of account is intrinsically superior to the other. Each is interesting and meaningful in its own right and sometimes as much can be learned from what is not said as from what is said. A different account given to a black interviewer does not invalidate that given to a white, although it may well cast it in a new light which will affect the interpretation. The effects of skin colour are, moreover, unlikely to be static but will vary with the context and questions which are asked (Cate Schaeffer, 1980). Whether or not it is more appropriate to employ a black or a white interviewer will depend on the circumstances of the interview and the content.

There has been little discussion in the British literature of race-of-interviewer effects, although there has been considerable coverage in America. A rare British reference in a study of West Indian immigrants in London reported no difference between black and white interviewers in interviewer-interviewee rapport (Rutter *et al*, 1974). Most of the American studies agree that items dealing directly with race attitudes expressed to an interviewer of the opposite race are almost always significantly more congenial than when expressed to an interviewer of the same race (e.g. Reese, 1986). Occasionally these effects spill into related questions but are occasional rather than typical and smaller in magnitude than for the direct racial questions. The literature suggests that the three categories of items most likely to show race-of-interviewer effects are those with explicit racial content, those with social desirability or prestige implications, and those inquiring about support for established political and economic institutions (Cate Schaeffer, 1980).   It is also widely believed, although with little experimental evidence, that response rates will be higher with same race interviewers (Tom W. Smith, Senior Study Director, National Opinion Research Centre, Univ. of Chicago, personal communication, 1987).

The most common explanations for these effects refer to the structure of race relations in American society which causes blacks to calculate their responses

---

[12] This is an example of possible consequences of an interview with ethical implications which go beyond the question of open and closed research discussed above.

to white interviewers in ways determined by the imbalance of social and political power between blacks and whites (e.g. Hyman *et al.*, 1954) or to the displacement during an interview of task norms by interpersonal norms: answers which are assumed to be hostile to an interviewer of opposite race are restrained out of politeness (e.g. Schuman & Converse, 1971). The American literature refers mainly to survey research and the results are not always clear-cut which makes it difficult to extrapolate. Far less has been written about qualitative ethnographic interviewing where it is recognised that all accounts are dependent on the contexts of their production and on the personal biographies of informants, factors which tend to be suppressed in analyses of conventional survey research.

In the current study, it was hypothesised that skin colour would be likely to influence the ways in which people respond, particularly when the subjects discussed impinge upon so-called 'racial' issues. It was assumed that:

(a)   a black interviewer would be more likely to share the experience of racial prejudice and discrimination with a black informant who would, therefore, feel more comfortable about discussing these issues than with a white person;

(b)   black people's suspicion and mistrust of white people in general will be extended to a white researcher and inhibit effective communication (Iganski, 1990);

(c)   if the view that all white people are, consciously or subconsciously, racist (*The Guardian* 11 May 87; Small, 1986a) is correct, a white interviewer would be likely to conduct an interview and interpret the data in a prejudiced manner;

(d)   the use of black interviewers would circumvent the social power differential which exists between white people and black people and which may be reinforced in the interview encounter.

For these reasons, two black interviewers of West Indian descent were engaged. Both were women in their late teens, local to the area and from working class backgrounds similar to the majority of informants. This strategy incorporated black people into the research process as co-investigators as well as subjects.

Contrary to expectation, the differences between the accounts given to the black interviewers and the white interviewer were not sufficient to warrant separate analysis. Twenty two of sixty three people were interviewed by the black interviewers and, where appropriate, the identity of the interviewer is indicated by initials in the text (PR = white interviewer, JA or PJ = black interviewer). On the whole, the accounts given to the white interviewer were more detailed and extensive which was probably a consequence of greater interviewing experience rather than skin colour. As the white interviewer, I also had the advantage of a certain 'stranger value' (Beattie, 1964). Even when discussing such sensitive subjects as racism, I found that being white was not always the handicap expected. Many informants were prepared to talk openly and at length about their experiences and opinions and several confided that they would not have had a similar discussion with another black person. As one person explained,

> I wouldn't have had a talk like this with another black person. I can discuss these sorts of things more easily with you. With a black person, you would just take it for granted.

In these discussions, I adopted the equivalent of a pupil role with the informant adopting that of teacher (cf. Donovan, 1986; Agar, 1980). People often spoke to me as a representative of white people in general and saw the research as a vehicle for conveying their views and experiences to a wider (white) audience. The guarantee of anonymity afforded a protection and, thus, an opportunity which is normally denied. In these encounters, we were speaking as a black person to a white person: the significance of skin colour became paramount but as a stimulant rather than a block to communication. On other occasions, people may have been wary of me as a white person and have felt more at ease talking to another black person, although, when asked, no-one admitted this. The significance of relative skin colour was not always static from start to finish of an interview and more was gained from considering it as an interactive factor in the dynamic context of each interview than by attempting to isolate it as a variable. The value of this approach was, perhaps, most clearly illustrated in the interview with the mixed couple discussed above.

When talking to the white applicants, my colour was often an advantage. I doubt whether some of the more racist comments would have been made to a black interviewer. Some white applicants' support for a policy of same-race placement, for example, masked a fundamental prejudice against black people[13]. The pattern of responses given to the two black interviewers was

---

[13] The following comment is an example:

I think it is right that each should look after its own. They are different from us. The boys mature sexually earlier than our boys do. I wouldn't trust a black teenager with my daughter.

(continued...)

similarly not always in the direction expected. Some informants were wary of talking to another black person about the issues covered in the interviews and two refused to co-operate when a black interviewer called but were willing to talk to me. Both indicated that they preferred to talk to a white person. Both were opposed to the new policy of 'racial matching' and feared to express these views to a black interviewer whose opinions they assumed would be strongly to the contrary.

The problem of validation   The main problem with much of sociology's treatment of interview data has been the over-riding concern with objectivity and control of bias and the illusory distinction between artificial and natural settings (Hammersley & Atkinson, 1983). The positivists' solution has been to try to create a standard context, whereas that of the interactionists has been to minimise interference by restricting the role of the researcher to that of observer or reducing the differences between researcher and researched to a minimum by embracing the member culture.   This kind of naturalism, however, is 'an unwitting inheritance of the positivist programme, albeit using different means to achieve the same unquestioned ends, that is, data which is as far as possible "untouched by human hands" – neutral, unbiased and representative' (Silverman, 1985:156). As Hammersley and Atkinson (1983) point out, the technique of open-ended or non-directive interviewing is, itself, a form of social control which shapes both the manner and content of people's responses (cf. Oakley, 1981). Ethnomethodologists, on the other hand, reject content analysis altogether and are concerned less with *social facts* than with the nature of *social processes* (Zimmerman & Pollner, 1971).   Members' 'commonsense devices for making sense of the environment' are presumed to be shared by interviewers and researchers alike; thus, 'the principles of good and bad interviewing can be read as basic features of social interaction which the social scientist is presumably seeking to study' (Cicourel, 1964:68). Ethnomethodological analyses, however, are grounded within an essentially functionalist Durkheimian/Parsonian social order (Silverman, 1985) which precludes discussion of relationships of power. The conception of social life is limited to the negotiation of meanings and the practical accomplishment of routine activities.

The incompatibility of these different approaches is more apparent than real. A 'realist' approach, Silverman argues, provides a useful synthesis in which 'the

---

[13](...continued)

On these occasions, I experienced an ethical dilemma between commitment to informants' anonymity and desire to expose racism which might harm children placed in their care. The compromise of informing the Team without naming informants will, I am sure, be considered unsatisfactory by many.

internalist concern with form and universality and the externalist commitment to content and variability' are treated as 'complementary rather than contradictory' (1985:170) since, 'for analytic purposes and in real life, form and content are seen to depend on each other' (172).

For positivists, validity is based on representativeness achieved through repetition of a standardised format. This attempt to create an artificial uniformity, however, ignores aspects of context which cannot easily be standardised and assumes that data generated in one context (the interview) can be generalised across time and across contexts. For interactionists, on the other hand, each interview situation is unique and validity is achieved through mutual understanding or 'intersubjective depth' (Silverman, 1985:162). Denzin's solution of 'combining methods and investigators in the same study' in order to 'overcome the deficiencies that flow from one investigator and/or one method' (1970:300), however, like that of the positivists, assumes a single over-arching reality.

An alternative suggestion has been resort to the research subjects' own pronouncements on the findings but, as Bloor (1983) points out, there is no direct correspondence between members' and researchers' accounts and structures and processes revealed in that of the researcher may be opaque to actors. Lack of interest in the topic, reluctance to voice disagreements, the artificiality of interviews, 'the occasioned and temporally bounded nature of the validation exercise' are among the problems outlined by Bloor (1983:171). In addition, the social distance between researcher and researched may influence the latter's accounts. They may attempt to guess the researcher's interest and to temper their responses and behaviour accordingly. Beliefs may change over time and context and serve a social and expressive as well as rational function. Despite these qualifications, the exercise 'can generate material highly pertinent to the analysis' by treating additional material 'not as a test (but) as data' (Bloor, 1983:172). A further justification, though one not mentioned by Bloor, is the opportunity for some sharing of power between researcher and researched. Member validation can also serve as a strategy for action research where the aim is not simply to record and analyse but to initiate or facilitate change (cf. Stoecker, 1991).

In the present study, the coding of the interviews and field data and subsequent analysis was carried out single-handedly[14], although the

---

[14] The first few interviews were transcribed and coded in full to develop the initial categories but, thereafter, following Burgess' advice (1984:121), were transcribed as a record of categories and themes indexed by tape count with only the most relevant material transcribed in full. As new themes emerged, many interviews were re-coded. Transcription, categorisation, coding and analysis were not separate exercises, following on from each other in chronological steps, but inter-dependent and often concurrent activities.

(continued...)

interpretation was discussed with the two black interviewers and, where possible, with informants. The preliminary findings were discussed informally with members of the Fostering Team and more formally when reports were presented to Team meetings, not so much as a check on validity as a means of collecting additional data, stimulating further analysis, involving participants in the research, and stimulating changes in policy and practice. As Nicki Thorogood points out, long interview sessions eliciting a wealth of information touching on many different aspects of informants' lives and experience are, themselves, tests of internal consistency and, thus, of validity and reliability (1988).

The way forward, according to Silverman, is to concentrate upon the moral and cultural forms which interviews display. 'Interviews', he suggests, 'share with any account this involvement in moral realities (and) offer a rich source of data which provide access to how people account for both their troubles and good fortune' (1985:176). The climate of change in which the present study was undertaken was suffused with moral themes in which workers were forced to come to terms with the fact that the 'good' practice of the past may be reinterpreted as malpractice in the present. The forging of 'a positive Black identity' inverted previous negative conceptions of 'culture' as a weakness or liability in to a positive source of strength and pride. It assailed the foundations of the social work enterprise with ethnic minorities, exposed workers to painful confrontation with their own prejudices, and challenged assimilationist aspirations for both workers and applicants. Overlying all was the unresolved dialectic between 'race', ethnicity and class. The following account attempts to reveal some of the ways in which the various players in this drama struggled with this complex of changing meanings to redefine their social and professional worlds. The object was to provide a plausible account which makes sense of people's experience while not claiming to be the only possible account.

---

[14](...continued)

The ethnomethodologists' use of several analysts to code blind the same data and comparison of these separately coded accounts as a check on validity was rejected, first, because, unless all those involved in the coding of the data have been equally involved in its collection, the background knowledge and keen sense of context of the field investigator is not equally shared. Second, the approach assumes a single over-arching reality of which there is only one true interpretation most closely achieved through consensus. (Note that it is the consensus of sociologists and not that of the research subjects which is sought.) From this, it follows that one person's divergent interpretation is less valuable or more likely to be `false' than the majority view (Silverman, 1985).

3 A new approach to child placement: The diffusion of same race fostering practice

Although 'racial matching' in fostering placements has sparked off one of the most heated debates in current child care policy, at the time of the fieldwork, changes in policy and practice had been patchy. Most local authorities, however, seemed to have been moving towards matching, however reluctantly. Some had formal policies, whilst others operated less openly but with similar effects in practice. In this chapter, some of the factors which have influenced these changes are explored.

It is significant that the new moves were occurring when the second generation of black people, born and brought up in Britain, were beginning to find their political feet (Howe and Upshal, 1988). The journal, *Marxism Today*, for example, described 'the emergence in the Labour Party of a different generation of black activists who took for granted that they should organise themselves as black people' (Sept.1985: 31, cited in Solomos, 1989: 151). The seeds of change came from America (Tizard and Phoenix, 1989; Gill and Jackson, 1983; Divine, 6 and 24 June, 1 July 1983) and germinated among a small handful of black social workers, most of whom had entered the profession in the early seventies and who spearheaded a campaign for changes in policy and practice in favour of 'same race' placements.

Much of the issue's emotive appeal lies in its salience for current 'race relations' and the debate has been carried beyond the confines of purely child care issues. With the leadership of organisations like the Greater London Council and Commission for Racial Equality, ethnicity and a separate identity as *black* people have emerged as effective platforms from which to agitate for political and economic power (Banton, 1987; Gilroy, 1987)[1]. The debate about the relative importance of class, culture and colour in determining the lot of black people in Britain today is as fundamental to the mixing–matching question as are the conflicting ideological positions of assimilation, integration, pluralism or separatism[2]. In many respects, the issue has become a testing ground on which black people can flex their newly developed and developing social and political muscle. The controversy embodies the attempt of a recently established minority which has been hitherto relegated to the status of second class citizenship (Dummett and Dummett, 1982) to gain equal access to the social, economic and political power structure and to assert its right to participate in the determination of its own destiny (Ahmed, 1988). The debate represents one of several fronts on which the struggle is being waged but one which is among the most bitter because it strikes at the heart of people's self–identifications and image of the society in which they wish to live and which, because it concerns the welfare of children, is open to manipulation and confounding of the issues (Roys, 1988; Young and Connelly, 1981).

Out–facing the two faces of power: strategies for change

According to Bachrach and Baratz (1970), there are two faces of power: the first is the ability to determine the outcome of conflict; the second, to keep particular demands outside the political arena. Lukes defines a third: the ability to keep potential issues out of the political arena in the absence of observable conflict. 'What one may have here is a *latent conflict* , which consists in a contradiction between the interests of those exercising power and the *real interests* of those they exclude' (Lukes, 1974: 24–5). Until the early eighties, the issue of 'racial matching' was not a subject for debate let alone action[3] and the question which springs to mind is how members of a politically–disadvantaged and relatively powerless minority have managed to bring it on to the social work and local political agenda? William Solesbury has identified three stages in the accomplishment of change (1976: 379–397):

---

[1] Cf. the struggle over 'Black Sections' in the Labour Party (Banton 1987; Solomos 1989; *The Guardian* 14 Apr., 5 May, 3 June 1987).

[2] See Smith (1985b) for a report of the debate on transracial fostering at the National Foster Care Association's membership seminar, 15 June, and David Divine and Paul Gilroy speaking on 'File on Four', *Radio Four* 23 April 1991.

[3] In the United States the controversy had erupted at least a decade earlier (e.g. Chimezie 1977; Grow & Shapiro 1977; Day 1979).

an issue must, first, command attention, second, claim legitimacy and, third, invoke action. In this chapter, it is argued that, although the advocates of 'racial matching' were successful in achieving the first of these three objectives, they were less successful in achieving the others.

Commanding attention

The most effective strategy is to seek the attention of those in a position to effect change or, failing that, to try to influence them indirectly. The black advocates of matching were aware that they had little chance of pushing the issue on to the national social work agenda and of commanding the attention of white social workers, if they could not claim popular support among black people. Their strategy was to educate black people about the issues, to rouse their sympathy and anger and enlist their support for change, to designate responsibility for action and, finally, to outline a plan of action.

They used the channels of communication aimed specifically at a black audience or readership, for example, articles in the black press, local radio programmes with a black audience and talks at local venues such as churches, clubs, community groups, and schools and colleges attended by black students (e.g. Divine, 1984). The *Caribbean Times* was one of the first organs to adopt the 'cause' of black children in care. An editorial comment in March 1983 stated, 'We have pledged ourselves to giving the issue of black children in care a mouthpiece as it has been stifled for too long'. As Social Services Correspondent, David Divine, a black social worker, wrote a series of articles in 1982 and 1983 in an attempt to mobilise 'grass roots' support.

Appeals were also made to black social workers within the social work profession. The *Caribbean Times* heralded the launch of the Association of Black Social Workers and Allied Professions (ABSWAP) with the following exhortation:

> The black community must be involved at all levels and its professionals, collectively, must strive to wrest power from the white service structures as power is the major platform upon which racism is exercised (8 April 1983).

Divine suggests that 'black people are particularly disserviced by the existing (social service) industry' and that 'black professionals... have a particular responsibility to seek to redress this' (1 April 1983).

These moves were occurring at a time when black social workers were entering the profession in sufficient numbers to group together locally for mutual support and to call for the formal establishment of an organisation to

51

provide a specific forum for the expression of their interests (Gilroy, 1987). The outcome was the formation of ABSWAP.

> (The Association) was spawned by frustration, anger, humiliation and deep concern by black professionals about the quality and relevance of services provided to the black communities. Increasing isolation in their work place because of their limited numbers and their increasing insight into how institutions set up to help individuals are actively disserving them, forced black professionals to come together. (Divine, 14 January, 1983)

At its launch in March 1983, Paul Boateng described the newly formed organisation as being 'at the cutting edge – the interface – of an increasingly harsh and oppressive state and the black community'.

The formation of ABSWAP was critical to the success of the new approach to child placement and the organisation was launched with the issue of black children in care as its inaugural theme. The explicit aim of the first conference was to 'raise consciousness' and the 'mixing – matching' controversy provided the theme around which members of the nascent organisation could unite. The level of concern aroused, the success of its emotive appeal and its significance beyond questions of child care practice can be guaged from the attendance of over a thousand people. ABSWAP gave black social workers a unity of purpose and provided an organisational base from which the campaign could take off. For many new entrants to the profession, their new–found status as middle class 'professionals' in a 'white' organisation weighed uneasily on their shoulders and they were torn between conflicting loyalties to their white colleagues and employing agencies and to the black communities (Divine, 1st April 1983; Liverpool, 1982; Rooney, 1982; Nixon, 1983; Stubbs, 1985). The conference helped to sweep away their ambivalence by affording an opportunity both to reaffirm their group loyalty as black people and to flex the newly–developed muscles which this new position of group power had given.

The matching issue became the chosen vehicle through which this new–found consciousness of power came to be asserted and tested. The fundamental issues underlying it were at the heart of a burgeoning 'Black consciousness' with reverberrations extending beyond the narrow domain of child care practice. The founding of ABSWAP was a key development and served as a forum for the continuing construction of a new consciousness and identity. Its launch was heralded as

52

a triumph and a celebration of black potential. In tandem with other individuals and organisations in our communities it will play its part in the authentic movement towards the liberation of black people. (*The Caribbean Times*, 8th April 1983)

The aims of the conference were evident from the organisation of its proceedings. Two speakers from America appealed to a sense of solidarity with 'our black brothers and sisters in America' and, through the concept of pan-Africanism, with black people the world over. The issues were, thus, firmly rooted within the international context of global politics. The meeting opened with an emotive call for solidarity on the strength of a shared cultural heritage and common identity as an exploited people. The success of this strategy was reflected in the massive standing ovation with which this first speech was received and which set the tone for the rest of the conference. By drawing from American experience and borrowing from arguments and strategies devised and implemented in the USA, parallels were drawn with the situation in Britain. American success in achieving a policy of 'racial matching' was held up as a model for action in Britain. The 'problem' of transracial placements was firmly set within the context of racism and discrimination as the prime determinants of black people's position and status within society (Constitution of ABSWAP December, 1982); rival explanations in terms of culture or class were summarily dismissed. There was virtually no publically expressed dissent from the views propounded from the platform which clearly struck a chord with most of the audience. The atmosphere was highly charged and almost festive but, although the conference gave expression to feelings deeply felt, it served less as a forum for discussion than an exercise in consciousness–raising (cf. FitzHerbert, 1984).

As a white member of the audience, I was aware of discontented murmurings among some of the white participants and many agreed with the view of the director of the National Foster Care Association, expressed in an interview for *The Times* (Hodgkinson, 1985), that 'the new militant movement is creating sharper divisions and more racial disharmony'. By no means all the white social workers who attended, however, were hostile. Many were fired with enthusiasm and came away questionning their own approaches. The conference seems to have been the catalyst which set in motion moves towards changes in policy and practice in a number of boroughs. This was confirmed in conversations with social workers from several boroughs and by some of the comments given in the postal survey to Principal Fostering Officers which is discussed in the next chapter.

The conference manifesto (ABSWAP, 1983) set the tone for subsequent debate. Past failure to recruit black substitute families was explained in terms of a failure to take into account cultural differences:

53

Irrespective of how well–meaning the white worker is, issues to do with family patterns, lifestyles, language and culture will prevent the worker from delivering an effective service – since he/she will not only be operating in an unfamiliar territory but also in the 'white world' so far as definition and interpretation of problems and events in the client's situation is concerned (pp.13–14),

white social workers' arrogance:

There is a blatant arrogance among most social workers and line managers when dealing with black people. They often operate from very little knowledge about the black client group, but, at the same time, want to give the impression that they know it all (p.10),

and 'institutionalised racism within local authority strutures':

whereby discriminatory practices have become a structural part of the way in which the organisation functions, e.g. service provision based on mono–cultural approach (and delivered by mainly white staff) making it difficult both for the individual practitioners to offer appropriate services to black people and for black people to be involved in the delivery of services (p.10).

Black identity was defined in both political and cultural terms but it was the multi–cultural focus which formed the basis for prescriptions for changes in social work practice. ABSWAP, thus, advocated the provision of 'an ethnic sensitive service' and the appointment of more black social workers who

can use their own background to provide an effective service and pass on their experience to their white colleagues – thus creating an ethnic sensitive service (p.14).

The elision of 'race' and a supra–ethnic culture (Gilroy, 1987; Morris, 1985) which, according to Gilroy, has its political counterpart in a variety of black cultural nationalism which relies on mystical and essentialist ideas of a transcendental blackness (1987: 65 following Marable, 1981, 1984), formed the basis of a sense of solidarity between black social workers and their black clients which transcended divisions of class and professional status. The analytical separation from class, however, in terms of antagonistic and competing models of social relations provided opponents of matching policy with the weapons of attack and the two camps were drawn into supporting artificially competing explanations of social change. Kay FitzHerbert's comments in an interview for 'New Society' are an example:

The claim that black children need a black background to establish their sense of identity is 'a load of dogma'. 'Lots of black people just want the same sort of life as the middle class – but they are just poor.' (Laurance, 1983a: 499)

or those of Scrape Ntshona, speaking in a debate about transracial fostering at the National Foster Care Association's membership seminar (15 June 1985):

It is nonsense to say that because there is racism in a white society every person is racist. The class battle is the problem. Racism is an instrument used by capitalists to divide workers. (Smith, 1985b: 4; cf. Sivanandan, 1983, 1985).

Attempts to command the attention of white social workers were made through articles in professional journals and occasional talks at professional gatherings. (John Small and Shama Ahmed, for example, were two of the most prominent activists in this field.) The tone was quieter and less exhortative than in the black press since it was not easy to gain access to media controlled by white editors who were constrained to select material which would appeal to a predominantly white readership. Access to mainstream media, national newspapers, radio and television, was even more difficult. There were occasional slots as topics of marginal interest but the bulk of coverage was limited to programmes with a mainly black audience. 'Rice 'n Peas' (Radio London) and 'Black on Black' (Channel 4, 25 Feb.1985), for example, both devoted a whole programme to discussion of the issue.

The national media provided a more effective forum for opponents of the new moves than it did for its advocates and the issue was presented in terms of a controversial debate. The convention of objectivity often meant that the liberal bias of the white journalist or reporter was subtley masked (Rhodes, 1984; Small, 1986a). At other times, positions were deliberately exaggerated for dramatic interest in order to present the debate as a battle between extremists and moderates. It was all too easy to portray the more vocal proponents of the new moves as militant extremists who were callously prepared to exploit innocent children for their own political ends and to portray the white social workers who supported them as their naïve and credulous dupes (Dale, 1987; *Daily Mail*, 25 Feb.1984; Taylor, 1984: 'The London Programme', LWT 6 June; Jessel, 1985: 'The Heart of the Matter', BBC1 15 September). The high profile adopted by some black proponents provoked hostile reactions from the 'white' press. The tabloids had a field day. For them, the arguments in favour of 'racial matching' provided a fine example of reverse racism and the fact that it concerned 'innocent children' was an added bonus. Banner headlines proclaimed their righteous indignation, for example, 'Black, white – and happy: the foster mother and the super star who disprove the left's latest theory on race'[4] (*Daily Mail*, 25 February, 1984) and the more extravagant comments of the policy's advocates were taken out of context and paraded with relish (e.g. Dale, 1987). Under cover of the convention of objective reporting, the more serious media were often only slightly less loth to express their opposition (e.g. Lawrance, 1983a,b).

Similarly, specialist and professional journals provided a forum for worried social workers and white foster and adoptive parents as evidenced by the spate of letters to *Social Work Today* and *Foster Care*. In the face of limited access to the national media, proponents of 'racial matching' made use of local forums to raise the issue at a local level and their efforts were initially directed primarily to the black population, although an increasing number of articles with a black authorship began to appear in the professional journals (e.g. Ahmed, 1980, 1982, 1986; Small, 1981, 1982, 1984a, b, 1986a, b) throughout the eighties.

Claiming legitimacy

This exercise in propaganda involved the subtle manipulation of language and exploitation of emotive terminology by both sides. Whereas the black proponents appealed to wider political issues and to a sense of 'Black pride', 'consciousness' and 'solidarity' and made liberal use of the language of 'us' and 'them' in order to promote a sense of group solidarity (e.g. Divine, 18 March 1983), opponents attempted to restrict the debate to the realm of child care by defining reference to wider concerns as neither relevant nor legitimate. Dale's views, for example, are an expression of the liberalism to which many black people were so opposed:

It is clear that those black children who are denied an available white family are at least in part the victims of a political ideology. The new conceptual apparatus surrounding black children – the 'black identity', 'coping mechanisms', and so on – take their starting point, not from observed and traditionally accepted needs of children, but from a political interpretation of social reality. In imposing that interpretation

---

[4] The article was about Justin Fashnu, the English footballer, who had been brought up by white foster parents. A similar article appeared five years later in *The Mail on Sunday* (27 Aug.1989) in which his brother, John, expressed a different view: `I love my white foster parents but life would have been easier with a black family' (Lightfoot 1989).

on to the needs of children, the commonsense view of good parenting –the provision of love, stability and understanding – is being treated with contempt. It is time that the interests of individual children were returned to their primary place. Not 'children' as a collectivity, still less a 'black' collectivity but individuals with individual needs. (Dale, 1987: 34).

In this extract, Dale reasserts the conventional separation of political from social work concerns and the primacy of the individualised, child–centred model of adoption and fostering (Stubbs, 1987). The liberal view is portrayed as simple 'commonsense' while that of opponents as 'escapist' or 'extremist and doctrinaire' (Dale, 1987: 1)

For most black and white people of reason and commonsense, a 'good home' has nothing to do with its racial make–up. Unfortunately, politicians and those with an escapist fascination for all–embracing ideologies, do not necessarily consider commonsense to be a reliable guide (Dale, 1987: 35).

'Adherents to both viewpoints maintain that they have the best interests of the children at heart' (Hodgkinson, 1985) but, whereas the supporters of matching consider the child's interests as a *black* child to be inextricably bound up with his or her other interests, opponents dismiss the child's 'racial' identity as irrelevant or, at best, secondary to other needs: 'It's not colour that counts. They're all children who need love and security' (*Daily Mail*, 25 February 84; cf. Dale 1987: 26; *The Guardian*, 31 Jan.1983; *Foster Care*, 1985a). Whereas proponents unite political and moral responsibility by defining the 'plight' of black children in care as the common responsibility of all black people (Divine, 11 and 18 March 1983), those in opposition appeal to the conventional separation of child care and family matters from politics and accuse the advocates of the new moves of using 'innocent children' as pawns in an attempt to achieve their own political ends (Hodgkinson, 1985; Dale, 1987)[5]. But, as Small has pointed out, 'it is a foregone conclusion that, as a group become socially and politically active, issues surrounding the survival of the specific ethnic group will take on political overtones' (1984a: 131). The power of the arguments of the opposition lay in their conformity with conventional thinking but some white commentators have, in their turn, been prepared to make use of political prejudices by equating the exploitation of

---

[5] 'I believe that developing child care issues into the political arena is dishonest – what we're doing is letting a political theory determine the development of a child.' (Bayliss, quoted in Smith 1985b:4).

innocent children with leftwing politics (*Daily Mail*, 1985; Taylor, 1984; Dale, 1987. See Rhodes, 1984 for criticism).

The argument also relates to different cultural styles. The opposed cultural and ideological methods of debate adopted by black and white people are examined by Thomas Kochmann who explains that

> (t)he black mode... is high–keyed: animated, interpersonal, and confrontational. The white mode – that of the middle class – is relatively low–keyed: dispassionate, impersonal, and non–challenging. The first is characteristic of involvement; it is heated, loud, and generates affect. The second is characteristic of detachment and is cool, quiet and without affect (1981: 20).

White, middle class commentators' use of more restrained language and the presentation of both sides of an argument is a cultural convention no less open to manipulation than the more direct style of the West Indian approach. Readers or listeners may be seduced into agreement with the author's or commentator's views although they have been led to believe that they have been persuaded by a careful consideration of the arguments and the evidence. In Vernon Harris's view,

> (t)o pursue the goal of open mindedness is tantamount to pursuing a mirage... The mind of an individual may indeed be open to new data, but this data is immediately integrated and modified by the set of *a priori* assumptions already held by the individual (1987: 18).

Such different approaches are open to different interpretations depending on the context. Within the 'white' context, the passion of the 'black' Afro–Caribbean style is not only out of place but illegitimate and it is all too easy to dismiss the arguments as the outpourings of hot–headed extremists on the basis of the language and style with which they are expressed and to justify the use of labels such as – 'hard–liner', 'militant', 'activist', 'extremist'. Dale, for example, writes about '"anti–racist" adoption policies pursued by extremist and doctrinaire local authorities, urged on by militant black organisations' (1987: 8). Ben–Tovim and his co–authors found a similar response in Liverpool where anti–racism became labelled as extremism. As they explain, it is not only the activities and style of the black approach but

> the content of anti–racist arguments, which is often dismissed as hysterical, outrageous or fanatical.... Anti–racism, since it challenges the prevailing norms inherent in institutional policy and practice, is thus inevitably regarded as extreme (1986: 105–6).

58

The issues were not only kept out of the forum of debate but, once admitted, were denied legitimacy. Institutional resistance to a policy of 'racial matching' has been widely reported (e.g. Ahmed 1988; Cheetham 1981b; Roys 1988) and, as Ben–Tovim and his colleagues explain, 'the respectability and apparent neutrality' of the official definitions 'have become deeply embedded in professional policy and practice' and 'serve both directly and indirectly to legitimise popular racist opinion' (1986: 105).

Naomi Connelly notes the strength of professional resistance and quotes a Director of Social Services speaking at a 1987 Study Day organised by the Association of Directors of Social Services:

> We all interpret things within our frame of reference. The more professional the training, the clearer the frame of reference and, thus, the more difficult to move (1989: 48).

The campaign in London was spearheaded by a few able, committed and even charismatic figures, among whom, John Small, David Divine and Patrick Kodikara figure prominently, and some commentators (e.g. Taylor, 1984; Hodgkinson, 1985) have even suggested that the entire movement can be attributed almost solely to the efforts of one man, John Small, who, thus, became a prime target for media hostility (Small, 1986b). The fact that these key figures were also in positions of some power (John Small headed the New Black Families Unit in Lambeth; David Divine was a Senior Social Worker in Tower Hamlets and later in Hackney; Patrick Kodicara was the leader of Hackney Council) meant that they were able to utilise the established power structure to put forward their views and to expedite changes. It is probably not coincidental that all three passed through Hackney on route to becoming the first black people to be appointed Directors of Social Services.

Invoking action

Three possible approaches to the threat of change have been suggested: (i) the search for agreement, (ii) management of the evidence and, (iii) no action (Benyon, 1984).

The search for agreement The advocates of the new approach met with hostility from several quarters, not least from white social workers who had placed black children transracially and from white foster and adoptive parents who had cared for them. In presentation of their case, one of the initial strategies for dealing with this hostility was the search for agreement. Proponents of matching attempted to divert the sense of individual blame by making it collective, the product of an institutionally racist society rather than individual racism (cf. Neale, 1987; Reid, 1985). In the words of one black teenager, 'Most white people have a little racism in them. They inherit it' (Orlebar, 1983; cf. Small, 1984b). By collectivising 'blame', responsibility for change also became collective.

The conceptualisation of racism as a collective burden led to the initiation of Racism Awareness Training (RAT), again, an American import (Katz, 1978). RAT came to be invested with a quasi–religious significance. It developed as a sort of conversion ritual from which people emerged cleansed and liberated. It was deliberately designed to be a difficult and painful process, a ritual ordeal through which more or less willing or reluctant converts had to pass in order to attain a state of raised 'consciousness'. The language of anti–racism which informs RAT has many religious overtones, is couched in terms of 'rebirth' and 'liberation' and makes explicit reference to both an in–group and an out–group, that is, 'conscious' and 'non–conscious' people[6].

The search for points of agreement led to the toning down both of the stronger claims of the advocates of 'racial matching' and of the language. Whereas much publicity was sought when seeking to command both professional and public attention and to gain legitimacy, efforts were made to keep the 'action', that is the implementation of changes, out of the limelight in a deliberate, if tacit, attempt to avoid incurring a backlash from the mainstream press and media. Even boroughs at the forefront of change kept a fairly low profile and were at considerable pains to deny that they were operating a moratorium on transracial placements in order to try to counteract some of the more rabid portrayals in the 'white' media (Small, 1986b).

Agencies engaged in greater visible consultation with black social workers in order to satisfy at least some of their critics; more moderate critics were co–opted onto working parties and committees and some proposals were at least partially implemented in an attempt to lessen the clamour for more radical changes. The details of these changes are discussed more fully in the next chapter. Such moves were both pragmatic, motivated by the desire to reconcile different and opposing groups or to avoid committing additional resources, and ideological, motivated by the desire to forestall more radical change. The responses of the national umbrella organisations representing social workers and foster parents (British Agencies for Adoption and Fostering, National Foster Care Association, British Association of Social Workers) were initially cautious. They were faced with the difficult task of trying to reconcile groups with opposing views and, at the same time, avoid alienating the

---

[6] For criticisms of this approach see Sivanandan 1985; Gurnah 1983; Jervis 1986; Alibhai 1988b; Banton 1985; Lee 1987; Owusu–Bempah 1989; Roberts 1988; *Social Work Today*, 16 Mar.1987, 11 May 1987.

majority of their members who were white. On the other hand, they were anxious to aviod being labelled as reactionary or conservative or, worse still, 'racist'[7].

Management of the evidence A second strategy employed in resistance to rapid change is *control of the type and quantity of evidence available*. The failure to collect or to publish statistics on the numbers of black and minority ethnic group children in care and on the 'racial' composition of placements (Roys, 1988; Cheetham, 1981b; Divine, 4 March 1983; Lindsey–Smith, 1979; Rowe, 1990) is an indication of how little importance was attached to the issue. It was also a product of the liberal 'colour blind' approach of the sixties and seventies (cf. Nixon, 1983), although some of those opposed to ethnic record–keeping were afraid that the figures could be abused if they fell into 'the wrong hands' (cf. Ely and Denney, 1987; Roys, 1988; Nixon, 1983). The fact that very few statistics or research findings were available meant that much of the evidence used either in support or in opposition was unverifiable or anecdotal and, consequently, subceptible to manipulation or to being dismissed as 'unscientific' (e.g. Laurance, 1983a; Dale, 1987).   Not surprisingly, since few black people have had access to research institutions, funds or resources, what little research that had been done in Britain had been carried out by white researchers working within the liberal framework of 'racial' assimilation. The only relevant research by black people was from the United States (e.g. Day, 1979; Chimezie, 1975).

The question of identity was particularly difficult to resolve (Brummer, 1988; *Foster Care*, 1986a). Before one can assert that a child's identity as a black person has been impaired, it is necessary to prove, in the first place, that a 'black identity' does exist and, in the second, that it is desirable. Neither is easily verifiable empirically since a personal identity is not necessarily a static and immutable entity and its establishment a once–and–for–all achievement

---

[7] BAAF and BASW have subsequently advocated a stronger policy line in favour of 'racially' matched placements and are, thus, at variance with the Social Services Inspectorate which warns against one particular factor, such as race, becoming a general overriding precondition in making a placement (Jervis 1990). More recently, following the furore over the removal of a black child from a white foster placement, there has been direct Government pressure, with the Minister for Health, David Mellor, warning that BAAF,s funding would be under review if it was seen to place too rigid an emphasis on 'same race' placements.

but the product of continuous interaction with the social environment[8]. 'What is so remarkable, in view of its importance,' according to Dale, 'is the paucity of effort spent on defining the term. All too often... its meaning is simply assumed and the term is used (or abused) as though it possessed a self–evidently scientific status' (1987: 14). Because it comprises political elements, it is easy for opponents to dismiss as a political ploy. Dale, for example, asserts,

> What is surely apparent is the essentially political nature of the 'black identity'... Even cultural differences between ethnic groups appear to be lost sight of in the interests of creating a political category out of blackness (1987: 17; cf. FitzHerbert, 1984; Modood, 1988a,b; Banton, 1987; Tizard and Phoenix, 1989).

Although black advocates of matching have been candid about their political aspirations (e.g. Divine, 10 December 1982, 14 January 1983; Ahmed, 1988), such aspirations have been dismissed as illegitimate. As Ahmed explains,

> In Britain, since the mid–sixties, politically conscious people of African origins (continental and the diaspora) and Asians (primarily of Indian sub–continental descent) have rejected the label 'coloured' (a dominant–society label) and substituted the term Black to proclaim and forge a political unity... Children need to be proud, not only of their culture but of their colour and race. The inadequacy of multi–cultural and anthropological approaches has been demonstrated by their failure to address issues of cultural and structural racism of British society. The term 'black' therefore has a specific political meaning in British society. (Ahmed, 1988: 9)

A second example of manipulation is the ability to *control how the available evidence is presented*. Critics of the most recent follow–up study of the British Adoption Project (Gill and Jackson, 1983), for example, have suggested that it is open to two different interpretations and that findings which could have been interpreted differently were glossed over, supressed or ignored in the text (Divine, 25 February, 18 March, 1983).

---

[8] Some of this complexity is illustrated in separate interviews with a brother and sister who were adopted into a white family ('File on Four', *Radio Four* 23 April 1991). The sister had little sense of a black identity and felt that she was 'black on the outside but white on the inside' but was quite comfortable with this identity. Her brother, on the other hand, identified himself very clearly as black and saw this as a crucial aspect of his personal development.

A third strategy is to *control which explanations are presented and which are to be considered legitimate* through control of the media – academic and professional journals, book publications and mainstream media. Rivals to the official explanations are either surpressed or discredited (cf. Ben–Tovim *et al.*, 1986). Black people's under–representation among foster and adoptive parents, for example, has been explained by their lack of interest and failure to apply rather than the failure of recruiting agencies either to encourage their applications or to approve them once they have applied (Small, 1981, 1982, 1984b, 1986a; Ahmed, 1980).

No action   Failure to act can take several forms: for example, outright rejection, delay by further investigation, or acceptance of proposals 'in principle' but failure to act by pleading lack of funds or resources. Advocation of the first course was the reaction of the tabloid press and of many white social workers and adoptive and foster parents but, as the pressure for change mounted, the call for further investigation (e.g. Gill and Jackson, 1983; Chambers, 1989; Tizard and Phoenix, 1989) came both from those who were genuinely agnostic and those who opposed the new moves. Lack of funds and resources was frequently cited as a reason for inaction (see next chapter) but this obscures the fact that the issue of implementation is essentially a question of priorities (cf. Connelly, 1989: 16)[9]. In theory, it is possible to reallocate resources, even if this means cutting existing services, although, in practice, this may prove more difficult than the creation of new services using additional resources.   The exploration of avenues to generate additional resources may, perhaps, be taken as some measure of commitment to change.
   Other excuses for inaction shifted the blame on to the shoulders of black people, themselves.   Such arguments are particularly pernicious since they promote a viscious cycle whereby, if no effort is put into the recruitment of black families on the grounds that they are not interested, potential interest is not tapped, few black families come forward, and the myth is perpetuated. Appeals to the scarcity of 'suitable' candidates make it possible to delay implementation of policy and highlight how flimsy the relationship between policy and practice may prove to be[10]. Of course, the nub of the issue lies in the particular definition of 'suitability'.   Many have argued that it is necessary to change the criteria by which suitability is evaluated (Brunton and Welch, 1983; Schroeder and Lightfoot, 1983; Schroeder, Lightfoot and Rees,

---

[9] 'If a resource is considered sufficiently essential it will usually be found' (Cheetham 1981b:50).

[10] '...by its practice you will know how a child care agency thinks: its rhetoric can be misleading' (Divine, 26 Nov.1982).

1985; Divine, 15 July 1983; Rhandhawa, 1985; Arnold and James, 1989; Small, 1984b; Ahmed, 1980). The lack of 'suitable' applicants may, thus, reflect less of any real scarcity than an unwillingness to approve black candidates. Similar arguments have been used in explanation of the failure to recruit black social workers (Liverpool, 1982; Rooney, 1982; Dominelli, 1988, 1989). Respect for the wishes of natural parents and children who do not want to be placed in a black family has also been put forward as a reason for inaction (Brown, quoted in Hodgkinson, 1985).

In sum, although those advocating 'Black parents for Black children' were successful in fulfilling the first of the stages identified by Solesbury as necessary to the achievement of change, the second and third proved more difficult. The small band of black social workers who spearheaded the campaign managed to command the attention of both social workers and the population at large but, although they were successful in claiming legitimacy among black people, especially black social workers, they were less so among the white population where their ideas were introduced into a climate of ideological hostility and presented a challenge to professional norms. Except for a few white social workers, attitudes ranged from ambivalence to open hostility. As a consequence, there has been no wholesale adoption of new policy and the implementation of changes has been patchy. This is revealed in the following chapter which examines in more detail the responses of individual boroughs.

4 Arrival on the local scene: The interpretation of ideas into practice

In order to evaluate the impact on policy and practice at the local level, a postal survey of the Principal Fostering Officers of each of the London boroughs was conducted in 1986. A copy of the questionnaire is given in Appendix 1. Although the response rate was disappointing with only 20 returned of 33 questionnaires sent out, despite reminders (see Table 5)[1], the replies reveal a range of different responses to the debate[2]. The opinions given are those of respondents and not necessarily the official view, except where explicitly stated, nor the views of other workers in the department. As the replies to the questionnaire reveal, the approach to 'racial matching' had been piecemeal, with some boroughs involved in a radical review of policy and reshaping of practice, while others had experienced little, if any, change.

---

[1] Some boroughs were making a political statement when they refused to answer the questionnaire by pleading lack of resources. Two of those most active in the introduction of changes were among those which refused for this reason. On the other hand, boroughs which had made little or no effort to introduce changes may have been disproportionately represented among non-respondents.

[2] The low response rate means that a numerical analysis would be misleading and the numbers are too low for any meaningful statistical analysis. It should be noted that a low response rate is not surprising given the controversial character of the area: direct evidence was bound to be scarce on the ground.

Table 5
Response rate

Questionnaires sent out	33
Replies	20
Refusals	5
No reply, despite reminder	8

The development of policy takes place on two levels. The first is formal and usually involves a public declaration of intent with a set of guidelines ensuring some degree of uniformity of practice and accountability to the community. Official policy, however, may be little more than political rhetoric (cf. Solomos, 1988; Connelly, 1989) or a statement of overall rationale which, in practice, leaves room for wide variation in interpretation[3]. The second level is less formal and concerns rules and guidelines in operation among colleagues but which are not usually available for public scrutiny. Some are more formal than others. They may or may not be written down and may be little more than a tacit agreement about what constitutes good practice. For these reasons, respondents were not only asked whether their borough had developed a formal policy but whether or not workers had developed their own informal policies or practice guidelines. Respondents were also asked to give their own subjective evaluations of the extent to which such guidelines were followed in practice and to outline the main changes which had occurred within their own boroughs and the main difficulties which they had encountered. The main findings of the survey are summarised in Table 6.

Formal policy and unofficial practice guidelines

Of the twenty boroughs which responded, only nine had produced official policy statements relating to the placement of black children in care, although in three more statements were in preparation. Others were ambivalent or opposed to what was perceived to be the 'political stance' of those campaigning for the abolition of transracial placements. Twelve respondents specifically reported that there was no embargo on transracial placements and seven boroughs had incorporated statements to this effect into their official policy.

---

[3] 'It is... not surprising that opinion can vary from social worker to social worker, let alone from local authority to local authority' (Divine, 22 Oct.1982)

66

Table 6
The diffusion of a new practice: a profile of the London boroughs

Borough identified by number	1	2	3	4	5	6	7	8	9	10
Official policy/guidelines re 'racial' matching	x	✓	*	x	✓	x	✓	✓	✓	x
Unofficial policy/guidelines	*	–	✓	✓	✓	*	–	✓	–	✓
– Extent of policy change	3	5	4	1	5	4	5	2	4	4
– Extent of practice change	4	4	4	3	5	5	4	3	4	3
– Relationship between policy and practice	3	4	4	–	3	3	3	4	3	2
Council Ethnic Monitoring Policy	*	x	✓	x	✓	x	*	–	x	x
Council Equal Opportunities Policy	✓	✓	✓	✓	✓	✓	✓	✓	x	✓
Black/Asian Councillors	✓	✓	✓	x	✓	✓	✓	✓	✓	x
Black/Asian social workers in Fostering and Adoption	x	✓	✓	x	✓	✓	✓	x	✓	x
Race/culture training	✓	x	✓	✓	✓	✓	✓	✓	✓	x
Plans for race/culture training	x	✓	✓	✓	✓	x	✓	x	✓	x
Race Equality or Ethnic Relations Committee[1]	x	✓	x	x	x	✓	x	x	x	x
% population from New Commonwealth and Pakistan	17.1	10.8	33.5	4.5	18.8	15.3	26.6	4.2	12.5	2.4
Political complexion of Council in 1986[1]	Lab	Lab	Con/Lab	Lib/SDP	Con	Lab	Lab	Con	Con/Lab	Con/Lab

Borough identified by number	11	12	13	14	15	16	17	18	19	20
Official policy/guidelines re 'racial' matching	✓	*	✓	x	*	✓	x	✓	x	x
Unofficial policy/guidelines	x	✓	–	✓	✓	–	*	✓	x	✓
– Extent of policy change	2	4	5	4	4	5	3	5	–	4
– Extent of practice change	2	4	5	3	4	5	4	5	3	4
– Relationship between policy and practice	4	3	–	2	3	4	2	4	–	3
Council Ethnic Monitoring Policy	✓	✓	✓	x	x	✓	x	*	x	✓
Council Equal Opportunities Policy	✓	*	✓	x	✓	✓	✓	✓	x	✓
Black/Asian Councillors	✓	✓	✓	x	x	✓	x	✓	x	✓
Black/Asian social workers in Fostering and Adoption	x	✓	✓	x	x	✓	x	✓	x	✓
Race/culture training	✓	✓	✓	x	x	✓	x	x	x	✓
Plans for race/culture training	–	✓	✓	x	x	✓	x	✓	x	x
Race Equality or Ethnic Relations Committee[1]	x	✓	x	x	x	✓	x	✓	x	✓
% population from New Commonwealth and Pakistan	15.3	25.4	–	3.6	20.3	19.8	10.7	16.9	3.8	15.1
Political complexion of Council in 1986[1]	Con	Lab	Lab	Con	Lib	Lab	Con/Lab	Lab	Lib/Con	Lab

One department, for example, stated explicitly that it did 'not want to be accused of being dogmatic on same race placements': another that 'We felt a dogmatic 'same race placement' 'stand inappropriate'; its official policy stating:

> In planning for the care of a child, its history, race, religion and culture are essential considerations, though they cannot override the need for security, which is a prime objective. The recruitment of more black foster and adoptive parents is a priority. The Department's policy will not allow a child otherwise suited to substitute family care to linger because of the lack of a family of the same race or religion. The Department does not therefore have a policy that a black child can only be placed with a black family (underlining in original).

But, although none was operating a moratorium, boroughs could be divided into those which had no official policy on 'racial matching' (8) and those adopting either a 'soft' (6) or a 'hard' (3) approach, that is, those which had merely expressed a preference for same race placements and those which had taken active measures to ensure that transracial placements took place as a rare exception. Most boroughs hedged their statements (whether formal or informal) with caveats, for example,

> An unusual feature of the (borough's) population is the existence of a large number of small ethnic groups: so that whilst racial matching will be a high priority there may be circumstances when it will be appropriate to make trans–racial placements.

For many, the question of how long it was appropriate for a child to wait for a matched placement was of prime concern (cf. Brummer, 1988), although no one was prepared to specify how long was too long. Clearly, this left considerable room for variations in interpretation in practice. What emerged was a strong commitment to family life beyond any considerations of 'racial' and cultural identity[4]. As one person commented,

---

[4] This commitment is echoed in official government pronouncements:

> We are... disturbed at the tone of some recent pronouncements on the subject and at suggestions that some adoption agencies may have over–reacted in refusing to place black children with non–black parents. If there are suitable black foster and adoptive parents, well and good: but it must be questioned, if there are not, whether such agencies are persuaded that it is better that a black child should linger in residential care than enjoy the benefits of family life. (*Children in Care*, House of Commons Select Committee, 1983, paragraph 313, p.cxxii)

Whilst race is always regarded as being a significant factor, the need to find a family for a child is always paramount, and overrides any considerations of race and culture.

In seven boroughs, this view had been enshrined in official policy. The weight given to 'racial' and cultural considerations varied considerably and, for some respondents (15), they were not necessarily important factors,

A child's racial and cultural background is taken into consideration along with many other factors when the child is placed with a family. Each child is treated as an individual and race is not always the most important factor.

Other boroughs were prepared to take a more hard line stance as the following policy declaration makes clear.

Within the services of this Council, transracial placements of children in need of substitute family care must be the exception rather than the rule ... Exceptions to this general rule should only occur in circumstances where the needs of individual children transcend the need to positively develop his/her own identity. Such exceptional placement should always involve families who live in multi-racial communities.

In at least three, there had been a tightening of social workers' accountability to the Council. One respondent, for example, reported that

Implementation of policy is to be monitored quarterly by the Social Services Committee ... exceptions must always be recorded, as must the reasons for deviating from the general premise and recorded in such a way that placements can be monitored.

In others, official policy left considerable room for variations in practice but workers on the ground were able to operate a fairly hard-line approach despite the woolliness from above. One person, for example, reported that

The Council and higher management have not been sympathetic but our unofficial policy is to offer the opportunity of same-race placement to each black child referred to us and seek to ensure this opportunity is accepted.

Some had faced opposition from the Council and had been unable to draw up official statements of policy for fear of antagonising elected members. This was the case for two of those boroughs which had pioneered developments in this field and reveals how official declarations or the lack of them do not necessarily reflect concurrent practice on the ground (cf. Connelly, 1989). In other boroughs, the gap between policy (official or unofficial) and practice was in the opposite direction.

> For the past few years it has been our unofficial policy to avoid where possible transracial placements ... So far, the existing unofficial policy has not been rigidly applied, so that when a child who has been transracially placed, comes before the Panel with a recommendation that adoption is in his/her best interests, the main consideration of the Panel is the welfare of the child, and adoption of such children by their foster parents is usually approved, unless there are grave concerns about the placement itself.

Six of the boroughs which had not produced policy statements, whether official or unofficial, were in the process of drawing up guidelines. Five respondents mentioned related changes which were in the process of being discussed, for example, 'to appoint more black staff, undertake racism awareness training, ensure equal opportunities, etc.' and three were awaiting reports from working parties. Much of the recent pressure had been to have the new changes in approach incorporated into a formal policy statement and, in at least one case, the initiative came from the Council itself. In two boroughs, there was no existing child care policy and the transracial placement issue seems to have provided the impetus which set in motion moves to draw up a child care policy. One respondent, for example, reported that 'the pressure has been to formulate a policy not to change an existing one' and another that 'there was no stated policy at all until the adoption policy and child care policy were written'.

Changes in practice

The main changes in terms of attitudes were, in the words of one respondent:

a. Acceptance of the principle of racial identity.
b. Awareness of the importance of racial identity.
c. Awareness of the need for support and guidance for children and families involved in transracial placements.

70

Others reported 'a move away from "well meant liberalism" to a more realistic, self-aware stance', 'a more sophisticated understanding ... of the different considerations in placing children of different ethnic backgrounds' and 'a recognition that cultural links and racism should be considered seriously in policy issues'. On the whole, there seems to have been much greater discussion of the issues at all levels. Thus, one person reported, 'The issue is regularly discussed at planning and decision making levels both in general and in specific child care cases'. Some changes were reported even in boroughs which received relatively few black or minority ethnic group children into care and where the issue of their placement was confronted as an exception rather than routine. One respondent, for example, reported that

> Last year we received three mixed parentage babies into care and this has raised the whole question of transracial placements. There has been a definite shift of thinking at all levels in the Children's Division.

As a result of these changes in attitude, mixed placements were reported to be much less common:

> Transracial placements were made commonly until a couple of years ago – generally because the racial mixes encountered in the borough are hard to match. Practice is now more assertive in seeking a good match for the child's race, religion and culture.

Changes in practice included:

a.   advertising in the black and ethnic press;
b.   improved links with black and ethnic minority communities;
c.   a more rapid response to applications;
d.   better links with other agencies;
e.   the training of workers in 'racial' and cultural issues;
f.   the recruitment of social workers from black and minority ethnic groups;
g.   greater appreciation of their skills;
h.   the differential treatment of black applicants.

Differential treatment was mentioned by three respondents. Two reported that they tried to ensure that, wherever possible, black families were assessed by black staff. One reported that the borough was moving towards separate black and white information meetings and preparation groups and another that preferential attention was given to applications from black people. Most authorities, however, seemed chary of initiating differential treatment and one

71

respondent explicitly stated that it was thought 'inappropriate to treat black applications differently from white'. Attention was drawn to the positive results of the changes in terms of the wider choice of black and ethnic minority families available and, in one case, a surplus was reported. Another person noted that 'disruption of black teenagers in black families is two and a half times less than for white teenagers in white families'.

Pressure for change

Respondents were also asked whether their department had been under any recent pressure to change policy and, if so, what the main sources of pressure had been. Those boroughs with significant concentrations of people from black and minority ethnic groups were likely to have experienced the greatest pressure for change (cf. Divine, 25 March, 1983).

The local population

The main influence seems to have been felt in terms of the numbers of black children received into care, in other words, in terms of the perceived size of the problem. Respondents from boroughs where there were low concentrations of black people specifically mentioned this factor as a reason for not having introduced changes. A few Fostering Officers and social workers reported that some black natural parents had expressed a wish for their children to be placed in black families but more often the opposite wish was reported. Only one person mentioned pressure from black foster parents, themselves[5].

Four respondents referred to pressure from black community groups, often exerted indirectly via the Council or political lobbies. One, for example, commented, 'We have a strong and efficient political lobby from the ethnic minority communities'. In other instances, the pressure seems to have been more direct. In some boroughs, social workers had been encouraged by their greater contact with black groups which had exposed them to the views of the black community. The process of change was, thus, self-reinforcing. As one person explained, 'The greater awareness within the black community of the issues and their positive response has encouraged us in our efforts'.

Pressure from community groups, however, is largely dependent on the organisation of the groups within the local area, their political activity and their access to elected members and to social services personnel (Ben Tovim *et al.*,

---

[5] This should not be surprising in view of the fact that, until the changes in ideas and practice had taken root, few boroughs could boast many, if any, black foster or adoptive parents.

72

1986). Where black organisations had no tradition of contact with Council Members or with the Local Authority service structure or where the Social Services Department operated relatively independently of Council influence and had little, if any, contact with local black organisations, the opportunities to exert pressure were limited.

Political influence

This seems to have varied considerably (Table 7). In one borough, there was 'a great deal of political pressure from the Council to change the policy' which 'generated a lot of ill feeling'. More often, both social workers and Council Members were in agreement. One person, for example, commented,

> Whilst there obviously is a political element in this ... I do not think the decision about the change of policy is political, in that it has the commitment of the professionals within the Department.

Table 7
Models of change

1.	Change imposed by Council in face of opposition from social service department.
2.	Both Council and Social Service Department in accord with the lead taken by the Council.
3.	Both Council and Social Service Department in accord with the lead taken by the Social Service Department.
4.	Change initiated by Social Service Department independently of Council.
5.	Change initiated by Social Service Department independently of Council but in face of known opposition.

In two instances, social workers had quietly developed their own policies and unofficial guidelines in the face of known opposition from Council Members and/or higher management but, in at least one case, the situation had resolved itself as the Council was won round to the new approach. Eight respondents reported 'no pressure from the Council, political or otherwise' and considered that the initiative had come 'entirely from practitioners'. Ten respondents, however, admitted to some political pressure but the degree which was felt to have been exerted varied from borough to borough. Seven thought that the impetus for change had come mainly from practitioners within the Department, especially from black social workers. Three attributed a greater role to the Council and/ or to lobbying from community groups.

Four factors seem to have been particularly important in respect of Council influence: the political persuasion of councillors, the presence of social workers on the Council, the presence of black councillors and lobbying from black and minority ethnic organisations. In some boroughs the political climate provided a favourable nurturing ground for the development of new policies as the following comments illustrate:

> The new Labour Administration has a large majority; after years of Liberal/Tory hung Council, this will make an impact and we anticipate a greater discussion in this area as to the needs of the ethnic minorities themselves.

> Until April '86 there was little political interest. This changed in April and we have a much larger proportion of young radical Labour people returned, many of whom are on the Social Services Committee and are social workers or equivalent. The whole climate is changing but this is only recently.

In each case, it was either the support for a new policy and pressure to introduce change of Labour councils or the opposition and inertia of Tory– and Liberal– controlled councils which was referred to. A policy of same race placement has been associated with 'leftwing' politics (Taylor, 1984; Dale, 1987; *Daily Mail*, 25 Feb.1984; Hodgkinson, 1985; Kerridge, 1985; Morris, 1986) and one commentator has even suggested the operation of a 'domino effect' whereby boroughs become contaminated by their more socialist and radical neighbours (Taylor, 1984). In the example quoted above, the presence of social workers on the Social Services Committee was considered to be a significant development in terms of changes in child care policy. The initiative seems to have sprung from the social workers and to have been exerted via the elected Council. Three respondents specifically mentioned the influence of black councillors and/or the activities of an Ethnic or Race Relations Adviser, Ethnic Minorities Forum or equivalent. Prior concern with racial and ethnic issues is likely to have created a climate of opinion within some boroughs which may have predisposed them towards the adoption of a placement policy of 'racial matching'.

Social workers

In most boroughs, the main impetus for change seems to have come from social workers. One or two workers who are committed to a new approach can effectively initiate changes by 'converting' their immediate colleagues. Their effectiveness will be influenced by their positions in the organisational hierarchy, the power which they are able to exert as individuals and the way in which control over resources is organised. In at least two instances, the impetus was brought in from outside, for example, from new workers. Three people mentioned a specialist group, for example, 'specialist workers in the Adoption and Fostering Sections' but, more often (14/20), the reference was to black social workers. As one respondent explained, 'Our black social workers group has gained in confidence and is applying pressure for change'. Again and again, references were made to black social workers who 'have found their voice', 'gained in confidence' and become 'increasingly involved in Working Groups etc.', in other words, to their collective organisation and higher profile as a distinctive group (cf. Connelly, 1989: 25; David Divine, speaking on *Radio 4*, 'File on Four', 23 April 1991).

In at least two boroughs, the lead seems to have come from the Adoption and Fostering Panels. One respondent, for example, reported that Panel members had stated that 'they would always try to recommend that a child is placed with a family of the same racial background when considering each child's individual needs'. Two others, on the other hand, reported that the conservative attitudes of their panel members was one of the main obstacles to change.

Several boroughs seem to have been caught up in a general momentum for change and described themselves as 'moving with the times'. Matching by skin colour and ethnicity seemed to have achieved a legitimacy within social work thinking and had become accepted as a general principle of good child care practice if not as a rigid policy. Respondents referred to 'increased awareness through public debate about transracial fostering' and 'the growing awareness within the social work profession of the issues for the child and family'. Two people referred to 'the existence of research, indicating that transracial placements were not in the best interests of the child[6], and another to 'our own observations of black children whose long term placement in white families had disrupted'.

Another significant factor was the organisation of child care services within the borough. In boroughs where central management is weak and the

---

[6] Unfortunately, specific references were not given. It is likely that an American study was being referred to as, at that time, there were no British studies which had reached this conclusion.

75

organisation of services is diffuse, it may be difficult to organise as a group to discuss and agree changes of policy and practice and to maintain the enthusiasm and commitment necessary for effective implementation. This may help to explain why some boroughs, which appeared to possess other favourable conditions, were slow to respond. In others, where adoption and fostering services were more centrally organised, social workers were better organised to develop their own initiatives. Where the fostering and adoption sections operated relatively autonomously, it was possible to effect an informal policy of same race placement independently of the views of higher management and elected members. This seems to have been the situation for at least two respondents and was also true of the borough of the case study. On the other hand, it may also have been easier to resist Council pressures for change.

Competition from other boroughs

At least three departments had been influenced by the 'demonstrable success of other agencies in finding black families', while others referred more generally to 'the general climate of change' or to 'a feeling that we ought to be moving with the times'. In addition to the impetus of example in escalating the spread of change, however, there was an element of inter-borough competition. The 'domino effect' (Taylor, 1984), referred to above, had a practical as well as a political dimension and was operative in terms of competition for potential applicants. Their stronger 'market' position enabled black applicants to choose between rival bids for their services and adjacent boroughs often found themselves competing for the same pool of potential applicants. Respondents complained of 'poaching' and 'competition for foster parents from other boroughs'. In order to attract and to retain applicants, boroughs were forced to take into account, in the development of their own approaches, the recruitment practices and terms and conditions offered by neighbouring boroughs. Competition between neighbours was, thus, a significant contribution to the general momentum of change.

The main obstacles to change

Respondents were asked what had been the main difficulties to implementing the new ideas. Once more, the value of family life resurfaced as a paramount consideration. Respondents were anxious to avoid 'the delay in placement of children where suitable families are not immediately forthcoming'. One Fostering Officer explained, 'Social workers will only wait so long to find the "right" family for a child'. Some people mentioned the preferences of children

76

and natural parents for a white family placement, while others referred to hostility from white foster parents. Others commented on the difficulty of achieving matched placements when the population of children coming into care was so ethnically and 'racially' diverse. As one explained,

> Many of our children don't come from the borough – their parents are passing through and we have a large student population of many races and nationalities which makes matching very difficult.

Another commented,

> In common with other inner London boroughs we have many children in care with complex racial parentage so the issue is not a straight–forward one of placement into an obvious ethnic minority community.

Problems in recruiting sufficient numbers of families from black and minority ethnic groups were reported, especially of short term foster parents. Problems occurred at both the initial stages of attracting applicants and at the assessment and approval stages and included 'lack of resources', 'cut–backs in services', 'lack of time to recruit specifically from minority groups', and 'failure to make contact with minority ethnic communities'.

A common complaint was the 'lack of Asian/black staff' and of 'black specialist family placement staff', in particular (cf. Connelly, 1989: 23). The following comment expressed a frustration which seemed to be general:

> I think a great many people, myself included, feel almost helpless at the size of the problem, at least without a concerted effort to obtain ethnic minority family placement and social work staff. The consequences in language development, cultural distance, and the difficulties posed in terms of rehabilitation when a black child comes into care are massive without appropriate ethnically sensitive resources.

Five respondents reported 'difficulties in the recruitment of black workers or workers with experience of working with minority ethnic communities'.

Social workers in boroughs where there was a large proportion of Asians, were particularly aware of their own ignorance of Asian cultural patterns and of the need for workers who had links with the Asian community. They tended to talk in terms of cultural difficulties and language barriers rather than in terms of racism. The changes in thinking prompted white workers to actively try to recruit Asian families and, thus, made them aware of their own shortcomings. As one explained,

It was at this stage that I became acutely aware of my ignorance of Asian cultural patterns and that a desire to recruit Asian relief parents was useless without Asian workers linked into the Asian community.

There was a distinction between those who conceived the need for black workers primarily in terms of 'a consultancy and advice–giving role' and those who believed that it was 'an impossible task for white social workers to get over the barriers of language and culture and come to terms with their own racism sufficiently to achieve the desired results'. Others conceived the problem in terms of white workers' own lack of experience and believed that this could be overcome be adequate training.

For some, the main obstacles were white workers, themselves. Respondents found it 'difficult to inspire workers with the necessary enthusiasm' and complained of 'worker apathy' and 'lack of commitment and sustained effort'. One person, for example, reported that there had been 'no sustained community based recruitment initiative'. 'Reluctance to change old ideas and practice', 'ethnocentric views', 'limited experience of black families except as clients' and 'workers' racism' (referred to in over half the replies) were also mentioned as obstacles to change. Three people also listed 'the undermining of workers' confidence', 'lack of training and feeling de–skilled without a frame of knowledge to replace the white ethnocentric teaching' and 'apprehension about being able to assess black families fairly' among the obstacles to change. Reluctance to approve certain types of applicant, for example, single adopters or working women, were reported, and, as noted above, two respondents mentioned particular difficulties with the attitudes of the Fostering and Adoption Panels.

For two people, the main obstacles were 'lack of direction from senior management' and a 'failure to produce clear policy or guidelines'. In some cases, higher management was openly hostile. One respondent, for example, reported that 'a recent consultation paper from the Director highlights the individual needs of the child and deprecates the "political" stance against transracial placement'. Such opposition, however, was often tempered by an official ethnic minorities or race relations lobby. Ambivalence or opposition from 'above', however, does not seem to have prevented movement on the ground, although it may not have been as rapid as in other boroughs where higher management and/or elected members have used their influence to impose changes. Finally, lack of progress was attributed to 'general inertia'; as one respondent remarked despondently, 'no race monitoring, no black workers, no equal opportunities policy, no energy to look for black families'.

'... patchy, piecemeal and lacking in strategy'?

A joint Association of Directors of Social Services/Commission for Racial Equality report published in 1978 characterised the response of social services departments to the existence of multi-racial communities as 'patchy, piecemeal and lacking in strategy'. The same could be said of the response during the early eighties to the issue of appropriate substitute care for black children received into care. Individual boroughs had clearly made more effort to develop a coherent strategy than others but the most common approach seems to have been a piecemeal solution of partial implementation. All but one reported some change in thinking and approach and some had incorporated beliefs about the desirability of preserving a child's 'racial' and cultural identity into their official child care policies. Others operated at a more informal level. None admitted to a moratorium on transracial placements and most included caveats and provisos which left considerable room for variations in interpretation in practice.

The impetus for change

In the reports published in 1981 by the Policy Studies Institute of a study of a sample of authorities (Young & Connelly, 1981; Connelly, 1981), it was found that social workers believed that the most important influence on their practice was 'the experience of working with ethnic minority clients' (cf. Nixon, 1983)[7]. Such perceptions, however, furnish only a partial explanation. They do not explain why the movement towards matched placements began to gather momentum in 1983 and not 1973 or even 1963, since many social workers had been working with black and minority ethnic group clients for over twenty years. Young and Connelly also mention the importance of 'ideas and understanding derived from colleagues from ethnic minorities'. The employment of black staff, however, was, often, itself indicative of a prior change in thinking away from the liberal notion of universal provision and equality of treatment or, as Divine has termed it, the 'like it or lump it' approach, (26 November 1982) towards at least partial acceptance of differential treatment for differential cultural needs. 'Political muscle in the black communities' was not mentioned but, in Divine's opinion, 'At the end of

---

[7] In her study of a social service department, Nixon similarly found that 'it was primarily as a result of the changing perceptions and consequent actions of individual workers that recognition of ethnic minority problems and special needs began slowly to percolate upward through the department' (Nixon, 1983:155).

the day ... this will be the key factor in making "cultural pluralism" a reality' (Divine, 3 December 1982).

'Political muscle' in the black community

The political influence of the black communities, however, depends on how and where it is manifest. Young and Connelly found that the most substantial progress was in authorities where there were active black councillors. In some boroughs in the current survey, black councillors played an active but not necessarily a primary role. In some, local black organisations were active but, in the majority of cases, their influence seems to have been limited. Some departments had made efforts to communicate with local organisations and representatives in an attempt to improve the recruitment of black families but these contacts seem to have been initiated by the social services rather than by the organisations, themselves. There was no mention of consultation with the local population about the desirability of a matching policy. On the rare occasions when consultation was reported, it was to seek advice about technical details of implementation.

The few black foster parents recruited in the past do not seem to have had much of a voice. Those who were members of local groups of the Foster Care Association were far outnumbered by white members, many of whom had fostered black children and were opposed to the new moves. Such organisations were used by white members as platforms from which to voice their opposition to the changes. This occurred in the study borough and is echoed in the many letters on the subject to *Foster Care*, the magazine of the National Foster Care Association.

The influence of ordinary people seems to have been even less apparent or effective. Many among the black population are shy of involvement with the Social Services (Dominelli, 1988). Others are involved as 'clients' and are therefore in a relatively dependent and vulnerable position and unlikely to challenge social workers' practices. Respondents referred to rare occurrences when black natural parents had refused to allow their children to be placed with white families but, more often, the opposite was reported. Concern among the black population does not seem to have been widespread and one Fostering Officer specifically referred to 'lack of awareness about the issues among the black community' as one of the main obstacles to progress. Current awareness and concern is some measure of the success of campaigners to publicise the issues.

The main impetus for change seems to have come from black social workers who formed a highly vocal pressure group. Their confidence stemmed from their collective organisation, both locally and nationally, under the banner of ABSWAP, and it was primarily through ABSWAP that 'the political muscle'

80

of the black communities was exerted. The extent to which its views were representative may have been a matter of debate (see Bagley and Young, 1980 and Simon, 1978) who reported ambivalence and hostility to a policy of 'racial matching') but the organisation, nevertheless, conceived of itself as acting on behalf of black people generally (ABSWAP, 1983). Collective organisation provided the means for the co-ordination of ideas and their outward diffusion from ABSWAP at the centre to the individual boroughs through their black employees.

'White' hostility

The pace of change, however, was slow. Few boroughs had engaged in the radical policy review demanded by ABSWAP (ABSWAP, 1983) and the approach of most was cautious and piecemeal, tempered by the antipathy of white social workers and management within and by the hostility of white foster and adoptive parents without. In their study of *The Local Politics of Race* in Liverpool and Wolverhampton (1986), Ben Tovim and his colleagues argued that the failure either to formulate or to implement anti-racist policies was a consequence of the twin ideologies of labourism and universalism. The first holds to the primacy of class above race as an explanation of social inequality and regards racism as a distraction from the broader class struggle; the second advocates identical treatment for all, irrespective of background. 'Both ... are colour-blind ideologies which ultimately refuse to acknowledge the unequal effects of racism and the need to tackle it on its own terms' (1986: 171). The possibility that institutional resistance may also be, in part at least, a result of political expediency and pragmatism is largely ignored in their analysis. The electoral consequences of introducing anti-racist policies, for example, and of antagonising the white population upon whose vote a council's continued existence in office is dependent may be seen to outweigh the potential benefits for a relatively small section of the electorate (Ely and Denny, 1987; Luthra and Tyler, 1988). In Ben Tovim *et al.*'s analysis the block is generated from within the organisation rather than being a response, at least in part, to pressure from the community without.

Such considerations clearly influenced the ways in which policy was developed in many boroughs where formal statements tended to embody the soft approach to 'racial matching'. Even those strongly committed felt a need to deny explicitly that they were operating a ban on transracial placements. At the level of practice, social workers were wary of antagonising their white foster parents or of alienating the community from which the existing pool was replenished. Both Cheetham (1981b) and Young and Connelly (1981), in their studies of local authorities' reactions to 'racial' disadvantage, found that one of the most frequently stated objections to initiating programmes of differential treatment or positive action was fear of a 'political backlash' and hostility from the white population. An ADSS/CRE report (1978) similarly found that 'fears of how the majority community will react inhibits policy initiatives'.

This recognition inspired a joint government/ local authority working group report (Department of the Environment, 1983) to advise that 'It is important ... to minimise conflict by way of consultation, discussions, education and training'. Far from accepting this advice, most boroughs seem to have carried out a finely balanced juggling act between satisfying political pressure and the black social workers in their midst and avoiding antagonising the white population by keeping a low profile. Ben Tovim et al.'s analysis fails to address the relative ease of access to policy makers and ability to influence policy decisions of the white community compared with the black. Although some of the ways in which black organisations become marginalised and pushed to the periphery of political action are discussed, the relative ability of comparable white organisations to retain their positions closer to the centre (cf. Holmes and Grieco, 1988) is not addressed.

The relationship between policy and practice

Ben Tovim and his colleagues came to the conclusion that

> the presence of certain policies and the absence of others is clearly related in practice ... Existing policies and practice come to be regarded as the norm (and) their 'naturalness' can only be upset or challenged effectively through policy intervention (1986: 172; cf. Pearson, 1989)[8].

The relationship between policy and practice, however, is not always one of exact correspondence (cf. Liffman, 1978; Divine, 26 November 1982; Solomos, 1988). The evidence presented in this chapter suggests that effective change can be achieved at lower levels within an organisational hierarchy without waiting for the lead from higher management or the Council (cf. Payne, 1979; Nixon 1983) or even in the face of known opposition (cf. Young and Connelly, 1981). Lack of a formal policy on matching, for example, did not mean that there had been no changes in practice. It was possible for workers to develop their own informal practice guidelines independently of the influence of higher management or elected members and to adhere to these more rigorously than to any formal policy (cf. Connelly, 1989). Alternatively, the aims of a formal

---

[8] Roy Pearson, from the Social Services Inspectorate, expresses a similar view: 'without a widely publicised written policy there (is) little chance of making substantial progress in providing ethnically sensitive services' (1989:13).

policy can be effectively sabotaged by workers in the field (cf. Nixon, 1983). Indeed, Nixon reports 'a natural antipathy' among social workers 'to proposals and directives which emanate from central management' (1983: 153).

Although the link between policy and practice may be fuzzy and change may occur in the absence of a policy initiative, it is, nevertheless, unlikely that it will be sustained without some form of policy directive. The strength of correspondence will be largely dependent on the degree of control which workers are able to exert over resources and methods of working and the strength of lines of accountability. The opportunities for sabotage can be reduced, for example, by a requirement that the reasons for not placing the child in a family of the same race be reported directly to the Council.

The lower down the hierarchy of the decision–making structure, the more effective such policy directives are likely to be, since 'the greater the number of links in the implementation chain, the more likely are divergences in practice to arise' (Young and Connelly, 1981: 158). As Young and Connelly point out, 'development is ... by no means universally imposed in a "top–down" fashion'. In common with the present study, they found that 'many important changes (were) initiated at the level of practice'. Sometimes, these were 'passed up to senior management to be elaborated or ratified at the policy level': at others, they were developed 'in the face of an apparently unsympathetic policy climate' (1981: 158; cf. Nixon, 1983; Payne, 1979).

As will be argued in the following chapters, the relationship between policy and practice is a complex one. The official statement of a principle does not guarantee appropriate behaviour (cf. Connelly, 1989). Smith and Cantley (1985) have argued that organisations themselves do not have goals, only their participants and that goals may differ between different participants, for example, between managers, service providers and clients. According to Richard Pinder, 'Social work practice is at the centre of a highly political process, in which workers are called upon to mediate between a variety of interests' (October 1980: 2). The demands of managing face–to–face interactions with clients may prove stronger determinants of social workers' behaviour than commitment to formal agency policy and the practical considerations which constrain practice for the individual worker are not necessarily the same as those for the administrator and policy maker (cf. Young and Connelly, 1981: 158).

Conclusion

As this chapter reveals, the development of policy concerning the placement of black children in substitute family care and the responses to it in practice have been variable and patchy, dependent on local conditions and personnel rather than any uniform process or common strategy (cf. Pearson, 1989; Connelly, 1989: 20)[9]. The pace, pattern and scope of change varied from borough to borough, with each borough acting relatively independently and little inter-borough communication or co-ordination (cf. Divine, 1988). Despite this, a number of common themes emerge which were also characteristic of developments in the study borough.

The first was the importance of the 'racial' and ethnic composition of the local population in terms of

a. the perceived size of the problem, ie the numbers of black and minority ethnic group children received into care and
b. the opportunities for 'racially' and ethnically matched placements in terms of the size and composition of the foster parent pool.

Several respondents reported that attempts to achieve ethnic as well as colour matching were frustrated by the ethnic variability of the local population. The ethnic and 'racial' composition of the local community was also a significant factor in transracial placements where there was a requirement for the family to live in a multi-racial area or to have social and/or kinship links with the child's ethnic community of origin.

A second geographical factor was the stimulus of proximity to other boroughs which had introduced changes, both in terms of example and in terms of competition for the same pool of potential applicants[10]. Another was the structure and organisation of fostering services: whether centrally-based or dispersed throughout area-based services. Central organisation and structures of information diffusion were important locally in terms of

a. policy development and gaining acceptance of the new ideas among colleagues and
b. co-ordinating implementation and gaining access to the black community.

A notable feature of developments in many boroughs was the impermeability of the Social Services Department to influence from the local community and

---

[9] 'A reactive *ad hoc* approach is all too typical of the general failure of our personal social services institutions to adapt their activities to the reality of a multi-racial society except in times of crisis.' (Pearson 1989:282).

[10] Informal networks operating across borough boundaries provided channels of communication for a flow of information about neighbouring borough practices. This enabled foster parents and potential applicants to exert a measure of choice in deciding to which borough they would offer their services.

the internal germination of change in ideas among practitioners and autonomous development of policy virtually independently of input from the local community. The influence of black social workers' collective organisation through ABSWAP was crucial and enabled the central co-ordination of ideas and their outward diffusion to individual boroughs via their black employees.

The introduction of change, however, was into a conservative climate of professional resistance from white social workers and hostility from the white community. Fear of a 'white' backlash in terms of (a) the possible electoral consequences and (b) the alienation of white foster parents provoked a cautious response in many boroughs. A culturalist rationale predominated. The 'problem' of black foster parent recruitment was interpreted in terms of cultural difference rather than socio-economic considerations. 'Race' was elided with culture and racism interpreted in terms of ethnocentrism and ignorance of other cultures rather than the structural relations of relative power. This brief portrayal of the London scene provides the backdrop against which the response of a single borough will be examined in more detail in the following chapters.

5 Discussing the details: Consciousness-raising within the Fostering Team

The previous chapter set the scene London–wide and provides the context against which the development of policy in a single borough is examined using social workers' verbal accounts. Within the borough of the case study, the new policy was developed more or less autonomously within the Fostering Section. The strategy employed among practitioners can be summed up as 'quiet consciousness raising' and the management of consensus. The result was a process of incremental change with the emphasis on 'flexibility' and 'balance'. The new approach emerged through negotiation and compromise rather than through direct challenge and the endorsement of a single clear policy. There were no clear winners or losers. At the time of the research, no coherent, concrete policy had been drawn up and formalised and policy decisions were, therefore, vulnerable to renegotiation, adaptation, revision and erosion. There are two levels, however, of acceptance of a new ideas and/or new policy: first, at the level of practitioners and, second, at the level of the community, yet the new approach was developed without a firm grounding in community support. It was introduced into a climate of ambivalence and hostility and imposed with little or no consultation.

The borough had many of the ingredients favourable to the promotion of change: both geographical – a significant black (mainly Afro–Caribbean) population and a disproportionate number of black children received in to care[1], structural – a centrally organised adoption and fostering service, and political – an Equal Opportunities policy, an Ethnic Relations Adviser and Ethnic Minorities Forum. It also had a Labour–controlled council which included several black councillors. Despite these factors, the influence of the local population and of the Council appears to have been minimal. Social workers in the Fostering Team were in unanimous agreement that the main impetus for change came from within the Team.

PR   Was there any pressure from the Council to make changes?

SW3 No, no, the reverse! Changes were already taking place before there was any pressure from the Council.[2]

SW4 I think, no–one else is doing anything about it apart from Fostering. I mean, there's been nothing. Nothing has come from above at all. There's a growing awareness and we involved the Race Relations Adviser a year ago in starting to look at what we should be doing because we felt there was a need. But it came from us rather than the other way about.

There was a general lack of awareness amongst workers about Council policy concerning ethnic relations.

SW4 This borough is fairly backward for a London borough which has a large black population.

PR   Why do you think that is?

SW4 I haven't the faintest idea. (laugh) Erm... I really don't know. It's strange, isn't it? I suppose it's something to do with the Council. I mean, I'm not terribly political. I mean, I'm not really aware of what the Council has been saying in the past years. I'm not quite sure what the Council are saying now, to be honest ... I don't know why because they seem to be fairly aware, generally. And they've had the odd Black Day, haven't they? But, somehow, policies just haven't been stated.

An enthusiastic Ethnic Relations Adviser and an active Ethnic Minorities Forum, however, significantly contributed to the pressure for reform.

---

[1] Children in care – quarter ending December 1983

British White	359	West Indian	161	Mixed	75
Other White	10	Other Non–White	42		

[2] Social workers are identified in the text by number.

87

Factors affecting acceptance within the Fostering Section

The structure of fostering services in the borough

The central organisation and autonomous operation of the fostering services clearly facilitated the introduction of changes. The foster parent pool was controlled by the Fostering Section independently of workers in the District Teams. The fostering social workers were responsible not only for placements but for the recruitment of foster parents and maintenance of the foster parent pool. The separation of services for fostering from services for adoption meant that the number of people who needed to be 'persuaded' in order for the new approach to be implemented was fairly small and the further subdivision of the Fostering Section into various teams meant that limited implementation could be achieved within even smaller units. In practice, there was considerable liaison between the different teams in the Fostering Section and some evidence of the operation of a 'domino effect', with one team following the lead of another. Communication with the Adoption Section, however, was surprisingly limited.

Working under the same roof, social workers from the Fostering Section were able to exert continuous pressures of persuasion and mutual encouragement. The large number of part-timers made this somewhat more difficult than had all the workers been full-time but much less so than had they been dispersed among the District Teams. The Section's central location and physical separation from area-based services meant that contact with social workers from the District Teams was limited. As a result of their physical separation, the fostering workers were able to control communication with and the flow of information to the outside world. They were able to develop their own policies and, to a large extent, to implement them without interference from the rest of the Social Services Department. There was thought to be little necessity for consultation or need to persuade those outside of the desirability of change.

The role of individuals

The role of individuals in promoting a change in both attitudes and practice appears to have been crucial (cf. Nixon, 1983; Young and Connelly, 1981: 94–5). Three social workers seem to have been the key instigators, two of whom were relatively new members. The new workers were less strongly socialised to the Team ethos and habituated to conventional Team practice, had formed less strong social and working relationships within the Team and were, consequently, less concerned about upsetting other workers than their longer–serving colleagues. Their status and position within the Team was less firmly entrenched and they may, therefore, have been less concerned about 'rocking the boat'. In addition, there seemed to be a general acceptance that new members come in with new ideas.

The unique role of individuals in the accomplishment of change (Weber, 1978) and the extent to which the new moves were the outcome of a fortuitous set of circumstances rather than emerging 'naturally' from conditions which would have evolved into the present independently of the individuals concerned are difficult questions to unravel. To what extent had outside pressures and the general climate of change set up a momentum which inevitably swept up the borough in its path? Was the Team being forced into a position whereby it became untenable to maintain previous policy and practice? Or was the impetus for change generated primarily from within? Opinions within the Team were confused. Although most wanted to believe in their own radicalism and instrumentality as agents of change, there was also a strong sense of 'moving with the times' and an awareness of the changing policy climate within London as a whole. According to at least one member of the Team, fear of a backlash from within the ranks of the social work profession, itself, was a strong motivating factor.

SW5   I think it's a nucleus of people within the Team (who were the main instigators of change) plus a fear of being criticised by other boroughs.

Although there was still hostility, 'racially' matched placements had gradually become more widely accepted. This change in the climate of opinion was due, in part, to the high profile of those campaigning for change, the practical success in finding black families of new initiatives such as the New Black Families Unit (Arnold and James, 1989) and of boroughs like Wandsworth (Brunton and Welch, 1983) and Ealing (Schroeder and Lightfoot, 1983), and increasing acceptance of the legitimacy of the concept of 'identity confusion' amongst transracially placed children. The influence of individuals was felt, perhaps, not so much in terms of the direction as the speed of change.

The personal motivations of the three principal activists varied according to their different personal biographies and experiences. One (SW1) explained that she had previously worked in a 'more progressive borough' where ethnic and 'racial' issues were accorded a high priority. Another claimed that her attendance at the ABSWAP conference on 'Black Children in Care' was the turning point: 'It had a major influence on me. It really made me realise how important this was as an issue' (SW3). The third (SW5) seemed to have been motivated partly by the general climate of change within the more radical boroughs, by the mood of anger among black social workers at the ABSWAP conference which she had attended (although she expressed reservations about some of the speakers' pronouncements: 'They had a right to be angry but some of it I just couldn't go along with') and by her increasing involvement with black people. 'As I became more involved in this area of work', she explained, 'and began going out to see existing black foster parents and applicants, I became more aware of the problems. My interest came with the work. As I became more involved, I became more committed.'

Strategies for change

Commanding attention

The strategy of individuals within the Team was deliberately low–key and designed to avoid head–on confrontations.

SW3　We didn't approach it head on. We didn't antagonise or confront people in a hostile way. It was just quiet consciousness raising. We were deliberately low key. We tried to raise it as a valid issue *before* raising ructions and I think it has paid off very well.

Relevant issues were raised unobtrusively at Team Meetings or brought to the attention of colleagues by putting items of information in their in–trays and by drawing their attention to recent journal articles.

One of the most vocal advocate of change set the tone for a meeting, at which the recruitment of black foster parents was on the agenda, by circulating an account of her own personal struggle with the issues[3]. This was one of the

---

[3]　*Vetting families from different cultures*

These are some of the difficulties I have encountered.

1. I have very little idea of what daily life might be like in countries that I know little about, so I find it hard to make sense of what I have invited people to tell me about their childhood and early years.
2. I know little of the expectations there are of both children and adults in societies outside my own. Does the eldest child in an Indian family have a special role? What are the different aspects of sex role etc. Who looks after whom?
3. Class/caste in other cultures – Do we have any ideas of where the family we are vetting fits in their home culture? Does it matter?
4. What is the perception of me as a white person with power in a specific issue – I get confused about this and my responsibilities.
5. Knowing few people from other cultures well, how on earth do I assess what is a cultural difference – say in attitudes to child care, and how it is carried out and who does it – and what is simply the way that the family operates? Does it matter that I can
(continued...)

90

very few occasions when questions of racism and power were raised. By admitting her own difficulties and weaknesses, she made it possible for others to accept gaps in their own skills and abilities. The account raises the notion of 'unconscious racism' and the sharing of collective guilt. Workers feared that a more assertive and confrontational approach would have risked being labelled as 'trouble-makers' or 'extremists' and having their views dismissed as too 'radical' or 'extreme'. It was thought that direct confrontation would have resulted in difficult and anguished scenes which would have risked alienating many members of the Team. Many of those interviewed attested to the painful process of confronting their own prejudice and of coming to recognise the deficiencies of their past practice. As one explained,

SW3 It's not easy realising that you may have acted in a racist way in the past and coming to accept your own prejudice. You have to come to terms with your innermost feelings and it can be very painful.

A more effective strategy was thought to be to try to persuade colleagues of the value of the new approach and to let them come to recognise their prejudice and deficiencies of their own accord and in their own time without coercion or confrontation. It was believed that they would be more likely to be convinced if allowed to come to their own conclusions without feeling pressurised into changing their ways.

Claiming legitimacy: consensus management

In order to claim legitimacy for the new approach, concrete evidence in the form of statistics on numbers of transracial placements within the borough was collected. This proved to be a much more arduous task than originally envisaged and those who undertook it felt embittered by the fact that the data eventually collected were not treated with the seriousness which they believed the effort to collect them had warranted.

---

[3](...continued)
never be sure?
6. How do I sift out racist attitudes I didn't even know I had from `professional judgement'?
7. Is it fair to take a long time over a vetting because of doubts about these things if I'm going to reject the family at the end?

91

SW3   We began to look at statistics in (the borough). (My colleague) and I
       literally spent days on it. But it was the only way. I felt it was a very
       bad use of social work time. It wasn't what we should have been doing
       but it was literally the only way to get them to realise how serious this
       issue was (in the borough). But it didn't come to much and that made
       us feel very bitter.

Appeal was also made to articles in official journals and by reference to
research. A trawl through the Team Meeting Minutes revealed that it was
invariably the same individuals who raised matters concerning ethnicity and
colour and who drew the Team's attention to relevant articles in the social
work journals. Another important factor was the ability to enlist the early
support of the Team Leader.

Those members wishing to promote change were constrained by the
prevailing ethos within the Team. The principal strategy for managing
working relationships was one of maintaining consensus, however fragile or
illusory, as opposed to resolution of conflict through direct challenge. Conflict
was considered pathological and to be avoided wherever possible (cf. Holmes
and Grieco, 1988; Burrell and Morgan, 1979). The following worker spoke
for the majority when she explained,

SW4   I would hesitate to have a policy, personally. I mean, if you make it
       (same race placement)   a policy, then it almost becomes divisive
       because it becomes too rigid. It is important to avoid conflict.

Policy, consequently, tended to be vague and flexible rather than firmly
clarified, leaving considerable room for variations in interpretation. The
emphasis was on points of consensus rather than conflict. Votes were rarely,
if ever, taken when policy decisions were made but disagreements were often
so wide that it was difficult to regard some decisions as the result of either
consensus or even compromise. What seemed to be operating was an implicit
agreement at least to display, if not adhere to, a consensus approach (cf.
Liffman, 1978). The importance of team cohesion and team functioning
superceded that of team policy.

This working ethos of consensus management as opposed to open challenge
meant that the evolution of policy was a gradual incremental process rather
than clear jumps from one approach or position to another. Policy and practice
were re-evaluated and revised in the light of changing ideas about the
placement of black children and in response to situations as they arose in
practice.

SW5 It was a gradual thing. I mean, as I started going out to meet existing black foster parents, applicants and community workers, it became clear that we needed to be more flexible if we were going to have sufficient black applicants and so, every time a piece of advice was given and it was brought back to the Team, we discussed it and things were changed – like religion, that was raised, and ways of assessing.

There were times when the Team as a whole discussed the issues but no single occasion when policy was comprehensively reviewed and firm guidelines drawn up and agreed. This piecemeal, incremental development has been noted by other observers (e.g. Young and Connelly, 1981; Cheetham, 1981b; Ely and Denney, 1987; Liffman, 1978). New elements were accrued gradually rather than resulting from an overall policy review or direct confrontation between conflicting approaches. Although members believed that there had been a radical change of direction, it was not possible to pinpoint a precise turning point.

The consensual approach, however, masked a simmering discontent but, as one social worker explained, this had never reached a head and erupted into the open.

SW5 I think there's been a stark contrast between those of us who wanted to move on much quicker than others and there's been a lot of impatience in Team Meetings. I think there's been a quiet rebellion. There's not been an open kind of thing but there's been sort of quiet apathy on the part of some people.
PR Would you describe it as a split?
SW5 No, I don't think I'd put it quite that way. No, I think those of us for whom this is the highest priority just go ahead and do it, really. But, it has often not been easy. There's sometimes been quite a lot of opposition to some things, really.

In other words, public consent or conformity masked a latent opposition which was expressed as 'a sort of quiet apathy'. It was easier to present a face of public conformity than to express open disagreement and decisions taken at Team Meetings were not necessarily, or only partially, translated into practice. Significantly, perhaps, those least committed to and most ambivalent about the new approach were the least likely to admit the existence of any serious discord within the Team.

The emphasis on issues of child care as opposed to the political implications of the new approach appeared to be consciously engineered. Certainly, most of the workers interviewed were as reluctant to address the political implications of the new moves as they were eager to point out that their enthusiasm was not, as they saw it, politically motivated. Members' conception of their role as non-political conformed with the widely held notion in social work that political goals are illegitimate (e.g. Dale, 1987).

Invoking action: Race Awareness Training

An attempt to achieve a more formal declaration of policy was made through race awareness training (RAT). Advocates of the new approach campaigned for RAT in the belief that it would provide the impetus for a clear declaration of commitment from the Team but, as one of them explains below, their efforts met with initial opposition.

SW3   In September 1983 we had a Joint Team Day (with the Adoption Team) at which we asked for a racism awareness course. (The Team Leader) told us that it was Council policy not to have one. But that was not true. Council policy was on the point of changing. We have worked consistently since then to have a course ... You know, we nearly didn't have the RAT and it took considerable pressure from four or five people to make sure it did happen. It could easily have been left and it was very much down to individuals whether it was run or not. The Team wasn't asked. There was just informal consultation with individuals and it needed very forcible expression of opinion that RAT was necessary. But the Team was not consulted.

RAT, they believed, would be the crucial turning point and agitation for RAT became the focus for their energies.

SW3   I think it is important for everyone to go (on a RAT course) because we need to work as a team. We have to work as a political unit. The aim is to change policy.

This concept of the Team as 'a political unit' was alien to many of its members, especially those longest serving, and it is significant that these words were spoken by a newcomer from a fairly radical and politically motivated department in another borough. At first sight, the RAT course, which was held in January 1985, seemed to have been successful in fulfilling expectations and stimulated the Team to produce the following manifesto or statement of goals:

1.   'Same race' placement policy by end the of 1985.
2.   Continuation of the advertisement campaign for black families until numbers reflect the number of black children coming into care.

94

3. Any new job vacancy in Team should be filled by a black applicant until there are at least 40 per cent black workers.
4. A revolution in recruitment and vetting programme as a priority above other work.
5. More regular meetings.

As one worker explained,

SW3 Out of the course came the current policy of same race placements.
PR   The Team had been moving in that direction before that, hadn't it?
SW3 Yes, but it was only after the course that it became a clearly stated policy.

Only later, when the hollowness of the Team's commitment was exposed by subsequent failure to follow it through, did it become clear to workers that their naïve faith in the efficacy of RAT to generate sincere commitment to change was misplaced. Within weeks, each of the stated goals had been eroded or discarded, resulting in disappointment and disillusionment. The first vacancy to arise, for example, went to a white worker[4].

One social worker confided her opinion that, although the course had 'pushed the Team towards a more effective policy' and 'made us aware of how little we'd really done', the aggressive confrontational style of the course leader had been counterproductive. By antagonising many members of the Team, it had ignited a resentment which had been smouldering for some time.

SW8 The course leader was quite aggressive and that put people's backs up and they became very defensive which was a bit unfortunate ...I also think that there is a little bit of er... rebellion that was begun then, that, well, there are other issues as well, like the fact that the Team was not consulted and not just the black issue.

Her opinion was confirmed in conversations with several Team members who objected to what they considered to be the course leader's aggressive and domineering aproach:

----

[4] SW4 There was discussion of a locum post and whether or not it would go to a black worker. It was felt that it should but already some members felt that it should go to a white person. It's a good example of how policies can be eroded. There was a Team decision for all vacant posts to be filled by black people until we reached a target of 40 per cent black members ... A worker is going on maternity leave and it was felt that, because it is a locum post, it should be a white worker and an approach has been made to someone who has worked in the Team in the past and that is the sort of thing that happens unless policy is made very clear.

SW4 I think it was more aggressive and negative than it might have been. I think there are better ways of handling it, personally. I think that I could have been made equally aware without it being quite so aggressive. She was particularly aggressive. She was very aggressive about the white power bit, you know.

SW6 She was very controlling and very much wanted agreement with everything she said. If you didn't agree with her, then you were racialist. I don't think she was very subtle about it. In fact, I think she more or less said, you know, 'That's it!', you know, (laugh) 'You're just not understanding what I am talking about because of what you are'. She was very reluctant to be interrupted too. If you disagreed, she didn't like it. She wanted it to go the way she wanted it to go.

and the strong political overtones of the course:

SW7 She dragged it all onto a political level which wasn't always necessary.

Others were more apologetic:

SW8 I'm not ready to start getting on a political horse (nervous laugh) because it isn't, I don't feel it's me.

RAT proved to be a double–edged sword. It is likely that the course, although, on the one hand, galvanising the Team into producing a clear, if hastily conceived, statement of objectives, on the other, stimulated a crystallization of the opposition. The lack of consultation, compulsory attendance, the course leader's aggressive and coercive style and the high profile which the course had lent to the 'Black campaign' aroused resentment amongst members who were not actively involved and who felt that other issues and their own concerns were being neglected. This was the platform upon which they mounted their opposition and which contributed to the disbanding of the Black Action Group (BAG) only weeks after its inception. The failure of the BAG is examined in more detail in the next chapter.

The Team policy of separating tasks and clients into distinct categories not only bracketed them off from mainstream activity but drew them into mutual competition for resources. The setting up of 'The Black Campaign' and, later, the 'Black Action Group' as distinct activities separate from the rest of the Team's work rather than an attempt to incorporate a 'black' perspective into all mainstream work excited jealousies and resentments. Although these tensions and conflicts revolved overtly around the issue of resources, this masked a deeper disquiet about the pace of change and the fundamental tenets of the matching rationale. The tacit commitment to consensus meant that confrontation was largely confined to the forum of RAT where confrontation between those with opposing views was subverted into personal confrontation with one's own prejudice. Dialogue was effectively suppressed.

Factors affecting acceptance within the local community

Simply to seek publicity, regardless of where it is directed, may be not only inefficient but detrimental to a cause. It may be as important to avoid the attention of specific groups as it is to command it of others.

Hostility from white foster parents

Social workers anticipated hostile reactions to a policy of matched placements from white foster parents, many of whom were fostering or had fostered black children in the past (cf. *Foster Care,* January 1985a,b September 1986a). They were faced with the dilemma of wanting to introduce changes which they knew would excite antagonism but, at the same time, not wanting to alienate existing foster parents nor discourage potential recruits from applying. Although there was limited consultation with black foster parents, there was little or none with white foster parents.

PR   Was there any sort of consultation with the community, for example, with community groups or foster parents?

SW9 Well, (my colleague) consulted black foster parents when she began to run her campaign. There was some with black foster parents but not with white. White foster parents were not consulted.

Discussions and conversations with white foster parents during taped interviews in their homes, meetings of the local Foster Care Association, training courses, Information Meetings and a variety of other occasions during the course of fieldwork revealed, at best, ambivalence towards a policy of 'racial matching' and, at worst, open hostility. Social workers corroborated these accounts from their own interactions with white foster parents.

The local Foster Care Association opposed the new moves, as was evident from the letters in its monthly news sheet. It provided the main forum for white foster parents to express their opposition and it was not easy for black members, who were in a small minority, to express dissent from the majority view[5]. As one social worker explained,

SW3 White foster parents will lose an image of themselves as helping the black community and therefore thinking of themselves as OK. They feel that they are being told that they are not good enough – which, of course, they are – and that work which they have done in the past is now being invalidated. As you probably know, there has been considerable hostility towards the way we are moving amongst many white foster parents. It does challenge all of us. It challenges white foster parents who feel that they are not racist and brings up the question of their own prejudices and that is uncomfortable.

The Fostering Team's rather timid and cautious approach was, to some extent, motivated by the desire to protect white foster parents from feeling threatened by the new moves. In at least one social worker's opinion, they were over–protected.

SW3 I think some people are far too over–protective of poor, hard–done–by white foster parents.

Equally important, although never openly stated, was workers' desire to protect themselves from white foster parents' wrath. During one anguished encounter, a white foster mother recounted how, when she first took in a black child, she had suffered abuse in the street and racist slogans daubed across her door. She was angry and upset not only because she believed that her motives and efforts were being devalued and distorted but because she felt deeply betrayed. In her view, those same social workers who had been very happy to place a black child with her in the past, were now telling her that the placement had actually harmed the child.

The views of the black community

A further consideration was that an assertive policy statement might alienate the very group on whom its success was dependent, that is, potential black applicants. Social workers were aware of ambivalent or hostile attitudes amongst the local black population from comments made by existing black

---

[5] At one meeting attended by the researcher, vehement opposition to policy of 'racial' matching was expressed by several white members. The only black person present did not give an opinion during the course of the meeting nor when the topic was discussed in the pub afterwards although she expressed herself eloquently on other issues.

foster parents but assumed that those holding such views would eventually be won round to the new ways of thinking and were simply the misguided victims of a 'false consciousness' of where their true interests lay.

SW5 It's just a matter of raising consciousness. Inevitably, there will be some opposition at first from people who are not sensitised to the problems but I don't think they will be very many and I think they will soon realise that this is the right way to go.

Workers were made forcibly aware of some black foster parents' misgivings at a consultation meeting to seek advice on how best to attract applications from black people. As one worker explained,

SW5 We arranged a meeting with existing black foster parents where we asked them what they thought about the advertising and what else they thought we ought to be doing ... and, it was from that instant, when we made our position clear, that we got quite a lot of negative reactions. I think they were suspicious about what we were trying to do. I think some of them thought that it was actually racist, that, you know, a child is a child and it's love and affection he wants and not to treat him differently because of his colour.

There seemed, nevertheless, to be a general reluctance on the part of black foster parents to voice their disquiet or to engage in open criticism. This may, in part, have been a strategy of conflict avoidance developed over years of experience of racist prejudice. As one social worker explained,

SW5 (The RAT course leader) talked about how one of the ways of coping with racism was to smile and say it's alright and to deny the problem because it's too painful and I think that's part of it, why they were reluctant to criticise.

On the other hand, foster parents were not consulted about the new policy nor were they asked about their views[6]. Elsewhere, it has been claimed that foster parents are afraid to speak their minds on the issue in the presence of social workers (Gardiner, quoted in Smith, 1985b).
The Fostering Team had been under little, if any, pressure from existing black foster parents to change its policy. 'It was very much us taking the initiative to ask them', one member explained. Among the black people who were interviewed during the course of the research, opinion about 'racial

---

[6] Similar complaints have been reported elsewhere (e.g. Smith 1985b).

matching' was divided, with most expressing some reservations. (See Chapter 7). On the whole, social workers seemed to underestimate the extent of ambivalence and hostility to the new moves amongst the local black population. One, for example, commented, 'I don't think there is opposition out there' (SW3).

Failure to consult the local community

Although there was no discussion about whether or not to publicise the new approach, the decision to keep a low profile in order to avoid courting opposition seems to have been taken by tacit agreement within the Team. No reference to publicity about the change in rationale concerning appropriate placement was made in the Team Meeting minutes. When asked about this, workers spoke of a fear of failure:

PR   To what extent has the new policy been publicised?
SW5 It hasn't.
PR   Was that a conscious decision on the part of the Team?
SW5 I really don't know. I think we're a bit afraid of setting ourselves up in case we fail, although that's never been made explicit. I mean, I would be a bit reluctant to say, 'Look, this is what we are trying to achieve', even though that's the aim (laugh) ... I think it's a question of going ahead and actually trying to do it rather than making too much of a noise about it.
PR   So, it wasn't a conscious decision not to publicise?
SW5 No, it's just not happened.

and a general muddled approach:

PR   Has there been any attempt to publicise the new policy?
SW3 Publicity, no, I don't think that there has been much, if any. We are not really very effective politicians in the Team. We rely on the Team Leader to do that.
PR   Has the question of publicity been discussed in the Team?
SW3 No, I don't think that there has been any discussion about it. Because we are really very muddled in the way we do things, it doesn't happen.

Only one person mentioned possible hostility from the community:

SW2 We don't have a firm policy as such to publicise and we don't want to antagonise people by too much publicity before we are ready.

The failure to publicise was reflected in the fact that the Team's commitment to end all transracial placements by the end of 1985 was unknown to any of the foster parents or applicants interviewed or even to the foster parent facilitators who took part in joint assessments (see Chapter 12). Placement policy seemed to have been changed without reference to local opinion or even to opinion within the rest of the Department. There was little, if any, consultation with social workers from the District Teams and no attempt to consult local opinion and, although a few black foster parents were consulted, it was about technical details of implementation of a policy which had already been decided. Similarly, public relations in respect of the changes with the local Foster Care Association were only undertaken at the group's own instigation and took the form of presentation of a *fait accompli*.

The new policy seems to have been initiated independently of any Council influence, although later the Council offered its support. The Fostering Team did not work closely with the Council and contacts were carefully controlled. As one worker explained,

SW6   We don't work at all closely with the Council or with the Director. In fact, we try to avoid too much contact.

The reasons for the failure to consult the local community were complex. There was no tradition of dialogue, forum for public debate (other than the local Foster Care Association) or machinery for consultation, save through the indirect route of lobbying the Council. Social workers considered themselves to be an unfairly persecuted group under constant threat of public censure and communication with the main forum for public scrutiny and debate, the Council Chamber, was restricted to a minimum. In addition, consultation with and accountability to the local community were not matters which were not considered to be particularly important in view of the taken–for–granted assumption that, as trained professionals, social workers know best how to interpret their clients' needs and how best to identify and provide the services to satisfy them (cf. Lacey, 1988b).

Members of the Fostering Team were more likely to be influenced by the climate of opinion within their own profession, especially by the highly vocal pressure from black social workers, and by the example of other boroughs and agencies, as the following conversation reveals:

PR   Did it (the initiative) come mainly from within the Team or were community views sought before you decided on the new policy?

SW5   Well, at that stage, John Small (Leader of the New Black Families Unit in Lambeth), I think, had written articles which our foster parents had reacted to – largely negatively, because it was white foster parents, but, nevertheless, the issues were much more publicised generally. And the pressure from black social workers who were publicising the issues, was much more evident. It was clear that social service departments had been criticised for not doing anything. It became a political issue by that time, really. And, I think the whole Team was aware of that.

Workers were far less immediately aware of the climate of local opinion and the ability of ordinary local people to exert pressure was limited. The group most likely to be able to exert direct pressure were the white foster parents and it was the reactions of this group which helped to temper the Team's approach (cf. Connelly, 1989: 10). Many Team members felt that it was difficult enough to gain acceptance within the Team without courting trouble by trying to seek outside legitimation.

Team ethos

A number of different elements of the Fostering Team's approach or ethos can be identified which shaped the development of the new approach.

Vulnerability to changes in personnel

The direction of the Team approach was largely dependent on the influence of individuals rather than on a framework of clearly stated policy. As one social worker expressed it,

SW3 It is quite worrying the way the Team works. If you are not feeling bright or miss something, things don't happen. Policies are very unclear. The fact that some of us are able to have influence means that it could just as easily work the other way.

As a result, it was vulnerable to personnel changes within the Team. 'What concerns me', one worker commented, 'is what happens when individuals leave the Team.'

SW3 At the moment, it is very much dependent on the commitment of a few individuals. We need more black workers which we haven't got at the moment but it also needs strong commitment from the Team as a whole and, the way things are done at the moment, it can't be guaranteed.

Reluctance to produce clear policy

Failure to produce a clear written statement of policy meant that Team initiatives were all too easy to retract or forget (cf. Pearson, 1989; Connelly, 1989). As one member commented,

SW3 It is one thing saying something at a Team Meeting and another having a very clear written statement. It is easy to retract things if they are not written down ... I think that it is a very bad thing that we haven't really made any attempt to publicise it. I think it would be much better to publicise openly.

Often, policy changes were simply 'lost' in the minutes of Team Meetings. As Connelly observes,

Decisions may be made, but because of uncertianty about just what is involved, or anxieties about embarking on implementation, there may be no follow-up and people gradually 'forget' that a decision was made at all (Connelly, 1989: 46).

The matter was raised on a couple of occasions and, in March 1985, a policy file was created in which all new decisions were to be recorded. When questioned about it, however, several members were unaware of its existence. New initiatives were liable to modification or reversal in favour of other issues which came to be perceived as more pressing or important, especially in times of resource constraints, as the following comment, made early in 1985, illustrates:

SW3 Already, the policy is coming under threat because of a shortage of white foster parents which has led to a diverting of resources away from this issue. Really, this shows a lack of commitment in the Team. It shows how easily a policy can become eroded.

The fate of the Black Action Group, discussed in the next chapter, was dramatic evidence of the fragility of the new policy.

Emphasis on child care as opposed to political issues

The conventional distinction between issues of social work and of politics meant that the latter were not adequately confronted or addressed. The issue of 'racial matching' was sanitised by decontamination from any overt political implications. This avoided confronting uncomfortable political questions and

103

bringing to the surface differences of political opinion among Team members. It also helped to legitimise the changes in the eyes of higher management who were wary of an overt political stance. The Team's apolitical stance and general lack of political awareness was a source of frustration to its more radical members who chafed at the slowness of the pace of change. A different interpretation is that it enabled social workers to restrict their field of action to an area in which they felt they could achieve some change as opposed to the wider field of socio-political action where they felt paralysed by the enormity of the problem (Corrigan and Leonard, 1978). Pinder (1980), on the other hand, has suggested that the institutional context within which they are constrained to work forces social workers to convert political problems into technical problems.

Consensus management

The strategy of consensus management, with its emphasis on points of agreement rather than conflict (Connelly, 1989), accommodated a plurality of views and enabled social workers with different rationales to operate within the same loose conceptual framework. But, although there was a superficial unity, this masked very real differences in philosophy and approach and left decisions vulnerable to variations in interpretation in practice. Liffman observed a similar process in operation in his account of the setting up of an experimental family centre in Australia in the early seventies. Policy decisions were 'often little more than a temporary surrender to the arguments of the most persuasive, forceful, manipulative or obstinate staff member' (1978: 138) and 'ideas accepted formally, either because of their persuasiveness or the politics of their introduction, were often ignored, modified or undermined by the ways in which they were acted on in practice' (1978: 62).

Although it could be argued that a plurality of ideological and political approaches promotes exchange of ideas, and that a fluid approach is more sensitive to changing conditions, enabling a more rapid response to changes in local needs than a situation of more rigid control, this is at the expense of tighter control over the implementation of policy. Free exchange of views, however, was restricted by a tacit policy of consensus management and avoidance of conflict. As one member put it,

SW6 In this team, people are too ready to say what they think is acceptable. People don't say what they feel so we tend to pussy foot around issues. We have never really discussed these issues (racism and work with black people) properly.

104

When asked about the Team's reaction to the use of black foster parents in joint assessments another explained,

SW7   I don't think you would call it violent. I'd say that some people were ignorantly opposed, if you know what I mean. If they had been pushed, there would have been much more fundamental disagreement. They may even believe in it on an intellectual level but, on an emotional level, it would be different. They don't let themselves feel on an emotional level and therefore never really sort it out in their own minds. We are too afraid of hurting people's feelings here so there is never any real challenge or discussion.

Elsewhere, it has been noted that a strongly held rule prevents social workers from questioning the actual way colleagues behave with clients (Pithouse, 1988). Greater discussion was also restricted by the political climate within many London boroughs which generated a fear of being branded as reactionary or racist. As one member commented,

I think some people are a bit afraid to say what they really think because they are afraid that the rest of the Team will think they are racist[7] .

In any discussion of the development of a new approach, it is important to ask whether, on the one hand, it is better to have a clear rationale so that everyone knows the theoretical, ideological and political framework within which they are expected to work and within which policy is formulated or whether, on the other, it is better to try to accommodate differences of opinion and approach by concentrating on points of agreement rather than conflict?

---

[7] The point has been made by a number of commentators, for example,

Many social workers, black and white, are deeply worried about what is happening to black children in care, but dare not speak out for fear of being called a racist. (Ben Brown of Dr Barnardo's, quoted by Toynbee, 1986)

In matters of race, social work has not quite reached the depths achieved in some education departments (Brent, for example) where any dissenting voice, however mild, is subjected to the mass pickets of `anti-racists'; nevertheless, the same process is at work. Where black children and families are concerned much is left unspoken, not because it might prove to be wrong but because, even if it should prove to be right, to speak it would bring the accusation of `racism'. (Dale, 1987: 4)

Fear of displaying ignorance or racist attitudes is a potent force which can disable and deskill workers at all levels. (Pearson, 1989: 112)

The assumption that conflict is necessarily pathological is itself questionable. Conflict may act as a promoter of change whereas an emphasis on consensus may inhibit it. On the other hand, although the strategy of attempting to maintain a consensus, however fragile, and the failure to make a public commitment to a clearly articulated formal policy meant a weakening both of the policy and its implementation, compromise meant that stalemate was avoided and some change was accomplished. When the field interviews were carried out, most of the social workers interviewed were still in a state of personal ambivalence and/or ideological confusion regarding the issues. A few had firm beliefs which they were attempting to promote as a Team position but the Team as a whole was not yet able to formulate through consensus a coherent rationale on which to base policy.

As Naomi Connelly observes, however, 'policies are not solutions' (1989: 30). A coercive approach, that is an attempt on the part of the leadership to impose change, would probably not have been effective, not least because it would have caused resentment among members. The dangers were revealed in the resentment, previously subdued, which blossomed in the aftermath of the RAT course. In addition, the opportunities for sabotage were considerable. It would have been difficult for the Team Leader to force approval of black applicants against the recommendations of the social workers who had conducted the assessment interviews. The failure to recommend black applicants could have resulted in an acute shortage of black foster parents producing a situation where black children would have had to be placed with white families or have remained in institutional care considerably longer than white children. Further, the desires of some black children, themselves, and of some black natural parents for their children to be placed in white families could have been manipulated and encouraged by individual social workers, considerably reducing the likelihood of a matched placement succeeding.

Lack of consultation and failure to publicise

The failure to extend discussion beyond the confines of the Fostering Section was primarily a matter of pragmatism. At the time of the field research, there appeared to have been no discussion within the Team as to whether or not a policy of 'racial matching' should be formally adopted and ratified by the Council and attempts to force the pace of change by holding RAT were counterproductive. The low-key approach had the initial advantage of minimising hostility which might have prevented or made it more difficult for the Team to put the new ideas into operation. On the other hand, the lack of public debate left them vulnerable to neglect and erosion. With little public accountability, a reversion to old practices would go relatively unremarked and, without a grounding in community support, the new approach may

106

become difficult to implement. This point underlines the importance of discussion beyond the confines of the Social Service Department and the involvement not merely of elected members and 'talking heads' but of the 'grassroots': the families and neighbours of children received into care, actual and potential foster parents. The imposition of policy without consultation reinforces the mistrust and resentment which, all too often, cloud relations between social service departments and the communities they purport to serve.

Not only had there been negligible consultation or dialogue but little attempt to publicise the new approach, save through advertising for black foster parents. Failure to raise the issues on home visits and, except peripherally, on the training and assessment courses was motivated by the desire to avoid alienating potential recruits and by social workers' own ambivalence. There was no such hesitancy when it came to stressing the negative aspects of fostering[8], although it could be argued that an open discussion of 'racial' issues and matching policy was just as important. The ability to work within departmental policy and guidelines and to appreciate the underlying rationale may be as much a prerequisite of the 'good' foster parent as the ability to cope with difficult children and their families.

The weaknesses of an exclusive in-house approach to policy development have been noted in other fields. In a 1986 study of local authority education policies, Troyna and Williams, for example, found that

> that the initiatives on policy formation have been taken largely by politicians and professional officers who have consulted the communities mainly for an endorsement of, not substantive contributions to, their policies. (Troyna and Williams, 1986)

An example of a 'top-down' approach which failed to include all relevant members of the community was discussed in the McDonald Inquiry report on the implementation of anti-racist policies in a Manchester school where an Asian pupil was murdered in a playground fight. The main criticisms were that 'policies were imposed from above, without substantial input from ethnic minorities, still less from working-class whites' and that they 'concentrated on the personal shortcomings of whites, an approach that derives from racism awareness training' (Wilby, 1988; cf. Roberts, 1988; *The Guardian* 3 May 1988), in other words. a 'behavioral' model of racism concerned more with changing individual attitudes than with changing institutions.

---

[8] Applicants complained that the negative aspects of fostering had been emphasised at the expense of the potential rewards.

RAT has been heavily criticised for 'the paucity of its theoretical credibility' (Jervis, 1986; cf. Gurnah, 1983; Sivanandan, 1985)[9], its confrontational and dictatorial style (Gurnah, 1983) and its equation of criticism with defensive prejudice (Jervis, 1986). Its basic tenets – that racism is a mental illness, that it is a white problem and that it is defined as prejudice plus power – have been dismissed as 'little more than superficial rhetoric' or 'empty sloganeering' (Jervis, 1986). According to Gurnah (1983), the first is based on a metaphysical notion of the ideal person; the second fails to recognise that racism is a relationship not a disease, while the third has not been adequately demonstrated. In Sivanandan's view, it confuses racism, which, 'strictly speaking, should be used to refer to structures and institutions with power to discriminate' and racialism, which is 'what individuals display'. 'Racism is not, as RAT believes, a white problem, but a problem of an exploitative white power structure' (1985: 27).

Several critics have pointed out that there is no necessary link between changing attitudes and changing behaviour. RAT's assumption that social conflict can be resolved by understanding ignores interest and fails to provide a clear strategic route from consciousness–raising sessions to political action. By 'ignoring political and structural components and concentrating only on the middle classes', it fails to distinguish between 'the different racisms of the different classes', severs 'oppression ... from exploitation, racism from class and institutional racism from state racism' (Sivanandan, 1985: 16). It diverts attention and energy away from political struggle and provides the state with a tool for managing black demands (Gurnah, 1983) by presenting institutions with a convenient package which merely camouflages racism by teaching white officials an 'acceptable' language. RAT's inward focus not only enables them to safely delegate their liberalism to enhancing professional status and adjusting verbal behaviour (Jervis, 1986) but can turn its effects inwards rather than outwards creating destructive divisions and tensions between colleagues rather than constructive collective action.

---

[9] According to Ahmed Gurnah, its theories, a combination of Marxism and Rogerian psychology, have been arbitrarily selected for their convenience with the result that 'illegitimate analytical leaps' are 'made from descriptions of capitalist phenomena to descriptions of psychological rationalisations' (1983:12).

Power and conflict

The ability to prevent conflict, according to Stephen Lukes, is one of 'the most effective and insidious' manipulations of power (1974: 123). Those in power are able to keep certain issues outside the arena of discussion and, where potentially conflicting positions are admitted, they are prevented from erupting into open conflict. This is achieved, first, through controlling the flow of information and the channels of communication and by circumscribing the field of discussion and action so that potentially oppositional issues are defined as irrelevant or illegitimate. Second, conflict is equated with pathology and sanctions are imposed and disapproval expressed against any form of behaviour or action that is perceived to be a threat to the general harmony. Third, opposing viewpoints are subverted and transformed into mutually compatible positions: thus, political-structural issues are converted into technical problems (cf. Holmes and Grieco, 1988) and power relations into personal relations. Such active strategies of conflict prevention, however, are never totally effective. The resultant 'harmony' exists as a precarious balance between the powers of those seeking to protect it and the powers of those attempting to subvert it and is maintained only at the expense of continued vigilance on the part of its guardians.

In the Fostering Team, these strategies resulted in the uneasy co-existence of opposing viewpoints. Debate was constrained by a dominant understanding of members' roles as non-political and confined within the conventional apolitical framework of child care and practice concerns (cf. Stubbs, 1987). Direct confrontation between opposing positions was avoided. Where change occurred, it was conditioned and channelled by the dominant interpretation and more radical changes which would have risked dividing the Team were averted. Strategies of conflict prevention were pursued both within the Team and between the Team and the outside world. Confinement of the debate within the Fostering Team and control of communication to and from the outside world meant that any changes were made virtually without reference to outside opinion and without grounding in 'grass roots' support. The new approach developed within the Fostering Team was, thus, vulnerable to subversion both from within the Team, itself, and from oppositional forces in the community outside.

6 A documentary account: Analysis of Team Meeting minutes

The development of Team policy in relation to the placement of black children can be traced from 1974 through the Team Meeting minutes. Although the record is incomplete, especially for the first five years, it contains the main developments in policy and practice over a twelve year period[1]. It paints a

---

[1] It would be naïve to assume that the account given in the minutes is a full and faithful record of what actually happened during the meetings. It would be better to think of it as a more or less distorted mirror. The minutes are not *verbatim* records but distillations of the main points which were raised. What these were was the judgement of the person taking the minutes and what one person would include was not necessarily the same as another would have done nor necessarily what the researcher would have considered the most relevant. The extent to which the record may have been biased by the recorders' personal views and interpretations, however, can only be guessed.

The minutes revealed very little about the context of the meetings or the nature of the discussions which took place. Often, only the final decision was recorded with nothing about how that decision was reached, the arguments for and against, the reasons why those against were rejected, which members put forward which arguments and so on. Little was said about how or why particular issues came to be raised on the Team agenda or about what went on between meetings. Some minutes were more detailed than others which may have given the false impression that some meetings involved fuller discussions and covered more relevant material than others. The actual recording of the minutes may have introduced a further distortion. Some may have been drawn from notes taken while the meeting was in progress and some workers' notes may have been more detailed than others, whilst others may have been drawn purely from memory.

(continued...)

110

changing picture moving from treating black children as culturally indistinguishable from white children (cf. Lambert and Streather, 1980) through to acceptance of a distinctive 'racial' and cultural identity. Despite the fact that a disproportionate number of black children compared with white was received into care in the seventies, black children were regarded as 'hard to place', tended to remain in care longer and fewer were placed in substitute families. Efforts were, therefore, concentrated on finding substitute families and, to this end, white foster parents were paid enhanced rates if they would accept black children. A dawning recognition that black children may have emotional and cultural needs different from white children led to the first tentative efforts to recruit black foster parents in the seventies. This grew into a questioning of the entire rationale for transracial placements after the ABSWAP conference of 1983 and the renewed campaign to recruit black foster parents with which this study began in 1984. As the minutes reveal, the process was not a smooth progression but a bumpy journey marked by timidity and compromise and, although the minutes refer to black children's 'racial' identity, the change was rationalised in terms of cultural difference.

Developments up to the first conference in November 1983 of the Association of Black Social Workers and Allied Professions

In 1977, long term foster placements for children under the age of ten were abandoned and a time limit of two years was set for rehabilitation with the natural family, after which, adoption procedures were to be set in motion. This policy was reaffirmed in November 1980 and permanency[2] (Morris,

---

[1](...continued)
Finally, it is not possible to know which issues were discussed and what decisions were taken at meetings for which we have no record. The minutes provide a skeletal outline of events and developments, of which some of the bones are missing and from which the flesh has fallen away with the passage of time.

[2] The possibility that children may remain in care indefinitely, in default of practical plans for them to return home, has been reduced by limiting parental rights after the expiry of statutorily determined time periods. A preference for clear–cut alternative arrangements of a legally 'permanent' nature has emerged (Ely & Denney, 1987:162).

'In the course of the last ten years, there have been a number of studies on children in the care of local authorities which have shown that, once a child has been in care for six months, there is only a one–in–four chance of him returning home before he is 18 years of age. Despite the fact that the child was the main client, work was geared towards the needs, wishes and sense of time of the adults in his life rather than to his own.
(continued...)

1984; Thoburn *et al.*, 1987; Vernon, 1985) became the cornerstone of borough child care policy.

The first discussion of 'racial' issues was in April 1974 and concerned a recent court ruling that foster parents who either 'refused to take in coloured children[3] or who 'had discriminated against coloured children under their care' would come 'within the scope of Section 2 of the (Race Relations) Act'. For the Fostering Team, the two most important questions were

1. Does this mean that, in the selection of foster parents, we must refuse applicants who are not prepared to take coloured children at the expense of obtaining a good foster home for other children?

2. To uphold the law, will it be necessary to make redundant those who will take only white children?

Black[4] children were considered 'hard-to-place' (cf. Rowe and Lambert, 1973; Brummer, 1988) and, for this reason, retainer fees were paid to foster parents who were 'willing to take a wide range of children and any colour'.

There was evidence as far back as 1975 that the Team was aware of the possible psychological and social problems of black children brought up in white homes and, in June, one Team Meeting seems to have been devoted to a discussion of these issues. Statistics were presented which revealed that many more 'coloured' children were referred to the Fostering Section than white children, although more white children were eventually placed in family care. This was followed by a discussion of 'coloured children in foster homes' sparked off by research carried out in the U.S.A. 'about the adoption of

---

[2](...continued)
Rehabilitation often did not take place because of the parent's unreadiness for it and often no alternative plans were made either because of repeated promises to have the child home or because of parental opposition to an alternative which would offer both legal and emotional stability of the child. For the last four years, the Department has been trying to apply the lessons learned by these studies' (Team Meeting minutes, November 1980).

[3] The word, 'coloured', was used to describe children of non–European origin until September 1976 when it was replaced by the term, 'black', although it does not seem to have dropped out of use until about 1983. One or two workers were still referring to 'coloured' children when they were interviewed in 1984. There seems to have been no Team discussion or official directive concerning 'correct' terminology, but the change seems to indicate a certain sensitivity to changes in language fashion if not also to the underlying conceptual changes which they signified (c.f. Banton, 1987).

[4] To the social workers in the Team, the term, 'black', was clearly restricted to people of Afro–Caribbean origin.

coloured children into white families and the effects this had on them when they grew up, their alienation from their own peoples and culture[5]. This was the first mention of possible identity problems. A distinction was made between those West Indians 'anxious to preserve their own culture' and 'others, especially second generation, identifying almost completely with their white neighbours'. No value judgement was made about the desirability of either a West Indian or a white identity but it was agreed that the child's identification was 'relevant to the choice of foster home and class of home'.

In recognition of these problems, the first mention was made of a need to recruit black foster parents and to review the way in which applicants were recruited and assessed. The different cultural profiles of family life of black people and white people were discussed and specific differences, such as the 'stricter discipline' in West Indian homes, were mentioned. It was assumed that, whereas 'West Indians at home use the extended family for the care of their children, when they come to this country, they tend to use the social services'[6]. The appointment of 'Liaison Officers', who would be involved in 'the fostering of non-white children, recruiting black foster parents, liaising with the District Teams and disseminating information', was also proposed.

Suggestions made at the meeting seem to have been taken up with some enthusiasm. At a meeting in August 1977, for example, several members expressed a willingness to become involved as liaison workers with black foster parents and interest was expressed in an in-service training course on West Indian children. The presence of a black social worker in stimulating interest at this time was significant. It is, perhaps, surprising that the borough did not participate in the London-wide 'Soul Kids Campaign' to recruit black foster parents which ran during 1975 and 1976 (ABAFA, 1977; Gayes, 1975/6). The reason recorded in the minutes was the difficulty of responding at short notice. Early commitment to the recruitment of black foster parents was reflected in the decision, in September 1975, to give council housing priority to black foster parents who required larger accommodation. In September 1976, a growing belief in a need to treat black foster children as a separate group, with its own distinctive needs, led to the arrangement of a meeting for black and white foster parents on the needs of black children.

The need to recruit more black foster parents meant that criteria which had previously been treated as clear reasons for exclusion were now regarded as problematic and raised the vexing question of dual and/or lower standards.

---

[5] Unfortunately, no reference was given.

[6] These beliefs were inspired by FitzHerbert's research (1967) which recommended that this tendency should be discouraged wherever possible. Her analysis has been heavily criticised (e.g. Denney, 1983; Jones, 1981; Holman, 1968).

The following incremental changes in policy were drawn up in response to situations which arose during the course of practice: applications from black single women to be given special consideration (July 1977); requirement for the social worker to see the marriage certificate dropped (December 1977); consent form to take up police references required (March 1981); working mothers to be considered as potential foster parents (July 1982); requirement of medicals for the over-sixties (July 1982).

Although there was general recognition of the difficulties faced by white social workers in the assessment of black families, there was nowhere any contra-indication to the belief that the necessary skills could be learned from experience. The allocation of work with black applicants and foster parents was, therefore, spread throughout the Team so as to give as many social workers as possible the experience of working with black people. The first 'Introduction Meeting' for black applicants was held in September of the same year in the Social Services offices by two white workers. All new black applicants were invited and allocated for immediate assessment. All applicants were invited to two Introductory Meetings and their cases closed if they did not attend but greater effort was made to retain the interest of black applicants who were further contacted by telephone.

The first conference of the Association of Black Social Workers and Allied Professions: a turning point?

The event which seems to have spurred the Team into action was the ABSWAP conference of November 1983. The worker who attended dated her commitment to same race placement and her determination to work for change from this time. For her, the conference was 'a major turning point' and it seems to have been a turning point for the Team also. Issues which had previously been comprehended and tackled in a somewhat unconcerted and piecemeal fashion were clarified and, through the conference, gained a legitimacy and significance which they had previously lacked. The conference provided the external impetus and sense of urgency needed to galvanise the Team into action. This is not to suggest that every member was equally committed to change but it was enough that a few were enthusiastic and, more importantly, that the Team Leader was supportive. In this initial enthusiasm, doubting and antagonistic voices were quelled.

Acceptance of the legitimacy of 'racial matching' and consequent need to increase black foster parent recruitment rekindled a flagging team spirit and united members in a sense of common purpose. In a field where rewards are sparse and difficult to define, it was an approach which promised quick and measurable results, i.e. the recruitment of more black foster parents and opportunity for more same-race placements. The initial flame of enthusiasm burned brightest amongst a small group within the Team who kept it burning for the rest. Without their sustained enthusiasm and commitment, it might simply have flickered and died. The minutes reveal that it was usually the same three workers who repeatedly raised issues concerned with ethnicity and colour.

The Team's enthusiasm seemed to rest in members' common belief that they were engaged in radical change but the chronology of developments up to the ABSWAP conference of November 1983 suggests that subsequent changes were not the dramatic departure which members believed them to be. The conference, nevertheless, marked some sort of turning point. Although changes in thinking and small concurrent changes in practice had been taking place over the past eight years, the conference speeded up this process and lent a sense of urgency which had previously been lacking. It was the catalyst which effected not so much a change in direction as a change in the level of commitment.

Some differences in approach can be detected. Prior to the conference, the 'problem' of the placement of black children had been defined in terms of cultural differences but the notion of a black identity independent of cultural differences came afterwards. Workers had not seriously questioned their ability to assess black families or to learn the necessary intercultural skills and, at no point, had the issue of racism been recorded in the debate. After the conference, they began to feel less confident and to recognise a need to recruit black workers but, though shaken, most appeared to retain a belief in their own professionalism and ability to acquire transcultural skills (cf. Brown, 1986). The idea that all white people are subconsciously, if not overtly, racist (Bernard, 1987; Dominelli, 1989; Katz, 1978; Carnall and King, 1983) had been growing nationally during the early eighties and, after the conference, references to the need for Race Awareness Training (RAT) began to appear in the minutes.

A report on the conference was given in March 1984. The principal message, that 'all black children coming into care should go into black foster homes', had been reinforced at the conference by the testimonies of two black speakers who had themselves been in care and of a black psychologist who had treated many transracially placed children with problems of personal identity. Further legitimacy was given by another worker from the Team who reported her attendance at a London Boroughs Training Course which had shown that 'even children in short-term foster homes could feel the same sense of isolation and alienation as children placed in care for a longer period of time with a family not of their own culture'. This stimulated a discussion of the implications of the conference message for Team policy.

115

The issue of dual standards ('how far we should impose our child care standards on black families or accept their different standards') was re-opened. Members believed that 'lack of knowledge or confidence about black culture or even what constitutes bad child care' meant that they were 'accepting different standards in a very *ad hoc* way without any consistency'. A worker who had run a course for foster parents of black children reported that 'black foster parents are not unhappy on the whole with (the Team's) approaches or relationships' but others in the Team pointed out that the foster parents on the course were 'probably the families who have "come over" to the white culture'. To compensate for white workers' lack of understanding of black families, 'a need for more positive discrimination to recruit black social workers' was recognised. One member suggested inviting the black psychologist who had spoken at the ABSWAP conference or a representative from Ealing Adoption and Fostering Services or Lambeth's New Black Families Project to come and speak to the Team. Both agencies had recently publicised the success of their efforts to recruit black foster and adoptive parents (Schroeder and Lightfoot, 1983; Small, 1982; Harbridge, 1981)[7].

No decision was taken for immediate action, although it was agreed that the worker who had attended the conference should liaise with two other workers to consider future developments. One of them produced a paper on 'The Needs of Black Children' which suggested the setting up of a Black Home Finding Unit (BHFU). This provided the stepping-off point for the BHFU Working Party to investigate the feasibility of the idea. The initial meeting comprised members of the Fostering and Adoption Sections, including both Team Leaders, and the Assistant Director of Social Work.

The fate of the Black Home Finding Unit

The analysis in this section is based on the minutes of Team Meetings and of the BHFU Working Party. A paper produced by the Council Ethnic Minorities Forum on 'Black Children in Care', various additional memoranda, documents and papers, and conversations with workers involved in the Working Party were also taken into account.

The failure to establish a BHFU was an example of inaction through procrastination and of the use of bureaucratic procedures to delay implementation (cf. Benyon, 1984). Submission of the Working Party's report was delayed and there was a failure to respond or to act on its findings, once it had been submitted. These delaying tactics encouraged the Fostering Section to develop its own independent initiatives. The anger and frustration of those

---

[7] At the time of the field research, neither of these suggestions had been acted upon.

workers who had been involved with the Working Party inevitably soured relations with higher management and they decided to concentrate their efforts among their colleagues within the Fostering Team.

Four models were considered by the Working Party.

Model 1   An independent unit would have to be of sufficient size to deal effectively with the tasks envisaged. A totally separate unit with its own managerial structure, administration and methods of working would provide an extensive service by finding appropriate placements for Black children in care with Black families and would preferably be community-based.

Model 2   This is a variation of the model of a totally independent unit (Model 1), namely the establishment of two separate units: one for Fostering and one for Adoption. The aims would be to provide family placements for children and to recruit and assess Black families. It was envisaged that, whilst the two units would function separately in their respective sections, they would be able to share information, expertise, community work, advertising and recruitment resources.

Model 3   Model three would comprise a loosely–knit group of workers drawn together with a common purpose for both the recruitment of Black families and Black children's placement, but still attached to the existing Adoption and Fostering Sections – and would be the development of a Black Home–Finding Unit, within the existing Fostering and Adoptions Teams. The proposed model would make use of some existing staff plus the employment of additional social workers to concentrate on the recruitment and assessment of Black families, and to provide a large proportion of the successfully recruited applicants with continuing support.

Model 4   This model has been described as the 'In House' model and involves the restructuring of current sections to allow for individual staff within each team to be identified and given responsibility for the recruitment and assessment of Black families.

Resource constraints and failure to achieve official ratification, however, meant that the initiatives eventually developed within the Team were along the lines of the model which the Working Party had considered least appropriate and had specifically recommended against (Model 4). Two of its most important recommendations – 'the need to employ black social workers' and 'full consultation with all levels in the department from higher management to field social workers in the District Teams' – were similarly not implemented.

117

Despite these failures, the Working Party's report helped to raise awareness of the issues and provided the conceptual framework for subsequent developments within the Fostering and Adoption Teams. The most important elements of this framework were:

1. recognition of the existence of a black identity[8];
2. a belief that a black family placement is the 'first choice for most black children';
3. a belief that black people's family patterns and life styles are essentially different from those of white people and that a 'white model of family life' is inappropriate to the assessment of black families;
4. confidence that cultural knowledge and skills can be learned through training;
5. the premise that all white people are racist;
6. faith in the efficacy of race awareness training;
7. reaffirmation of the primacy of family life above considerations of 'race' and identity.

The Working Party never claimed that a black family is always the most desirable placement or that black children brought up in white families would fail to develop an adequate black identity. To the contrary, they specifically pointed out that it is 'wrong to imply that those Black children who have been placed with white families will be totally disadvantaged by their "white upbringing"' (Final Report of Working Party) (cf. Brown, B. and Reeves,C. quoted in Hodgkinson, 1985). Specific recommendations were made against the adoption of a rigid matching policy. The reasons given were that it was important to consider both the wishes of the child and of the natural parents when making a placement and that children of mixed race 'have a right to a multi-cultural environment'[9]. Although, in the original paper presented to the Working Party, the term, 'black', was 'taken to include children of "mixed racial" background on the premise that all children who are not white have a need to identify with that part of them which is black' and that 'non-white children are regarded as "different" no matter what the shade of their skin', children of 'mixed race' were subsequently treated as a separate category. The reasons for not recommending a more rigid policy included genuine reservations and a pragmatic desire to avoid confrontation. The only recommendations for consultation with black foster parents concerned technical matters of implementation and not the ideological rationale, itself.

---

[8] The definition of 'blackness' was based on the needs of the Afro-Caribbean community.

[9] This seems to have been an euphemism for placement in a white family.

118

Recommendation against a rigid policy was coupled with recommendation for the provision of integrated services as opposed to separate provisions for black people. These points were also made independently by the Ethnic Minorities Forum. Its 'Proposed Structure for the Home Finding Unit' suggested that it should be 'part of the existing fostering and adoption service' and 'provide as broad a service as possible'. The arguments presented in the final report of the Working Party against 'a totally separate unit with its own managerial structure, administration and methods of working' (Model 1) were, first,

> concern at the prospect of an Independent Unit ... where the philosophy and strategy is based on an apparently different premise from that currently existing within the Adoption and Fostering Sections

and, second, that

> establishing working relationships between the Black Home–Finding Unit and the Adoption and Fostering Teams... would be extremely difficult to achieve in these circumstances. There is a danger of one service being considered superior to the other and the consequent competition may well affect both recruitment and quality of service provided. It is therefore the considered view of the group that an entirely separate service would not be in the interests either of the Black community or the Department.

The potential for an innovative and challenging role seems to have been regarded as a distinct disadvantage and, in recommending against the establishment of a separate service, the possibility of 'a different philosophy and strategy' was specifically mentioned.

The advantages of the favoured model (Model 3), which would have utilized 'existing staff within each team who would be given a specific brief to be involved in the BHFU on a part–time basis', were 'the maintenance of common practices and present standards', 'integration with other workers and existing systems' and 'a strong management line', in other words, the machinery through which to exert control. The 'independence' of a separate unit and its supposed 'weak and confused line management structure' were listed as reasons for recommending against it.

It was, nevertheless, recognised that 'the use of predominantly white workers could perpetuate difficulties in communication with the Black community' and 'would not involve the use of any fresh input'. 'Fresh input', however, was entirely conceived in practical terms:

The importance of the grapevine and connections within the local Black community is (*sic.*) a vital source for reaching Black families and this can be undertaken more naturally by Black social workers than by their white counterparts. Because of shared identity and experience, a Black worker may often be better able to look beyond some of the barriers that exist between Social Services Departments and the Black community. (Final Working Party Report)

Issues of black representation and power sharing within the organisational hierarchy were not raised. The employment of black workers to reflect the racial mix in the community was mentioned only in passing in the initial paper presented to the Working Party on 'The Needs of Black Children' but the concern was with visibility rather than with the political issue of access to the power structure. The main consideration was pragmatic and involved the desire to change the image of the service as a predominantly white organisation in order to gain the trust and confidence of the black community. At no point does the difficulty of recruiting suitably qualified and experienced black social workers seem to have been discussed, despite the fact that the official reason for not employing them within the Fostering Section in the past was the paucity and poor quality of applicants[10]. The definition of 'suitability' seems to have been accepted as being without problem and the delicate issue of the relevance of cultural competence and 'life skills' *versus* professional training and experience was not addressed. Another recommendation, identified in the initial paper and repeated in subsequent meetings but neither acted upon nor included in the final report, was for 'consultation at all levels in the Department and with black organisations'. In summary, although the Working Party did much useful work in laying the groundwork for subsequent development of policy within the Fostering Team, it failed not only in its principal objective – the establishment of a black home finding unit – but in two of its main recommendations – the employment of black social workers and consultation within the Department and with the community. In addition, the Team was forced to develop its approach along the lines of the least favoured of the four models which the Working Party considered (Model 4).

At no stage did the Working Party find any group who felt that this model was a viable proposition to deal with the problems of the borough's Black Home–finding (Final Report of Working Party).

---

[10] personal communication from Team Leader.

The development of a policy of 'racial matching'

Rather than an all-out commitment to ending transracial placements, the main emphasis seems, initially, to have been on providing help and support for existing white foster parents of black children in the form of workshops and training sessions. Social workers were wary, however, of making them compulsory (Team Meeting minutes, July 1984). Those in favour of a more stringent policy considered themselves to be 'a crusading minority' and, although the Team was not overtly divided into two opposing camps, there was an undercurrent of tension between the radicals and conservatives. One of those least enthusiastic, for example, spoke of 'the dangers of rushing into radical changes of policy without sufficient thought', and thought that 'the case against transracial placements had not been adequately proved'.

Ideas about the value of matched placements, however, gradually took firmer root and a commitment to ending transracial placement was made in February 1985 in the aftermath of the Race Awareness Training course. Other plans were shelved in order to concentrate effort on the achievement of this objective by the end of the year. This commitment was at best equivocal and accepted with reluctance by at least some members of the Team and its fragility was revealed by the ease and rapidity with which it was later abandoned. No future date for ending transracial placements was set. Similarly, when a 'Record of Transracial Placement' form was introduced in May of the same year, there were recurrent complaints about under-recording. It was pointed out that the forms 'ought not to be regarded as some sort of test' and that 'transracial placements ought not to be regarded as either a good or a bad option', even though this undermined the original purpose of phasing them out. 'If staff have no personal motivation to introduce changes', Naomi Connelly remarks,

> ... they sometimes feel justified in ignoring the policy, or 'forget' to implement significant aspects of it, or don't get around to it due to pressure of other work (1989: 32).

The weakness of the commitment to ending all transracial placements by the end of the year was partly a consequence of the weakness of its conceptual underpinnings. The Team had not reached any universally agreed definition of the term, 'black' and, although 'racial' and cultural factors were accepted as important dimensions of a child's identity, they had not been fully explored. In order to avoid open conflict, some of the more thorny questions were circumvented and, therefore, remained unresolved. In April 1983, for example, one member brought to the attention of the Team the case of a black family who had expressed a willingness to take a white child. The Team had no

121

policy on the placement of white children in black families and it was thought unlikely that a black family would be considered. The question of whether or not the white child had a right to a 'racially matched' placement and the possibility that he or she might suffer identity confusion if placed in a black family were not raised. Similarly, the question of whether or not it was appropriate to approve black applicants who refused to take white children and, *vice versa*, white applicants who refused to take black children was not discussed. The placement policy for black foster homes clearly differed from that for white. As one social worker explained, 'white foster parents are expected to take both black and white children', although 'now, they would very rarely be asked to take black children'. No such expectation, however, existed for black foster parents.

The issue of the placement of children of mixed parentage was, similarly, never fully resolved (cf. Jervis, 1990) and different workers continued to hold different views (cf. Heywood, 1990). At a Team Meeting in November 1985, which was attended by the researcher, for example, one worker expressed the opinion that 'it is both emotionally and politically better for the child to go to a black family because, essentially, as a mixed-race child, it would be regarded as black'. Hers, however, was an unpopular view. The contention that children of mixed parentage are regarded by society at large as black (Small, 1984a, 1986a; Kelly *et al.*, 1990[11]) was ignored and the issue of racism evaded. Instead, various factors which were thought to militate against placement in a black family were suggested. Members lamented the lack of clear policy. One, for example, referred to a case involving two small, mixed-race children with a white mother and a black father who was 'not much on the scene'. The placement was planned for the short-term and there was thought to be little likelihood of it continuing into the long-term. 'Instinctively, I would look for a white placement,' the worker explained.

But, then, I began to wonder what was the Team policy on mixed-race children. Would placement with a white family count as a transracial placement? I wondered what I was supposed to put on the transracial form. Does it count as a transracial placement or not if the children are mixed-race?

It was generally agreed that the colour of the family was not important in the short term whereas, for long-term placements, the child should go to a black family. Where 'the significant parent figure' was white, however, it was

---

[11] 'In Britain if you are not white you are black regardless of whether you are Asian or have one parent black/white. Politically you are seen as black and you are accepted as such by both the black and white communities' (Kelly *et al.*, 1990:30).

considered 'more appropriate for the child to go to a white family.' The colour of the substitute family was agreed to be of little consequence to young children while, for older children, the child's own wishes were thought to be important. Other considerations included the wishes of the natural mother (cf. Brummer, 1988), the child's social background and friendship patterns, the 'racial' mix of the home locality and the shade of the child's own skin, in other words, whether or not he or she could 'pass as white'. The social worker who had favoured automatic placement in a black family later confided, 'People here are still "hung up" about the question of skin colour. There's still the idea that the paler you are the better'. Differences of opinion were felt to be too strong for the Team to be able to reach any agreement regarding a clear policy on the issue and, as on other occasions, a decision was delayed by appeal to 'the urgent need for research into mixed–race children and the effects of placement in black or white families' (Team Meeting minutes, November 1985)[12].

At the same meeting, another worker asked whether the policy was 'to look for black homes for any child which was not white, such as Asian, American Indian, Turkish, Vietnamese?' and, again, the plea was made for clearer guidelines. Most agreed with the worker who commented, 'a black family wouldn't have a clue with those races (*sic.*)'. Since placement in a family of the same ethnic origin as the child was considered to be an unlikely possibility and black (i.e. Afro–Caribbean) homes had been ruled out, the preferred placement was obviously in a white family. No–one explained why a white family was thought to be a better placement and better able to cope with cultural differences than a black, why a 'racial' and ethnic identity was thought to be less important to non–white children who were not of Afro–Caribbean origin than to children of Afro–Caribbean origin, or why racism was thought to have less impact. There was no mention of John Small's argument that, since white society treats all non–white children as black, such children are best placed in a black family if they cannot be placed in a family of their own ethnic origin (Small, 1984a; Kelly *et al.*, 1990).

The decision about which aspects of the child's heritage were to take precedence rested on the individual circumstances of each child. In this way, the individualized, child–centred ethic of treating each case on an individual basis (cf. Stubbs, 1987) was maintained and conflict avoided by allowing workers scope to interpret cases according to their own professional judgement (cf. Chambers, 1989) and prejudice (Divine 22 Oct.1982). The Team as a

---

[12] That the social workers, themselves, considered mixed–parentage children primarily as black is evident from the fact that the question of whether or not a placement was transracial only arose in relation to children placed in white families and not in relation to children placed in black families.

whole shied away from the political considerations which underlay Small's arguments about the nature of racism and rejected the 'blanket rule' which would have been the logical outcome[13].

'The Black Campaign'

As a result of these changes in attitude, black foster parents came to be more highly valued as a resource and, in May 1984, a specific recruitment campaign was launched. It was this campaign which provided the focus of the field research effort. It was, thus, scarcity, rather than any fundamental conceptual change, which motivated the various changes in approach which took place over the ensuing months and, in unspoken recognition of this, there was general uneasiness among workers who feared that they were being forced into lowering standards in order to boost recruitment. Practical changes occurred in four main areas: advertising and publicity, the processing of applications, the conduct of assessments and the criteria upon which the assessment decision was based.

Advertising and publicity and the processing of applications

In March 1984, the decision to make 'advertising for black foster parents for children aged between 0 and 5... a high priority' was taken, prompted by the new acceptance of 'racially matched' placements as the most desirable option for black children in care. A group of interested workers met over the next two months to consider strategies and, in May, a recruitment drive was

---

[13] Much of the problem stemmed from an inadequate definition of 'black'. Few people of West Indian origin are 'pure black' in the sense of having a pure African ancestry, therefore, the term, 'mixed race', has little relevance as a physical or hereditary description. An alternative, proposed by John Small (1984a), is the term, 'mixed parentage'. This refers to the child's biological parents and refers as much to social as to physiological factors since children of mixed parentage may be physically indistinguishable from their 'black' peers. By virtue of having both a black and a white parent, the child is presumed to have exposure to two different social and cultural spheres, hence the notion of being caught 'between two worlds', and of marginal or inbetween status (Melville 1983). He or she is 'mixed race' only in the colloquial sense as a consequence of social and personality characteristics erroneously ascribed to his parents and the 'two worlds' between which he or she is presumed to be caught are not necessarily constructed on cultural difference: both parents may share the same culture but be separated by differential experience of racism. The debate was between those who believed that the child's 'racial' identity is socially prescribed (e.g. Small 1984a; Reid 1985) and those who believed that it is a matter of choice (Staffony 1986; Philips,M. interviewed for *The London Programme*, LWT 29 June 1984, quoted in Smith,R. 1984; 'File on Four', *Radio Four* 23 Apr.1991; Foster Carter 1986).

launched. Its success, in terms of numbers of enquiries, was reported in November when it was calculated that over a hundred enquiries had been received[14]. The campaign stimulated a number of new departures in advertising and recruitment methods which are discussed in more detail in Chapter Seven.

Assessments

Workers' doubts about their own competence led them to question the way in which they conducted assessments. There was a move away from the conventional interrogatory approach motivated by concern with the way in which information was elicited (the nature of the questioning and the phrasing of the questions) and the type of information sought (which questions were asked). In each instance, workers were responding to applicants' reactions to the assessment. In the past, when they had been less concerned about recruiting black foster parents, the assessment encounter had been one-sided, with social workers dictating the terms: now, applicants' bargaining position had changed and they were in a better position to influence the way in which their assessments were conducted. The issue of questioning was raised in September 1984 when the Ethnic Relations Adviser, who had been invited to the meeting, pointed out that,

> for many immigrants, questioning is a frightening experience. It is associated with being sent home. The police always ask for a passport before dealing with any matter referred to them, for example, if people complain of harassment (cf. Donovan, 1986; Dominelli, 1989).

It was also noted that 'many black applicants have a strong reluctance to give personal information' and that 'older applicants don't like being asked personal questions about their past'. This reticence was explained in terms of cultural differences:

> In the West Indies, one can be seen as a failure if one admits to having discussed things outside the family,

and the solution was seen to lie in better explanation of the reasons for asking such questions:

---

[14] Unfortunately, it was impossible to calculate exactly how much more effective the new approach had been, since there was no prior record of enquiries from black people.

125

Our reasons for asking for personal details from applicants should always be clearly explained to them and we need to explain more carefully our reasons for delving into their family histories.

The question of 'why we ask for this sort of information and whether we really need to do so' was also raised. Some members thought that the Team should be 'looking for applicants' ability to be flexible' and thought that it was 'easiest to get a feel of this by discussing the way they handle their own children, rather than asking them about their past'. Others were of the opinion that 'talking about their past could be a good vehicle for discussing attitudes and a possible predictor of likely suitability'[15]. Workers were torn between their belief that childhood experiences affect a person's psychological and social development in later life and the exigencies of the face-to-face interaction with the applicant. It was easiest to avoid asking questions which were likely to provoke a hostile response and their concern was as much about managing a potentially difficult encounter as it was about eliciting appropriate information. These pressures marked a general move away from concentration on past experience towards greater emphasis on the present. By February 1985, it was reported that 'everyone queried the relevance of such information and generally felt it more important to focus on the present situation'.

No real consensus about the value of the approach, however, was reached during the course of the field work and the weight placed on questions about personal details and past life was left to the judgement of individual workers. The relevance of questions about childhood, for example, remained an area of contested terrain and, in November 1985, was reintroduced onto the Team agenda[16]. The Team Leader suggested that the 'psycho–dynamic model of assessment was probably not so important now' and that the Team ought, therefore,

> to rethink the value of asking questions about childhood and the purpose for which we are asking them.... Now, other things – confidentiality, how well (applicants) can work with the Department and with natural parents and so on are important. Now that fostering has changed, we are looking for slightly different qualities.

---

[15] This latter view conformed to conventional wisdom and is supported by research (see Dando & Minty (1987) for the latest restatement).

[16] This discussion had been stimulated by a report of the preliminary findings of the research which had been presented to the Team earlier in the week.

Another tenet of 'good practice' which came to be questioned was the need to interview husbands and wives separately.

> Some couples are reluctant to be seen separately. We should question why we do this... Individual interviews probably originally arose from the need to discover whether both parties really wished to foster. We needed to see the 'joint personality' of the couple, but also how they were as separate individuals ... If applicants are reluctant to proceed separately and this reluctance persists, then we should be flexible.

An important change in approach was the introduction of group assessments. At a study morning in February 1985 a decision was taken to offer a choice of individual or group 'vetting' to new applicants and to review the approach after six months. It was suggested that black applicants, in particular, would 'find vetting easier in a group and feel more threatened in individual situations'. The main reason for switching to group as opposed to individual assessment, however, was economic since groups were thought to be more cost effective in terms of staff time. In the Spring, the Black Action Group decided to discontinue individual assessments in favour of groups and the first all–black course was run. It consisted of weekly two–hour sessions and was planned to run for six weeks followed by a joint home visit with a social worker and a black foster parent.

Another significant change was the introduction of joint visits. The issue was first mooted in March 1984 but was not put to the Team for discussion until July when the decision was taken to use black foster parents on joint assessment visits for a trial period of six months. Since they were engaged on the strength of their presumed cultural skills, they were initially used only in the assessments of black applicants. This led to problems because it was not always possible to identify beforehand which applicants were black. It was, therefore, decided in November to include a question on 'race' in the application form. Later, the practice of joint visits was extended to white applicants as well as black. These developments are discussed more fully in Chapters Eleven and Twelve.

Changing ideas about family life

The perceived shortage of black foster parents resulted in the dropping of certain prohibitions against acceptance and a relaxing of requirements or, in the language of the Team, 'an increase in flexibility'. The challenge to the old ideas about 'suitability' thus came from the new pressure to recruit black foster parents rather than from any fundamental change in ideas about what makes a 'good' foster family. It was the solutions to practical problems which

127

stimulated changes in ideas and, as each practical change was made, the previously-accepted model of family life was further undermined. To counter the accusation that they were merely lowering standards, the Team was forced to justify the changes on grounds other than supply and demand (cf. Brunton and Welch, 1983). The resort was to cultural differences rather than to any consideration of possible structural causes of inequality which might also have handicapped black people in the selection process as members of a socially, economically and politically disadvantaged group.

The various changes that were introduced included extending the catchment area for recruitment beyond the previous twenty mile radius, dropping the requirement of legal marriage and reducing the minimum duration of a relationship for it to be considered stable, dropping the prohibition against working women and single applicants, accepting the use of co-carers for children placed with women who worked, restricting the categories of crime which would debar an applicant to serious crimes and crimes involving violence and/or children, and extending the acceptable age range for applicants.

The setting of suitable age limits exemplified a series of recurrent problems. The age limit was increased to sixty and continued to be revised upwards in response to the pressure of applications from older applicants, but not without obvious reluctance on the part of the Team. In March 1985 it was extended to sixty-three and a month later to sixty-five, only to be reduced to sixty-three again two weeks later. These rapid changes resulted in considerable confusion. The extension of the age range was a radical departure from what many in the Team believed to be 'ordinary family life'. For them, there was a clear distinction between the roles of parent and grandparent, with the caring and nurturing role being primarily the responsibility of the former. The challenge to these ideas came from a pragmatic response to the changing dynamics of supply and demand – 'It was felt that the Team must change policy if it wishes to provide black families for under fives' (July 1984) – rather than from any radical revision of the conceptual basis of the model. With each pragmatic acceptance of change, however, the conceptual model was further undermined. In order to quell misgivings about compromising standards in the enthusiasm to increase recruitment, it was suggested that the Team needed 'to accept that there are differences for black applicants and that the different criteria do not mean a second-class service' (August 1984). There was, nevertheless, a general reluctance to treat black applicants differently from white and, in September 1984, 'it was decided that it was not appropriate to have different rules for black and white applicants regarding age limits'.

One of the dangers of the emphasis on cultural differences was the simple equation of cultural with inter-generational differences. A black foster parent, who had been invited to a meeting in November 1984, for example, pointed out that 'young black mothers do not like their children looked after by much older women who may economise on clothing and aren't interested in fashion (e.g. who would buy clothes several sizes too big for the child)'. Similarly, 'most older black families would expect the foster child to attend church and, although this is very important to them, it is not acceptable to teenagers'.

Throughout, the emphasis was on 'flexibility' and the Team appeared to be reluctant to set firm guidelines. A consistent policy was repeatedly rejected in favour of 'flexibility' and, again and again, policy decisions were accompanied by the caveat, 'but this can only be a guideline, and each situation has to be assessed individually' (September 1984). In this way, a compromise solution was reached which avoided open conflict and the issue of appropriate standards was shelved rather than adequately resolved, with the danger that some workers would continue to operate in ways contrary to the spirit of the new approach. On the other hand, a flexible approach enabled the Team to adapt rapidly to changing circumstances by relaxing or tightening the conditions of acceptance in response to changing perceptions of placement needs. It also allowed greater scope for workers to exercise their own autonomous expertise and judgement and, thus, to retain the idea of their own 'professionalism'.

Pithouse (1988) has noted that social workers are capable of holding contradictory assumptions simultaneously. Although social workers in the Team believed that they were operating a new 'ethnically sensitive' approach by taking into account cultural differences, in practice, they were often reluctant to implement an approach which broke the tenets of non-discriminatory practice. Workers believed that, by adhering to the rhetoric of cultural pluralist practice, they were collectively engaged in a new principled enterprise. The rhetoric of cultural pluralism provided the moral high ground which served to bolster solidarity as a unified moral community and, thus, to quell dissonant voices. But it often seemed to exist on a level independent of the actual conditions of practice where the universalist model continued to hold sway. According to Barney Rooney, 'fashions in expressed attitudes tend to be more ephemeral than the attitudes themselves. Much more stable', he notes,

is the fundamental identification within which that attitude is formed. Identification here refers to an affinity or an emotional tie which influences the impartiality of organisations in discharging their functions to all members of society (Simon, 1965; cf. Lipsky, 1980). It is out of this identification that the confused objective of integration, the confused process of integration, the commitment to normal process, all arise (1982: 91) (References inserted).

The demise of the 'Black Action Group'

The Black Action Group (BAG) was set up early in 1985 in the aftermath of RAT in response to the Team's stated commitment to 'ending all transracial placements by the end of the year'. As one of the workers involved in the group explained,

> In order to achieve this we have decided to extend the advertising campaign to the end of the year and a small group has been set up with five members who will concentrate their energies entirely on the recruitment of more black foster parents and will no longer do any more white vettings.

Within weeks of its inception, however, the BAG was disbanded, ostensibly in response to an acute shortage of white foster parents. No plans were made for its reformation after the crisis had been resolved and the objective of ending transracial placements by the end of the year was quietly abandoned.

The formation of the BAG conformed to the 'logic' of the organisational structure of fostering services within the borough. The pool of children needing placement was subdivided according to age and mental or physical disability, and the work of recruiting substitute families and child placement was allocated to specialist workers or sub-teams. Once black children had been recognised as a distinctive group, it was 'logical' within the structure of work organisation to allocate responsibility for the recruitment of substitute families to a sub-team which operated more or less independently of the work of other sub-groups or of the Team as a whole. The decision to treat black applicants as a distinctive group from white, thus, flowed partly from the recognition of cultural differences and partly from the structural logic of work organisation within the Team.

In this way, work with black applicants was compartmentalised rather than dispersed throughout the Team. It became a specialist area outside of 'normal' practice, something 'exotic' rather than routine. Not only was it effectively placed outside the practical experience of many members of the Team but outside their responsibility. Any general commitment to the aims and objectives of the BAG was weakened from the start and the existence of a double-stranded approach was perpetuated. The BAG was, thus, established within a framework of competition for resources and competition between rival approaches to practice.

The shortage of white foster parents became acute in the spring of 1985 and a 'White Action Group', or 'WAG' as it was jocularly called, was set up to deal with the 'crisis'. Underlying the 'joke', however, was an undercurrent of largely unvoiced reservations about the direction which work in the Team was taking. The designation of the WAG was not the casual gesture it appeared. The group was set up as a rival rather than a complement to the BAG and revealed the extent to which thinking in the Team had become polarised into 'black' issues and 'white' issues. Work with black foster parents had come to be regarded as separate and distinct from work with white and reflected both the co-existence of and antagonism between the two rival strands of thought of the old and the new approaches to child placement. The establishment of the WAG provided a basis from which to reassert the old values and approach and the success of this bid was played out in subsequent developments.

It was not until faced with a situation of resource constraints that the Team's commitment to the aims and objectives of the BAG was really tested. Early in 1985, the shortage of white foster parents and of staff to recruit them resulted in the cancelling of foster parent reviews until further notice, the shelving of assessments and the cancelling of a workshop for toddlers. By Spring, the situation had become acute and, in May, the decision was taken to divert some members of the BAG back into mainstream work. Effectively, this meant the end of the group, although it was not until September that it was finally disbanded and responsibility for the assessment of new black foster parents handed over to the Under-Elevens Team. At no point was the placement of white children in black families suggested nor was the implicit decision challenged to give same race placement for white children higher priority than for black. In effect, the goal of same race placement for white children was pursued at the expense of black.

It is significant that these back-tracking moves were taking place at the time when opposition to the policy of 'racial matching' was beginning to organise. White foster parents within the borough were becoming more vocal as they became more aware of the direction in which the Social Services were heading and social workers were able to draw on this groundswell of discontent in their arguments against the continuance of the BAG. It was suggested that potential white applicants were put off from applying because they thought that the borough was only interested in recruiting black foster parents. Considerable hostility towards the black campaign was reported among white foster parents and the white community in general. It was decided, in consequence, to tone down the advertising targeting the black community and to emphasise the need for all types of applicant. Previous experience, however, had shown that such non-specific advertising not only failed to draw in black applicants but tended to discourage them[17] and that a reversion to past advertising practice would effectively discriminate against them.

---

[17] 'Advertising to be as personal as possible avoiding blanket advertising as this has been shown not to work. Blanket advertising can be used as a back-up only' ('Summary of Advertising Campaign, May to Nov.1984'; c.f. Schroeder & Lightfoot 1983; Arnold 1982).

131

The arguments for redeployment were made on the technical grounds of staff shortage and need to attract white applicants rather than in terms of opposition to the rationale of same race placement, itself, and inter–colleague resentment of the high profile which the 'Black Campaign' commanded within the Team. There was discussion about whether or not to hold mixed or all–black training and assessment groups in the future but it was recognised that the decision to concentrate on mixed recruitment meant that the numbers of black applicants would be too low to make it possible to run an all–black course. One worker suggested that the black group's concerns should be given first priority but she was quickly told by the Senior who co–ordinated the group that 'we can't be too precious about this black group. We mustn't forget what is going on in the rest of the Team'. Her comment highlights the precariousness of the BAG's position and the undercurrents of ambivalence and resentment within the Team despite its superficial show of solidarity and commitment to the group's aims after the Race Awareness Training day.

The fate of the BAG was a bitter disappointment to those of its members who had been deeply committed to its aims. The demoralisation and sense of failure and consequent loss of energy and enthusiasm was as much a setback to future developments as was the U–turn in policy. The goal of ending all transracial placements by the end of the year and the practice of differential treatment on the grounds of differential needs seemed to have been lost at a stroke. The BAG, however, limped on until September and many of the innovations pioneered within the group, for example, joint assessments, became standard Team practice.

Influences on the development of policy

Permanency and 'professionalism'

The cornerstone of borough child care policy rested on the concept of permanency. Paul Stubbs, however, has described 'a whole set of problems with "permanency models"[18] which ... tend to present structural–political issues as if they were neutral–technical–professional' (1987: 481). Peter Ely and David Denney observe that

---

[18] For a critique of permanency models see also Hillman 1986; Jordan 1985; Parton 1986.

132

The convergence of 'permanence' ideology, bureaucratic practicality, economic stringency and the paramouncy of the interests of the child has enhanced the powers of social work agencies and the importance of their interpretation of the child's best interests, at the expense of the 'rights' of parents (1987:162).

Adoption and fostering practice involves the reallocation of children according to notions of justice and welfare and consequent making and breaking of families. As one of the workers in Stubbs' study expressed it, 'You are playing God if you say "this child must have a new family"'. According to Stubbs, social workers have learnt to deal with the demands of their role by the development of, what he terms, a 'new professionalism'. He describes a 'strong commitment' to their own professional competence to make such decisions 'within a model which plays down material and ideological structures, including racism' and illustrates his point with the following quotation from a senior social worker: 'There are a whole number of criteria, if you like, a checklist... that a professional experienced social worker really ought to be able to use about a family, whether it's black or white' (1987: 481). In other words, professionalism[19] is located within a technical framework of standard rules which can be applied across all situations.

This 'new professionalism' represents a coherent response to increasing pressures, which include shrinking resources, an emphasis on statutory functions and increasing managerial control (Stubbs, 1987: 482; Jones, 1983) and amounts, in Stubbs' view, to an argument for 'a more limited, clearly defined, decisive role for social workers, bracketing off broader structural, material and organisational issues' (Stubbs, 1987: 482). This narrow compass ensures that the structures and processes of disadvantage and oppression which lead to disproportionate numbers of black children being received into care (Ahmed, 1980; Roys, 1988), are not examined (Divine 26 November 1982). The stress on professional competence means that factors deemed to lie outside the sphere of professional responsibility are ignored or dismissed. Professional concentration on the technicalities of individual placement is at the expense of concern with broader issues at the level of population and social structure.

It has been suggested (Pinder, 1980) that social workers have little choice in this constriction of their role which forces them to convert political–structural issues into technical concerns. Pinder, however, is less concerned about the structural conditions of inequality than the problems of 'institutional constraint'. 'The issues confronted by social workers in areas of

---

[19] Connelly found that 'a common criticism is that "professionalism" is too narrowly defined'. In the view of one white adoption and fostering worker, 'a lot of racism is hiding behind white professionalism' (1989:48).

133

ethnic diversity', he argues, 'stem not so much from the "difference" of the client as from conditions of practice' (*op cit.* p1). 'Most important of all' is 'the contradictory relationship workers have with their own authority' and 'the sense of inauthenticity' which this produces. In a later paper (Pinder, 1981b), he suggests that workers 'attempt to "deal with diversity" by falling back on a practice that cuts through it by '"settling" issues with reference to supposedly universal norms which all parties "must" acknowledge'. Pinder and Stubbs are largely in agreement about the end result – social workers' increasingly narrow conception of their own professionalism, and the cause – 'institutional constraint' (Pinder, 1980) and 'the increasing pressures on social workers in the contemporary period' (Stubbs, 1987), but they seem to disagree about the degree of voluntarism involved. According to one Director of Social Services, quoted by Connelly,

> We all interpret things within our frame of reference. The more professional the training, the clearer the frame of reference, and thus the more difficult to move (Connelly, 1989: 48).

Team ethos

The mesh of understandings amongst members or Team ethos had a number of significant elements which had consequences for the way in which policy was developed. Fundamental was a shared understanding of conflict as pathological (cf. Burrell and Morgan, 1979; Holmes and Grieco, 1988) and consequent belief in the importance of consensus. The emphasis was, therefore, on the common ground between members rather than on the differences. A second element was members' understanding of their role as non–political. Third was a focus on the solving of practical, as opposed to philosophical or conceptual problems, and consequent tendency to convert structural–political issues into technical ones (cf. Holmes and Grieco, 1988). A fourth factor was commitment to flexibility in deference to workers' claims to professional autonomy within the tradition of individual casework. As Young and Connelly have observed, 'Diversity in practice is... sustained by an acceptance... that many aspects... are 'off limits' for policy makers'.

> The boundary between policy and practice is an elastic one. However, its precise location is never determined by the fiat of policy makers but has to be negotiated within the context of professional claims to autonomy. (1981: 158)

Goal limitation

Social workers' notions of 'professionalism' and the generally conservative ethos of the Team led to the early circumscription of goals. The reasons why the initial proposals for the recruitment of black social workers were abandoned and such political considerations as black representation, access to the power structure and participation in decision–making were not pursued are complex. One explanation for this 'slippage in organisational goals' (Holmes and Grieco, 1988: 4) was the Team's structural dependency (Etzioni, 1961) and need to frame goals in ways which are compatible, consistent and congruent with the dominant requirements of higher management (Holmes and Grieco, 1988). Faced with the rejection of its proposals by higher management together with financial cut–backs and resource constraints, the Team decided to concentrate on objectives which could be more readily achieved. The result was the limitation of goals to an easily quantifiable objective – increasing the recruitment of black foster parents – which could readily be presented as an index of successful practice.

In order to maximise the likelihood of acceptance, goals were conceived in terms of least disturbance to the *status quo* and defined in non–political terms. The objective of increasing the supply of black foster parents was grounded in the need to place black children in black foster homes and was presented as a technical/professional decision. At no time had the argument been made in structural–political terms, for example, in terms of positive action to counteract the effects of racism and/or to redress past imbalance in recruitment or to incorporate black people into the service structure as service providers as well as service users.

Limitation to the narrow goal of increasing black foster parent recruitment resulted in the 'problem' of contact between white service structure and black community being conceived in terms of surmountable technical problems caused by cultural differences. Black people's experience of the social services, however, was often limited to that of an agency of social control acting on behalf of other agencies of control, the education authorities, police and law courts, to implement sanctions and punishments, supervision orders, care orders and so on (cf. Dominelli, 1989). The nature of this relationship between white service structure and black clientele was not addressed.

The emphasis on cultural differences meant that the black and white communities were treated as different and separate groups and that similarities in their situations were ignored. The tactics of 'divide and rule' were played out effectively, if not consciously, with the collusion of at least some members of the black community itself who agreed in a cultural interpretation of their circumstances. This point has been made forcibly by Sivanandan. 'Multiculturalism,' he argues, 'deflected the political concerns of the black

135

community into the cultural concerns of different communities, the struggle against racism to the struggle for culture' (1985: 6). The ways in which racism may condition black people's contacts with the social services and, in particular, their chances of becoming foster parents, were similarly not adequately confronted. Where racism was tackled, it was reduced to a personal subconscious level. Goals were, thus, defined in technical/ professional, non-political terms and confined to easily quantifiable objectives – the increased recruitment of black foster parents – achievable through technical improvements in social work practice – over-coming cultural differences and misunderstandings.

Incremental development

Throughout, the emphasis was on practical considerations. Small adjustments to policy and practice were made in response to situations which arose during the course of practice. This piecemeal, incremental development has been noted elsewhere (Young and Connelly, 1981; Cheetham, 1981b; ADSS/CRE, 1978; Ely and Denney, 1987). Lindblom (1965) has argued that agencies do not have the time or the resources to start with a clearly defined goal, evaluate all the different methods of achieving it and choose the most effective. Rather, they start from existing activities and policy and examine the effects of small changes or increments. They make successive limited comparisons which allow them to adjust sensitively to their environments through a process of trial and error. Pinder has suggested that the notion of 'practice' is more appropriately read as 'practices' and that 'a diversity of styles characterises the day-to-day operations of practitioners'. For the most part, 'new tactics and strategies emerge piecemeal, products of the worker-client exchanges and the surrounding negotiations which together make up practice' (1980:1).

Within the Fostering Team, these incremental changes took place within a climate of ambivalence and division despite the apparent consensus. Policy development was a process negotiated between members and marked by deferment and compromise rather than rational planning, and was influenced as much by the constraints of internal politics as by the exigencies of practice. The emphasis on flexibility and deference to professional autonomy as a means of diffusing or avoiding conflict meant that the reins between policy and practice were loose. Thus, although policy development may have been an introverted process carried out within the arena of Team Meetings, it was in encounters with applicants that many of the details of practice were moulded. These processes are examined in more detail in the following chapters.

7 Supply and demand: The shaping of recruitment procedure

In the past, the social work response to black communities' needs has been to focus on black people as the passive victims of racism and discrimination and to ignore the ways in which they, themselves, have been able to influence their situation (Cheetham, 1981b; Pinder, 1983). In the present study, the black applicants who responded to the campaign to recruit black foster parents were able to use their 'market' position and the fact that they were offering a scarce resource to influence the recruitment procedure in a number of ways.

Why black people did not apply in the past

When asked why so few black people had applied to become foster parents in the past, the main reasons put forward by those who had responded to the campaign were:

Lack of information about fostering and about application procedures

Although unofficial and unpaid fostering existed in the black community as a form of community self–help (Ahmed, 1980; Ely and Denney, 1987), the concept of formal fostering was alien to many people. As one woman explained,

Why I think most coloured people don't go in more for (formal) fostering children (is because) it is something new to the older ones. Because, back in our country, we don't have much (formal) fostering ... So, it's really something new to us because we didn't know about fostering until we come here.

There was no tradition of fostering for the local authority and the low recruitment of black foster parents in the past meant that there were few role models to follow. Black people had little access to the informal grapevines and communication networks through which information was circulated in the white community and their exposure to publicity and advertising, which was targeted at the white rather than the black population, was limited.

Mistrust of the social services

Many people mistrusted the Social Services as a 'white'–dominated organisation and believed that they would be discriminated against (cf. Arnold, 1982; Stubbs, 1987; Ely and Denney, 1987). In one man's words, 'It's no good for us because they (are) not interested in black people'. Second, the Social Services were perceived, and had been experienced by many, as an agency of social control. Past encounters with social workers had often been in their social control rather facilitative role (cf. Williams, 1988; Roys, 1988; Dominelli, 1989). As one informant explained,

I   Well, they have made a lot of mistakes in the past.
JA   What sort of mistakes?
I   Well, they've gone in and taken the children away when it wasn't right. Yes, they've made a lot of mistakes like that. And you only see them when there's trouble. A lot of people, they don't take much with social workers.

A belief that black people would not be considered to fulfil the criteria of acceptability

There was a belief that applications were judged according to the conventional standards of the nuclear family and middle class affluence and that black applicants would have little chance of acceptance. One applicant explained,

I   Well, on the leaflet, I would definitely tell them (other potential applicants) 'You don't have to be rich. You don't have to own your own home, you know'. I would let them know that... so, I think a lot of people need some more explanation.

138

PR   You think that is important to get that across, do you?

I   Very important because, even if you find people that come in more, that
        keep them back ... 'No, I don't have enough room. No, I don't have my
        own home. I can't foster children in a council house.' and things like
        that. They want more explanation and... um, even like you would share
        a room with another kid, they probably think, 'Oh well, they have to
        have their own room because, um, welfare will come and... you know.'
        So, I think a bit more information.

The following comments were typical:

> ... and some of them think they have to have money in the bank and
> they have to save and things like that. You'd be surprised to know what
> some people think.

> I saw it once on the TV and... I didn't notice it much because I think,
> 'Oh well, it's for people who have a home of their own and things like
> that...'

> ... because they were saying that they wanted people who are working
> and, you know, good financial situation and yet I know about 40% of
> the black population is unemployed.

> I thought, yeh, well, they are going to say, 'Well, yeh, you ain't having
> no kid because you're a single mum. You ain't working and how are
> you coping with your first child?' That's what I thought.

The bureaucratic application procedure

Many people were deterred by the application procedure which was
bureaucratic, drawn-out and impersonal. In the past, this lengthy procedure
had been used as a test of applicants' commitment to fostering[1]. As a member
of the Team explained,

> In some ways, the length of the application procedure was used to
> screen out applicants who were not really committed to fostering.

---

[1] Similar attitudes have been observed in other boroughs which have launched recruitment
drives for black foster parents (Schroeder & Lightfoot, 1983; Brunton & Welch, 1983).

139

Most of those interviewed had not been aware of the borough's policy of short term fostering when they applied and some withdrew their applications once they discovered that long term fostering placements were not an option. As Liz Brunton and Mary Welch found from their experience in Wandsworth, the 'belief that adoption should be the plan for most (younger) children in preference to inclusive fostering is challenged by black fostering and this is not easy for us to accommodate'.

> In our experience, black foster parents often manage inclusive fostering so as not to create tension and confusion for the child, seeing it as a natural arrangement. Adoption poses financial problems and unease when natural parents are in the picture and not in agreement. (Brunton and Welch, 1983: 17).

Changes in the recruitment procedure

In order to recruit more black foster parents, the Social Services were forced to adopt a more sensitive approach and to adapt their procedures to the disposition and physiognomy of the black community. The new campaign, thus, provided the stimulus for a number of departures in advertising and recruitment methods. These are summarised in Figure 1.

A targeted approach

One of the first changes was a move away from the previous blanket advertising coverage towards a more targeted approach. This included advertisements and posters appealing specifically for black families and featuring a photograph of a black foster family. Advertisements were placed in the black press, for example, the *Caribbean Times* and the Carnival edition of the *Westindian World*, and posters were put up in places frequented by black people, for example,

> small posters were placed by co-operative businesses in commercial stores that black people were most likely to use, e.g. West Indian hairdressers, grocers, greengrocers, bakers, chemists and confectioners across the borough (Report to Team Meeting, November 1984)

Figure 1
The recruitment of black foster parents

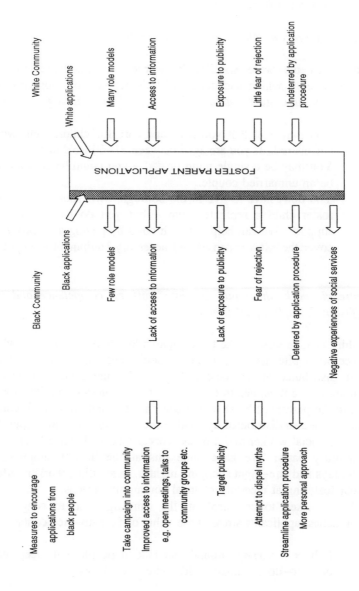

141

In June 1985, an Open Meeting was organised to which anyone interested in the fostering of black children was invited, whether or not they wished to apply to become foster parents[2].

Dispelling preconceptions about acceptability

Advertisements were specifically worded to counteract the 'myths' or preconceptions which had deterred black people from applying in the past. The following extract was taken from one of the campaign leaflets:

You may feel that you love and care for children but would not be considered. If you are aged between 21–60 we'd like to hear from you. You may be a single mum or dad – you could be at work or you may be an unmarried couple.

You don't have to live in the borough, own your own home or give a foster child a separate room – but you do have to offer love and support. We can help out with costs by paying a weekly allowance to cover the extra expenses and necessary equipment – even beds.

Outreach work: the limits to white workers' competence and information diffusion through informal networks

A third change was to take the campaign 'out into the community' rather than expecting applicants to come to the Social Services as in the past. Leaflets were distributed at the local College of Further Education, local libraries, community centres, health centres, doctors' surgeries and the Housing Office and to the pastors of West Indian churches to hand out to their congregations. They were also distributed by hand at the local market and shopping centre by a white social worker and a black worker who had offered her services on a temporary basis: 'We have done this at the busiest shopping times i.e. Saturdays and late–night shopping nights'. In addition, workers offered to talk about fostering at meetings of local community groups.

When asked to comment on the campaign and to suggest alternative approaches, applicants stressed the value of face–to–face contact.

I think if you go around and talk to people and meet people like a door–to–door campaign, it's better, you know.

---

[2] This was held in response to a report on the campaign presented to the Team by the researcher.

The door-to-door approach was an accepted method of campaigning for recruits, since it was used by the churches. Word-of-mouth was considered to be the most effective means of advertising:

But you would impress people more by talking to them, people talking to each other. Word-of-mouth would be better.

and the snow-balling approach, the most effective method of information diffusion:

I would start by going round and asking people. Getting people that I know and that knows others that would be interested.

I would get a few mothers to come round to somebody's house and let us have a good talk and then, from there, each one to each one. So a lot of people will get to know.

Such informal gatherings or 'tea parties', each week in a different person's home, were an important element of the social life and, thus, cohesiveness of the female community.

In sum, reliance on external sources of publicity, albeit targeted at the black population, was thought to be less effective than the utilization of internal communication networks already in existence within the black community. In order to locate and infiltrate these informal networks, however, it was necessary to gain the confidence and trust of the black community. For these reasons, the worker running the campaign admitted that, as a white worker, she had probably gone as far as she could in making contact and that it would need a black worker to make further advances (cf. Arnold, 1982; L.B.Wandsworth 1986d).

Informal networks were important not only in the dissemination of information about fostering and about the application procedure but as a means of support for existing black foster parents who were excluded from the informal support networks operating among white foster parents. Ironically, the move toward same race placement would sever the links cultivated between the two communities by an inclusive approach to transracial fostering which encourages contacts between the white foster family and the child's natural family (Holman, 1975). On the other hand, with the establishment of mixed training and assessment groups and the recruitment of more black foster parents, the relative impermeability of the networks of communication in the two communities may begin to break down.

A more personal approach

At the outset to the campaign, it was decided to make the advertising 'as personal as possible ... with a named person for interested applicants to telephone' (Report to Team Meeting, November 1984). The personal touch was important in both the generation and retention of interest. Many people seemed to regard both the speed of social workers' response and their willingness to visit them personally as a test of their commitment to recruiting black foster parents.

> They should come and interview us individually first before they call us all together for a meeting. If the Social Services had come to me instead of me having to go to them, maybe, I would have a little girl now (i.e. would not have withdrawn my application).

> It's a pity they are so slow. They want you to go to them instead of them coming to you.

Where, in the past, workers had judged applicants' willingness to attend meetings or interviews as a test of their commitment, the tables had been turned and they found themselves having to make the first moves.

A more streamlined approach

The tenor of the advertising had led applicants to believe that they would be welcomed with open arms and many resented what they considered to be the lengthy and delayed process of assessment and the amount of 'red tape' involved.

> If they is so desperate for foster parents, why all this long delay. They come to visit you once, they come again and its the same questions over and over...

> And you know what? She (the social worker) was here again yesterday and she made me fill out another form. I can't see the point of it. What's it for? They probably don't even bother to read it anyway. It just gets filed somewhere. Just more jobs for them so they can waste tax payers' money.

Some even suspected a 'racial' motive for the delay.

All this delay and waiting. If they were really interested to have black people doing the fostering, they wouldn't take so long and they wouldn't put so many things in the way.

Steps were, therefore, taken to make the process more streamlined, with fewer stages and a faster response time. The following changes were made soon after the outset of the campaign.

a. Usually when applicants contact the Department they are sent an initial form which they complete and send back to the Department. They are then invited to an Information Meeting where the day–to–day demands of fostering are discussed. During the campaign, these initial forms have been filled out over the phone and applicants invited to the next meeting straight away... This has meant one less form to complete and procedure is speeded up...
b. Formerly, if an applicant was sent two invitations to a meeting then failed to turn up, there was no further action. Since the campaign started, these applicants have been followed up by phone.
c. If application forms were not returned, the applications were not followed up but, since the campaign started, they have been followed up by phone. (Report to Team Meeting, November 1984)

A decision was also made to review the application forms. After the campaign had been running for eight months, a report was presented to the Team which included the following recommendations:–

a. Recruiting procedure needs to be as personal, direct, flexible as possible. It needs to involve as little bureaucracy as possible.
b. Continuity – applicants should deal with as few people as possible so that applicants deal with people who are familiar to them and the whole procedure is therefore less threatening.
c. The assessment procedure should not be long and drawn out as, if applicants are left hanging around, we may lose them[3] [4].

---

[3] The minimum number of home visits was discussed in September when it was decided that 'the initial meeting was instead of the first home visit' although 'at least four contacts with the family were still necessary'. Later, the number of home visits was reduced further with the introduction of group asssessment.

[4] Two further recommendations were made, neither of which were fulfilled:

(continued...)

145

Reactions to the campaign within the black community

Reactions to the targeted approach varied. Some people were suspicious of social workers' motives.

> It's just to have a few more black faces so they can say they is concerned for the black folk. But they're not really interested in letting black people through. It's a lot of talk but you won't find many black folks get through.

Others were surprised that the campaign had been aimed specifically at them:

> I was surprised that they were asking for **black** people to foster, I mean, that they mentioned colour, that they were actually using the word, **'Black'**, and asking for black people. That really came as a shock to me. I didn't expect it.

Most, however, were reacting to the call for black foster parents to care for black children, as the following comments demonstrate.

> I saw it in the *Jamaica Gleaner* ... There are more black people who are doing fostering now. And it's a good thing: all these children needing homes.

> Until I saw the advertisement, I didn't know about all these black children needing families.

Despite the success of the targeted approach, many people expressed reservations about the underlying rationale and concurred with the respondent who declared that

> It doesn't matter what colour the child is, whether it is black, white, pink or blue. A child is a child. It's love that counts.

There seemed to be some contradiction between people's specific response to the advertisements for black foster parents for black children and their

---

⁴(...continued)

(d)   Applicants should be recruited as far as possible by black social workers and black foster parents at each stage of their application.

(e)   Where white social workers are involved in assessing black applicants, cultural issues need to be explored by discussion group.

146

reservations about a policy of same race placements. The following exchange between a mother and daughter is an illustration.

Da. You have to do things on individual merits, really. It is important to consider the situation, why the child is being fostered in the first place and why it has to be taken away from its parents and go to somebody else. You have to look at each child individually, regardless of colour.
Mo. Yes, because, at the same time, if the child has to be fostered, and there's only a white family available, I don't see why ...
Da. It's better than being put in a home. Much better.
Mo. That's right.

Some people were openly hostile:

> I couldn't carry a campaign saying black children should go with black parents. Whatever we going to say, they only different here (pointing to skin): underneath, we are the same. I don't see why people should look at other people skin.
> So, I would say, spread it out and let's get together more, you know what I mean. It would seem as if you was racialist if you was only to put them with black family, put black with black and white with white. But, if you put white with black and black with white... it would work better. All this racialist would stop because we would get to know that we need each other.

Others were more favourably disposed. One person, for example, explained,

> They grow up like white people and do all them things like white people but, when they reach a certain age, they find that their skin is against them, that they are different. They become conscious... It is bad for the child to be raised up from a baby in a white family... At the end of the day, the child is not accepted by that white society because its skin is black. All white culture: it don't have no black culture... You feel you want to help. I wanted to take these children and give them a good home and a good bringing–up so that they can learn their own culture.

But most were ambivalent and the following comments were typical:

> We are meant to be living in an integrated society: that's pushing us further apart.

I have already said that I don't believe in segregation. If the whites have it (the black child), I would (give it to them). Why not? Sometimes, they lead better lives. After all, black people give their children to white child minders and they give them better lives than black people would. They take good care of them and treat them well.

They should mix it up, you know. Because... um, there are plenty other people going to look in it, you know. So, why white children don't come to black people? You know, they should. They have to do a lot to make this thing work.

The placement of mixed-parentage children seemed to cause special difficulties, as the following comment illustrates:

If I had a white mother who had adopted a black child, could I tell that white mother that her child would have to go with a black parent? I didn't hear them speaking anything about mixed kids. What about the mixture, the one with the black father and the white mother? I didn't hear them tell me who the child is to go with. What about them? What about mixed marriage? Some of the same people who are saying that black children should go with black people are mixed marriage. I would like to know who they would want their one to go to?

Nearly all were opposed to a rigid same race placement policy and it seemed as if, for some, opposition to differential treatment could only be maintained by denying the relevance of culture and black identity.

Oh no, I'm not the kind of a black woman that look at people colour. I don't business what colour anyone make it.

I don't believe in segregation. Some people may believe in it but I don't. No, I don't agree with that policy because I don't believe in segregation.

Although it was on a reconsideration of the importance of racism and of cultural and ethnic identity that the policy of matching was founded and to which black applicants owed their stronger position in the fostering 'market', these issues were not highlighted in the advertising campaign nor were they broached by either social workers or applicants in either of the two Information Meetings attended by the researcher. Social workers seemed reluctant to raise the issues and many of the applicants interviewed, far from utilizing their ethnicity to consolidate their position, were dismissive of the

148

relevance of culture and hostile to the introduction of ethnicity into the fostering process. One woman, for example, remarked,

> It doesn't matter what culture you are. It is being able to give a child a home that is important. As long as you can love and care for that child, that is what is important. It doesn't really matter what culture that child is.

The relevance of a 'Black identity' shared with all 'non-white' people was even more strongly opposed. 'What is 'Black identity'?', one man demanded,

> What's having 'Black identity'? We all eat, drink, sleep. Black people must realise that they aren't any different. I don't know what they mean by 'Black identity'.

Another commented,

> No, I wouldn't agree with that, where they would loose their black identity, I wouldn't say that. Isn't that a, um... a bit racialist, don't you think?

Other people were proud of their cultural heritage and pleased that it was being taken seriously, although they did not necessarily think that it was a particularly important consideration when placing a child in a foster family. Many thought that it was unrealistic to expect black children brought up in Britain to share their own Caribbean heritage. One woman, for example, described how she would cook rice and salt fish for herself but sausages and chips for her children.

Many people seemed to maintain close-knit ethnic ties in their private lives, as the relative closure of their informal social networks and channels of communication demonstrates, but to reject ethnic differentiation in the public sphere (cf. Jayaweera, 1991). Thus, although they responded to the targeted approach on an emotional level where they had not responded to the more general advertising in the past, they rejected the campaign's underlying rationale of racial and ethnic differentiation on a public ideological level.

Conclusion

The features which characterised the initial stages of the campaign, that is

a. the ability of black applicants to influence the conduct of the recruitment drive as a consequence of their stronger 'market' position;

b. their ambivalence about the underlying rationale and consequent underplaying of issues concerned with 'racial' and cultural identity;

c. their suspicion of differential treatment on the grounds of skin colour and cultural distinctiveness;

d. the tension between their private preferences for ethnic cohesion and their public opposition to differentiation

set the tone for the assessment process in general and form continuous threads which run through the following chapters.

The campaign's objective of increasing the recruitment of black foster parents in order to increase the number of 'racially matched' placements was accomplished, although the underlying rationale of 'racial' and ethnic differentiation was often not acknowledged. Despite their rejection or partial rejection of the underlying theory, however, and their reluctance to mobilise their ethnicity or political identity as black people to consolidate their position, applicants were able to use their 'market' position to influence the campaign in a number of ways which had implications not simply for black recruits but for fostering applicants in general.

A number of writers have warned against the dangers of labelling and of assuming that black people are simply the passive victims of racism and discrimination (e.g. Pinder, 1981a; Solomon, 1976; Cheetham 1981a) and have shown how black people have often been able to employ their ethnicity to their advantage in encounters with social workers (Pinder, 1983; Ballard R., 1979). Ethnicity, as Wallman (1979) has pointed out, is not a static and immutable condition but a resource or handicap, the relevance of which has to be negotiated in each encounter and can be mobilised or resisted according to circumstance. The assumptions about the relevance of ethnicity of the social workers running the recruitment campaign were both challenged and compromised by the applicants who were able both to challenge the terms of the assessment encounter and to shift the frame of reference from a specifically ethnic and cultural orientation towards a consideration of economic and material circumstances and a more general reappraisal of family assessment skills. These processes are examined in the following chapter.

8 Assessment and the challenge to cultural pluralism

In order to retain a sufficient 'stock' of foster parents of various kinds to ensure a sufficient measure of choice to avoid hasty and inappropriate placements (as occurred in the placement of Jasmine and Louise Beckford) (Parker, 1988), Departmental policy was to recruit into a pool rather than on the basis of individually tailored placements. This meant that, unless a home for a particular child was being sought, much of the preliminary stage was 'conducted in rather general terms' (*op cit.*: 15). This encouraged reliance on a model or ideal type of family life as the standard against which potential recruits were assessed[1]. The model adopted was the popular stereotype of white, middle class family life with its division of labour between male and female roles and its underpinnings of material affluence.

---

[1] At least one specialist agency has abandoned this approach altogether. Parents for Children argue that 'The children's needs are so varied that we do not see how we could 'approve' people in the abstract as potential parents – it makes so much more sense to approve the placement of one particular child with one particular family' (*Parents for Children First Year's Report 1976/77*).

Workers commented on their past reliance on 'conventional white, middle class family norms'[2] (c.f Brunton and Welch, 1983; Dominelli 1988; Brummer 1988; Divine 25 Mar. 1983) and believed that one of the most important changes of the recent campaign had been a move towards 'a more flexible and culturally-sensitive approach'. The cultural pluralist approach, however, not only called into question social workers' cross-cultural skills but conflicted with their liberal commitment to assimilation. As John Solomos observes,

> the most resonant themes in contemporary racial discourses are not concerned with absolute notions of racial superiority, but with the threats which black communities are seen to represent to the cultural, political and religious homogeneity of white British society (Solomos, 1989: 127).

What had seemed appealing in theory, thus, proved more difficult to implement in practice (cf. Ely and Denney, 1987). The 'surface gloss of appropriate language use' (Connelly, 1989: 18) masked a deeper ambivalence and, for some, a lack of commitment. In focusing on the ways in which the conventional model of family life discriminates on cultural grounds, workers ignored economic and class considerations and failed to address the nature and impact of racism (cf. Roys, 1988). Providing 'an ethnically sensitive service' was thought to be a simple matter of adjusting practice to take into account cultural differences, with applicants the passive beneficiaries (Connelly, 1989)[3], rather than a two-way process negotiated within a context of unequal power. The question of relative power between black, working class applicant and white, middle class professional was not addressed.

The concept of 'family'

The notion of 'family' is one of the most potent ideological concepts of our time. As Barrett and McIntosh put it, 'the realms of the "natural" and the socio-moral are nowhere so constantly merged and confused as in our feelings

---

[2] In a recent survey of 2694 foster homes, Bebbington & Miles found that

Foster families typically include a woman in the 31–35 age group, live in homes with three or more bedrooms, are two parent families with one parent working full-time and the other not, and they have older children only (1990: 283).

[3] '...discussion and work continue within a framework which is department-centred, so that the role of people in local black communities is seen in terms of reacting to departmental initiatives' (Connelly, 1989:16).

152

and thoughts about the family' (1982: 26). The conventional stereotype is that of employed husband and his dependent wife and children. It prescribes the relations between husband and wife, parents and children, and the division of labour between the husband's 'work' outside the home in his role as 'breadwinner' and the wife's domestic duties as wife, mother and home–maker. Its strength does not lie in its prevalence as a structural unit – in 1985 the married couple with dependent children represented just 29% of all households and married male employees with a wife at home looking after two dependent children represented only 8% of the labour force (Howard, 1987) – but in its power as an ideological construct. The model is essentially functionalist (e.g. Parsons, 1949) and derives from the biological concept of Darwinian fitness (Rappoport et al., 1977) and, because it embodies assumptions about 'how families ought to be' (Robertson Elliot, 1986), is both morally coercive and avoids important intellectual and empirical issues (Lambert and Streather, 1980).

The family is portrayed as a 'grass roots' institution and the main bastion against state interference in people's lives (Mount, 1982)[4]. An attack upon the family becomes an attack upon the people (Mrs Thatcher 6 June 1986). The class–based (David, 1986; Barrett and McIntosh, 1982; Burgoyne, 1987), sexist (Oakley, 1987; Barrett and McIntosh, 1982) and ethnocentric (Satow and Homans, 1981) character of much of this moral rhetoric is disguised amid claims about the conventional family as the 'natural' and 'fundamental unit of society' (letter to *The Guardian*, 24 February 1985). The coercive elements of family ideology are turned, by political sleight of hand, into the defence of 'ordinary people' and what is rightfully theirs, in other words, the right to enjoy a 'normal family life'. Every shade of the political spectrum has claimed 'the family' for its own so that 'every party (has become) a party of the family' (*The Guardian*, 6 June 1986). An idealised version of the family has come to be perceived 'as the institution that can cure all our social ills, a metaphor for some private and public paradise lost' (Ellis, 1981)[5]. In the demise of the family is located the source of all our social woes, hence the perennial concern

---

[4] 'The working–class', according to Ferdinand Mount, 'is the true defender of liberty and privacy' within the family (1982:7:175). Certain Marxists and feminists have made similar claims, although for different reasons: Morgan (1979), for example, sees the working–class family as a repository for revolutionary values and Humphries (1977) as the basis of the cohesion and solidarity necessary to class struggle. In a different vein, Betty Friedan (1982) has defended the family as a source of protection for women allowing them to express their individuality in the face of state intervention and pressure to conform to socially–defined roles. Other strands of what Judith Stacey has called 'conservative pro–family feminism' promote the family as the seedbed of the nurturant values of motherhood as opposed to patriarchal values (Thorne, 1982; see Oakley, 1987, for discussion).

[5] Mrs. Thatcher, for example, described it as part of 'the great open site of human freedom' and that 'little bit of heaven on earth' (Conservative Women's Conference, 1986).

that 'the institution of the nuclear family, fundamental in the design of our society, is crumbling' (*The Guardian*, 24 February 1985).

Woman's role within the family is traditionally conceived as one of nurturance and subordination to the authority of her husband and of her own needs and desires to those of her husband and children. The 'ethic of the sentimental nuclear family' (Oakley, 1987) and especially that of the mother–child bond is enshrined in religion, biology (Mount, 1982; Murdock 1968; Linton 1949), psychology (Richards, 1982), sociology (Robertson Elliot, 1986; Oakley 1974), media imagery (Barret and McIntosh, 1982; Oakley, 1987) and government policy (Zaretsky, 1982; David, 1986; Nissel, 1980; Henwood *et al.*, 1987). Its existence is predicated on the needs of society (usually men in society) (e.g. Parsons 1949) and the needs of children (see Berger and Berger, 1984 for a recent restatement) and, although it is portrayed as woman–centred (e.g. Mount, 1982), women are not regarded as having capabilities, needs or desires independent of their caring/nurturing role. In the words of Ann Oakley, 'The era of enforced conformity of women to happy housewife and mother stereotypes is still with us' (Oakley, 1987: 15).

In contrast with men's paid employment, the role of wife/mother is sentimentally revered as a vocation which demands women's 'exclusive personal loyalty' (Wainwright, 1978). A conceptual distinction is drawn between the 'public' world of male employment and social life outside the family and the 'private' domestic world of family life. Housework and child care were not regarded as 'real work' but as the natural duties of women which it is their biological destiny to fulfil (Mount, 1982). The proportion of a woman's time budget spent in the home was therefore taken as a measure of her worth, not only as a wife, mother and home–maker, but as a woman.

Although the rise of 'the sentimental nuclear family' and of 'the cult of Motherhood' is a relatively modern phenomenon (Oakley, 1976; Hewlett, 1987; Burgoyne, 1987; Gillis, 1986), societal ills continue to be interpreted in terms of a sociobiological imperative and concern about 'the family' and, more specifically, about women's role within it. Women who have transgressed the public/private divide by engaging in paid employment – 'working women', 'working wives', 'working mothers', for example – have been defined as a 'social problem' (Oakley, 1974). 'If the Good Lord had intended us to have equal rights to go out to work, he wouldn't have created man and woman', Patrick Jenkin declared in a television interview on 'Man Alive', when Secretary of State for Social Services in 1979.

During the 1960s the optimistic belief that society in general was becoming not only more affluent but more egalitarian was reflected in a sentimentally rosy portrait of 'ordinary family life'. The family on the back of the cornflakes packet and in the T.V. ads. became a symbol of national well–being of the new consumer society. This sentimental ideal, as Burgoyne has pointed out,

154

is based on the conceptual separation of emotional from material considerations; thus, real happiness is thought to lie within the close personal relationships formed within the nuclear family (Mount, 1982). Economic and material concerns are considered to be not only secondary but potentially damaging to this portrait of emotional well-being. In the spirit of the well-worn adage, 'Money can't buy happiness, ..."materialistic" becomes a dirty word and we all join hands in agreement that riches do not necessarily lead to happiness' (Burgoyne, 1987: 13).

The importance of the economic and material side to 'family life' has been exposed in a study of stepfamilies in Sheffield by Jacqueline Burgoyne and David Clarke (1984) which 'illustrates how the connections between access to material resources and emotional well-being affect families of all kinds' (Burgoyne, 1987: 13). According to Burgoyne, the artificial separation of emotional from material considerations has encouraged

> the widespread belief... that family life is, in some senses at least, the same for everyone; a universal experience and thus a kind of lowest common denominator and potential source of national unity... It is all too easy for politicians, policy makers and others to believe that the persistent and deepening social divisions within our society have little effect on the essentials of family life because they seem to have very little to do with economic inequalities. (1987: 13)

The conventional family and fostering

Through fostering, this bourgeois ideal was preserved. Children's social and moral welfare was protected by removing them from 'broken' and 'inadequate' homes (usually the homes of poor people whose family arrangements differed from the conventional norm) and placing them in homes which, in the eyes of those making the placements, most closely conformed with the bourgeois ideal (George, 1970; ABSWAP, 1983b).

From the conceptual separation of the emotional from material and economic aspects of family life it is a small step to believing that the psychological and relationship problems of poorer families are unrelated to their financial or material circumstances and derive, in some way, from flaws in their make-up or the personalities of their members. Deviations from the popular stereotype have come to be regarded, at best, as an indication of inadequacy and, at worst, as pathological. Social workers placing children for fostering and adoption have recruited families from the middle and more affluent sections of the working classes (Bebbington and Miles, 1990), on the assumption that emotional and material well-being go hand-in-hand. Recent

155

research on transracially adopted children, for example, emphasised the material advantages, educational and social opportunities of their middle class upbringing (Gill and Jackson, 1983)[6].

Not only were the economic underpinnings but the conventional separation of roles preserved. Recruitment posters featured photographs of a happy two-parent family smiling down from their comfortable haven of domestic bliss. As Marion Lowe has pointed out, 'the role of foster carer is inextricably linked with women's traditional place in the home' (1989, v iii; cf. Rhodes, 1989; Dennison, 1987)[7]. Advertisements and newspaper features, concentrate on foster mothers rather than foster fathers and emphasise the mother's warm, nurturant qualities rather than the organisational and 'professional' skills which the fostering task increasingly entails[8].

---

[6] This was underlined recently in the judgement in a United States court which removed parental rights from a surrogate mother and transferred them to the family with whom she had made a contract to bear the baby on the grounds that she would not be able to offer the child the same material security and advantages (*The Guardian*, April 1987).

[7] That fostering is still regarded as essentially 'women's work' is made conspicuous in an article in *Foster Care* (Dennison, 1987) which begins, 'In the beginning there were foster mothers...', and where the argument is made for the greater involvement of foster fathers in the care of foster children. According to the writer,

Many fathers seem reluctant to change, and the ability of being able to drop into a full caring role without losing any of their masculinity in the process is a very real threat indeed, not only to themselves as people, husbands, fathers/males, but also (*sic.*) to their traditional roles in life...

'Throughout history', he explains,

the traditional role of the husband/father has been one of provider, decision maker, boundary and discipline keeper, not only within the home but also within the community...Many men have... been reluctant to take on the caring role...

As a consequence, 'the acceptance of foster fathers as part of the caring team has left many foster fathers uncertain as to their true role in the family'. The writer implies that women are more emotional, less practical and less objective than men and, therefore, less competent to take part in important decision making. In other words, the foster father arrogates to himself the more 'professional' managerial and, in the writer's eyes, more prestigious role. He talks, for example, of 'compensation for any lack of status (the foster father) may feel' and advocates 'a supportive but not servile' role in relation to his wife. The foster father is encouraged to take on the dominant role in interactions with the public world - in reviews, case conferences and so on - in an attempt to preserve intact the boundary with the private domestic world of the family and the woman's role within it. To the foster mother fall all the mundane tasks of day-to-day child care and the emotional involvement which is believed to be both woman's strength and her weakness. As the writer correctly perceives, recognition of the potential contribution of foster fathers is a new development, hence the concern with the demarcation of male/female roles within the foster family and with the maintenance of conventional boundaries (Rhodes, 1989: 94-5).

[8] The conflict is most apparent when it comes to parting with a foster child who has spent some time in the foster mother's care when ties of love and affection deemed so fundamental to the motherhood role are broken. The failure of a short-term foster mother's attempt to adopt a black child who had been with her almost since birth recently highlighted the conflicts involved in the role (Kirton, 1989; *The Independent*, 28 Oct.1989; Gaffeney, 1989; Mills

(continued...)

156

Previous lack of involvement of foster fathers has, perhaps, contributed to the often patronising stance of many social workers towards foster parents. Foster parents complain that they are not consulted and often not even informed about decisions affecting the children in their care. The relationship of social worker to foster parent was one of professional and expert in child care to well-meaning but unqualified helper. The foster parent's skills and experience were devalued and unrecognised compared with the professional knowledge and expertise of the qualified social worker (Letter to *Foster Care*, March 1986b). In other words, the social worker adopted the male role of decision-maker and often also of provider and disciplinarian. The social worker was often the main link with the public sphere outside the family, taking decisions about the child's schooling, medical care and so on, whereas the foster mother's role was not considered to extend beyond the motherly duties of providing physical care, warmth and affection in the domestic space (Rhodes, 1989: 95).

The conventional stereotype of white, middle class family life not only discriminated against black people at the level of both culture and location in the class structure and the relationship between professional social worker and foster carer reinforced the unequal power relationships between white and black people in the wider society. The economic insecurity of many black families (Cheetham, 1982b; Commission for Racial Equality, 1981; Smith, 1976, 1981; Runneymede Trust, 1976; Home Affairs Committee, 1981), combined with society's intolerance of cultural differences (Roys, 1988), association of minority cultures with deficiency (Keddie, 1978; Solomos, 1988) and failure to acknowledge the significance of racism (Solomos, 1988), resulted in their relegation to the category of 'problem families'. Not only were their children removed disproportionately into care (ABSWAP, 1983a; Arnold and James, 1989) but they were placed in white rather than black substitute homes. The new ideas about 'racial' and cultural matching, however, have stimulated a drive to recruit substitute families from a section of the population previously under-represented in the foster parent pool, that is, among people who do not necessarily conform with the conventional stereotype on either a cultural or material level and whose family patterns have previously been categorised as pathological (Roys, 1988). In order to recruit more black foster parents, social workers were forced to revise their ideas

---

[8](...continued)

1989). Here, the traditional mothering image proves inadequate. The 'good' foster parent is one who does not form bonds with the foster child which cannot easily be broken. There is an implicit recognition that fostering often requires a 'professional' attitude towards the foster children which does not necessarily mirror the popular conception of a mother's relationship to her children. (see *A Child in Trust. The report of the panel of inquiry into the circumstances surrounding the death of Jasmine Beckford 1985*, London Borough of Brent, Blom-Cooper, 1986).

about suitability and about fostering as a vocation or charitable service rather than a job. They were confronted not only with the problem of how to accept as equivalent standards which would have been considered inferior by conventional criteria but with the equally difficult question of whether or not to adopt different standards for black applicants than for white.

The pluralist challenge

Attempts to resolve these questions relied on arguments of cultural relativism rather than class. This was partly a consequence of the rationale which underlay the recruitment campaign which portrayed black people and white people as members of distinctive cultural groups and partly a consequence of the popular conception of 'the normal family' as a template for social organisation rather than as an economic or consumerist unit (Burgoyne, 1987). The artificial separation of emotional from material life and consequent denial of the model's economic underpinnings was mirrored in the dissociation of culture from class and focus on the ways in which the model discriminated against black applicants on cultural rather than on economic grounds. This cultural analysis, although superficially appealing in theory was often difficult to sustain in practice (cf. Ely and Denney, 1987[9]) and ran into difficulties on a number of counts.

Inter-cultural competence

Social workers' commitment to cultural pluralism often seemed to have little grounding beyond the level of rhetoric. This was partly a consequence of their lack of confidence in their own powers of discernment and ability to make judgements about another culture (cf. Cheetham, 1981a,b) and this was most severely tested over the question of acceptable standards of discipline. The supposedly unrealistic expectations of children, over-rigid regimes and harsh punishments imposed by some West Indian parents were a persistent cause of concern (cf. Nixon, 1983; Brunton and Welch, 1983) and it was in this area that workers, perhaps, felt most ill at ease and unsure about their own abilities to make appropriate judgements. One, for example, described her confusion when an applicant she had recently visited had, 'in one minute, talked of the importance of talking and reasoning with the child and, in another breath,

---

[9] Ely and Denney found that, although 'white workers may intellectually assent to 'cultural pluralism' and understand that other ways of defining situations may be as valid and held with a conviction equal to their own, they generally find it hard to put into practice' (1987:112).

spoken of "a good beating never doing a child any harm"'[10]. Another confided,

SW4 It's matters of discipline I find difficult. I sometimes think I am simply imposing my own 'white' standards but, then, there's the danger of accepting things which, really, are not acceptable.

This lack of confidence and 'tentativeness, tantamount to de-skilling' which is 'evident in relationships between white social workers and black clients' (Blythe and Milner, 1987: 20; Connelly 1989: 9,13) has been noted by other writers (Parker, 1988; Roys, 1988). Brummer has suggested that 'social workers' fears of being perceived as racist can lead them to applying '"a rule of optimism", to losing a balanced judgement and fudging hard decisions' (1988: 119; cf. Blom-Cooper, 1986).

Value conflicts

The question of discipline highlighted the problem of conflicting values and of knowing how far it was justifiable or appropriate to compromise conventional standards (cf. Brunton and Welch, 1983)[11]. Multi-culturalism was not the simple matter of 'live and let live' which many had been seduced into believing but a difficult process of adjustment involving clashes of principle, often deeply held (cf. Cheetham, 1981b). Resolution is a matter of negotiation and compromise, rarely easy and, sometimes, even impossible. The recent eruption of violent demonstrations over the publication of Salmaan Rushdie's 'Satanic Verses' is a dramatic illustration of the passions which can be aroused. Like religion, issues concerned with family life and the care of children comprise some of the most cherished and deep-rooted values in a society.

Ahmed (1981b) has explained how many clients' perceptions of social workers as agents of social control may lead to difficulties, especially where the social workers are seen as the purveyors of a dominant British culture and

---

[10] The contradiction was, perhaps, more apparent than real. It may have been only in the social worker's own eyes that the two modes of discipline were opposed and mutually exclusive.

[11] Brunton and Welch (1983) found similar difficulties in Wandsworth:

If we are properly to assess black families... we need to adopt a totally different model of the 'successful family' and to discard our white family model. This has proved enormously difficult and prompts workers to fear that double standards, or a compromise in standards, are being adopted. Factors common in black families and traditionally seen as undesirable in white applicants have caused the greatest concern (cf. *Community Care*, 13 July 1989).

tradition. Such difficulties have led Roskill to suggest that 'social work with ethnic minorities highlights the relativity of value systems and the extent to which these are culturally determined. It raises very difficult questions as to whose value systems should prevail, the social worker's or the clients" (Roskill, 1979: 18 cited in Nixon, 1983: 143; cf. Cheetham, 1981b; Nixon, 1983; Connelly, 1989: 49).

Pluralism or assimilation?

The recognition that different standards did not necessarily mean having to accept lower standards did little to alleviate workers' deep concern about operating a dual approach. Their problems seemed to stem from their inability to square their pluralist ideas with their liberal commitment to assimilation/integration. Workers spoke of their reluctance to adopt differential criteria of acceptance:

SW8 I am not very happy about using different standards to vet black families. In fact, I think it may be quite a dangerous move and I think that a lot of us here are rather worried about the way the Team is moving. After all, we all have to learn to live together if we want to be an integrated society and that is pulling us further apart. I don't think it is necessary to have different standards. You ought, really, to be able to work to the same basic set of guidelines. After all, in the end, you are really looking for the same basic things, whether the family is black or white.

and their intuitive dislike of working with black people in a different way from white:

SW4 I don't feel, as an individual, that there's an awful lot one can do other than, perhaps, be aware, really, and sort of just treat blacks the way one would treat anyone else which is, hopefully, what one has done. But I am sure that she (Race Awareness Training Course Leader) would have said differently, that one shouldn't treat black people the same. But that's my feeling.

Differential treatment was seen as the thin end of the wedge which would lead to 'racial' separatism (cf. Rooney, 1981).

SW2 I think that we ought to be able to work together. I do not think that separating it off, only black with black and white with white, is a good thing at all. That would be dangerously like apartheid.

160

At least two workers considered the need for differential treatment to be a temporary measure which would be obviated as black people became assimilated into mainstream society. As one of them explained, although it may be an appropriate stance at the present time, black separatism was, in her opinion, only a transitory phase.

SW3   Black separatism is probably an appropriate movement for the black community at the moment.
PR   What do you mean by that?
SW3   It means that I am an optimist, a long term optimist. I can't see things changing in the near future but I am a long term optimist.
PR   I still don't quite understand.
SW3   Well, I think black people have to be forceful and aggressive, if you like. I think that they have to get angry in order to get things done in the short term. It is necessary in the short term to go a bit separate, perhaps, but not in the long term.

Such attitudes are characteristic of views among white social workers in general and Phillip Roys (1988: 214) has suggested that the assimilationist perspective is the dominant paradigm in most social service departments (cf. Rooney, 1982; Stubbs, 1985).

Culture or class?

According to Roys, 'the model of cultural diversity... adopts a naïve belief that minority cultures can be isolated from political and economic realities' (1988: 221). Social workers' reluctance to acknowledge the relevance of a family's economic circumstances was most clearly revealed in their changing ideas about good parenting and appropriate parental roles. Black families confronted workers with patterns of domestic organisation which did not conform with the conventional stereotype and, as the campaign progressed, they were forced to re-evaluate their ideas. During the first six months, the age limit was extended to accommodate older women whose families had grown up, and applications were considered from unmarried couples[12], single parents and working mothers. None of these changes was made easily. Single parent

---

[12] Once marriage was waived as a requirement the definition of a 'stable relationship' raised difficulties, as the following extract from a Team meeting in September 1984 revealed:

We agreed that the ability of the relationship to withstand stress is what we needed to look at, and discussed whether there could be definable guidelines to do this. We concluded that asking that couples should have been together for three years was longer than necessary: probably, one year would be more appropriate, but this could only be a guideline, and each situation had to be assessed individually.

161

families, for example, were regarded as incomplete and potential 'problem families' and the decision to approve was not taken lightly, especially if the mother worked (cf. Blunden, 1988). As one worker explained,

SW5 There's been a real problem with single parent families. You see, it's very hard to get over the idea that a family needs a father figure and, then, most of them go out to work, and there's the problem of who looks after the kids. You see, many of these kids came into care from single parent families.

Many applicants who worked were loth to give up their jobs since the fostering allowances were insufficient to compensate for loss of earnings. Social workers were, therefore, forced to reconsider their ideas about 'suitability'. Once it was accepted that a mother may work without necessarily neglecting her children, there was the question of co–carers and a re–evaluation of the importance of the mother–child bond. How much should a mother be permitted to share her nurturing role with another person or persons? Should the same criteria of acceptance be applied to co–carers? At a Team meeting in May 1984,

It was acknowledged that many black mothers worked, and that we would be prepared to include in the advertisement another person, not immediately in the family, who would be involved in child care. It was decided that people looking after under fives should not work more than the equivalent of 3 full days.

The degree of help with housework required of children, often a necessity where mothers went out to work, was another cause for concern, as one social worker explained,

SW5 Sometimes the kids are expected to stay at home to do the housework, especially the older girls, and they may even skip school. They are expected to work in the house when the mother goes out to work but we wouldn't expect our kids to work like that.

The need for black foster carers prompted the decision to recruit from among the unemployed and this resulted in a similar reassessment of conventional views about men and women's 'proper' roles and of the assumption that families where the husband is unemployed are inadequate and prone to 'problems'. Through unemployment, the husband was thought to be deprived of a major source of his male identity as breadwinner and head–of–household which sets up stresses and tensions within the marriage.

162

As one worker explained, 'We wouldn't normally have considered a family where the husband is unemployed, ...because it puts a strain on the whole family'.

The fact that large numbers of black applicants would have been excluded by conventional criteria forced workers to compromise or to abandon previous standards of material affluence and to re-examine their notions of good parenting and male/female roles. Although the changes were essentially pragmatic responses to the new demand for black foster parents, they were justified by the need to take into account cultural differences. In relation to single parents, for example, the Team Leader noted that 'We must take into account that it is culturally acceptable for West Indian women to go out to work' and that 'the role of the father in many black families is not as important as in white families for cultural reasons' (Team Meeting Minutes June 1984). Single parenthood, common-law unions, working mothers, multiple care-taking and different approaches to child-rearing were regarded simply as cultural characteristics of the West Indian community rather than as possible adaptive responses to economic circumstances (Dex, 1983[13]). The emphasis was on cultural characteristics as opposed to socio-economic circumstances and on black applicants' difference from white applicants as opposed to the common ground between them. The possibility that white applicants in similar economic situations might have been discouraged from applying to foster or, having applied, been similarly discriminated against, was not considered. The dominant concern was with the application of different standards to the two groups.

By contrast, applicants interpreted their situations in economic rather than cultural terms or deficiencies in parenting skills. Some thought that they would be disqualified because they lived in council accommodation, received Supplementary Benefit or were unemployed. Falling below the material standards of what they believed to be social workers' model of 'normal family life' may have deterred many people. Several gave this as a reason for not

---

[13] We must avoid offering values and attitudes, etc. found in the sending society as an explanation for certain behaviour or responses in the metropolitan society, giving them the status of 'West Indian characteristics'. This would be a very incomplete (if not racist) sort of explanation if it did not also include a discussion of why this particular aspect had come to be a significant distinguishing characteristic in the receiving society and why other values or forms of behaviour had declined in importance. By taking a view in which individuals and groups can actively respond and interact with their (new) environment, rather than being a bundle of 'inherent' characteristics, we should be able to guard against such partial, unsociological, and what can easily fall into racist explanations (Dex, 1983:58).

163

having applied in the past[14] Important symbols of affluence were the 'family home' and the 'family car' (Rhodes, 1989):

> I didn't apply before because I thought that they wouldn't take you if you lived in a council flat.

> They're not interested in black people. They want the person with the big house and car. There's no way a black person will get in or, if they do, it's the one with the car like the white, with the big house and garden for the kids to play and a car to take them out. They not really interested in black people.

> White people may think that black people aren't interested in this fostering but it isn't true. I can tell you a lot of black people is interested. It is just that when they get to it they won't get through. They (social workers) just isn't prepared to put the effort to let them through. I know there is some black people doing fostering, one or two here and there, but that is just to have a few black faces. And they are the ones who have a big house and all that, like the idea that social workers have, the ones with the big house and the car and money in the bank. But not most black people, they won't get through.

> They wouldn't look at us. How you going to take the kids out without you have a car and all them things? No, they wouldn't look at us.

> If the Fostering Department send an interviewer to see anyone, and when they see that the person they come to see have a four or five apartment house, a car at the gate, they would think, 'Ah, here is someone!' There would not be any trouble for a black person getting the fostering, you know. That is the way I see it.

Similarly, the main obstacles to the recruitment of single parents or the unemployed were thought to be financial rather than psychological. The fact that many West Indian women went out to work was considered to be a consequence of economic necessity rather than cultural preference. As one

---

[14] A few suggested that the borough's advertisements had been misleading and saw them as a face–saving device which betokened little genuine commitment to recruiting black people as foster parents (See Chapter Six). Bebbington and Miles have recently shown that there is some justification for this view. Fostering Officers, they note,

> often believed that the typical foster family profile had changed in recent years, with many single parents or unemployed couples now fostering. (Our data) show this to be a myth (1990:291).

164

woman explained bluntly, 'If you is a single mother, you has got to work'. Neville Adams found a similar disparity in views in his study of black children received into care in Lambeth: the children's parents tended to interpret their problems in material and financial terms whereas the social workers looked for cultural and psychological explanations (1981; cf. FitzHerbert, 1967). As Brummer observed,

> These discrepant attitudes of problem definition have not been confined to ethnic minority groups... but the issue of race has often amplified the findings of other studies (1988: 118).

Financial considerations were undoubtedly a factor in some people's decision not to pursue their applications. Several people had made enquiries to other boroughs which were offering higher rates. Others said that they would consider moving to another borough which paid higher rates or if they found that 'this borough messed you about', was slow in making payments or reluctant to give people their proper entitlements. They reasoned that, once accepted, it would be easy to change to another borough. Their stronger 'market' position enabled black applicants to choose between rival bids for their services and, as the new ideas gained legitimacy, the borough found itself competing with its neighbours for the same pool of applicants (cf. Chapter Four). It not only risked losing potential recruits but existing foster parents in whom it had made considerable investment in recruitment and training.

Fostering was thought to be a suitable occupation for women who did not go out to work and short term fostering, in particular, was considered a skilled and demanding occupation which ought to be remunerated accordingly[15]. At least eight people had given up or were intending to give up their jobs in order to take up fostering. They would, thus, have been giving up part or all of their incomes and some had expected to earn roughly the equivalent by fostering. Three people had been made redundant or been forced to give up their jobs for other reasons and were considering fostering as an alternative. At least two people, however, had decided to abandon their applications and seek a job instead because they thought they would not be able to manage on the rates which the borough paid. Others had dropped out and gone back into full- or part-time work, although they did not give the low rates as their main reason.

---

[15] Several people compared the rates paid for fostering unfavourably with those paid for childminding:

> They pay more for a childminder to look after a child during the day. But, if you take a child into your home all day and in the night, they pay you less. Why is that? You have got every responsibility of that child.

> If you were childminding, you'd get the same money for only a few hours a day whereas for fostering you have them all the time.

workers, on the other hand, tended to treat fostering, like motherhood, :ation rather than a job and applicants for whom the financial incentive was clearly important were regarded with suspicion (cf. Lowe, 1989). As one of them explained, 'You have to be careful about people who take on fostering for the money'.

The failure to address racism

In order to offer help, Roys maintains, 'social services institutions must... be sensitive... to the processes of racism' (1988: 221). The model of cultural diversity, however, ignores the question of 'race' and both applicants and social workers appear to have found the subject difficult to broach on either an individual level, on home visits, or in a group setting, during training courses (see Chapter Ten). Although black foster parents were sought partly on account of 'their ability to teach black children the survival skills necessary to combat racism' (Team Meeting minutes, Nov.1985), issues concerned with racism were rarely, if ever, raised during assessments. Although workers paid lip service to the issue in theory, they appeared to discount it in practice.

This may have been, in part, a response to applicants' own ambivalence. As with the question of cultural distinctiveness, many found the issue of racism difficult to handle[16]. A second reason was workers' taken–for–granted assumption that black applicants naturally possessed the necessary survival skills. A third was the conception of the family as a private island existing independently of the economic and political life of the society in which it floats and able to protect the child from the vicissitudes of the world without (cf. Small, 1984a 1986b) Much of the problem lay in the lack of any coherent analysis of the impact of racism on either a societal or individual level and the consequent failure to develop an appropriate strategy for dealing with it. An

---

[16] There did not seem to be any clear consensus and opinion was divided between three broad groups:

  i. those who believed that racism in British society was of fundamental importance to the lives of black people and that only black families could empathise with the child and give him/her the confidence and skills necessary to cope with it;
  ii. those who believed that sympathetic white families could help black children to overcome racism and that trans–racial placements were one way to combat it and, finally,
  iii. those who believed that counteracting racism should not be an important factor in the placement decision, including those who believed that class was a more important source of discrimination and prejudice than skin colour.

Most of those who claimed that neither culture nor racism were important seemed to be motivated by a desire not to be perceived to be different, not to 'rock the boat', almost as if a denial of the existence of racism was one means of eradicating it. The issue not only threatened people's position in society but their personal identifications. The same people often confided personal experience of racism at later points in the interview and, significantly perhaps, many said that they had coped with it by ignoring it.

166

unsuccessful attempt was later made through the initiation of Race Awareness Training (see Chapter 6). To most workers, racism was an alien concept which had no place within the conventional framework which had guided practice in the past (cf. Ely and Denney, 1987; Ahmed, 1982; Roys, 1988; Dominelli, 1988).

Applicants' self-presentations

Developing 'a more ethnically sensitive service' is a two-way process and not simply a matter of social workers changing their ideas and approach to take into account cultural differences. Far from being simply the passive victims of a discriminatory assessment procedure, black applicants were active contributors able to adjust their self-presentations according to what they believed to be social workers' notions of 'normal family life'. In the past, this had been the conventional two parent bourgeois family, but new ideas about the importance of cultural identity meant that a presentation in terms of the conventional profile was no longer always appropriate. These new ideas, however, were slow to take root. First, mistrust, born of past experience, generated a 'credibility gap', with many applicants doubting both social workers' sincerity and their ability to change (cf. Dominelli, 1989). Second was the time lag between the changes in social workers' thinking and the ability of applicants to make appropriate response, during which an awareness of the change filtered down to the black community. Third was the counteracting influence of the mass promotion of the popular stereotype by politicians and the media (Barrett and McIntosh, 1982).
Whichever strategy they chose, applicants risked prejudicing social workers against them. If they chose to remain loyal to their cultural roots, they risked being discriminated against on both cultural and economic grounds. On the other hand, a presentation in terms of the conventional 'white' profile was no longer appropriate where social workers placed importance on cultural and ethnic identity. Similarly, where the conventional model stressed stability and harmony, evidence of past ability to cope in times of stress and hardship was now to be regarded as an indication of current ability to cope in a crisis. As one worker explained,

SW3 Sometimes the people you had reservations about had experienced difficulties in their lives and had learned to get through them which often made them more able to cope when problems arose with foster children.

Black applicants' likely confusion about the appropriate model of family life to adopt as their guide during the assessment placed them at a disadvantage

167

compared with their white counterparts who could rely more securely on the popular 'white' stereotype. The latter were also more likely to have been familiar with the conventional view of fostering as a charity or service as distinct from paid employment and more likely to have known how to manage presentations of themselves in ways acceptable to the social workers. Each side knew the 'rules of the game' and how to play them. The emphasis during interviews, thus, seems to have been on the impact which taking in a foster child would have had on the family as a social rather than as an economic unit[17]. Financial considerations seem, by tacit agreement, to have been played down or denied and charitable and motherly motives stressed. One black applicant, for example, commented,

> What I really wanted to know about was the rates that they paid you but it wasn't discussed. I didn't ask about it because I didn't want her to think I was only interested in it for the money. But it's things like that you really want to know about to know if you can afford to do it.

In this way, the fiction of fostering as an approximation to 'normal family life', as something independent of and uncontaminated by material and financial considerations, was preserved. For many black and working–class families, however, this fiction was becoming increasingly difficult to maintain.

Black applicants' attempts to present themselves in accordance with white middle class standards encouraged an emphasis on material well–being and reluctance to talk about the past, especially their childhood years. Hostility to questions about their early years was typical:

> Their questions were useless. Most of them I couldn't see the point of at all. Most of them would have been better not asked. They just offend people and they don't serve no purpose. They've got nothing to do with how good you are at fostering a child. It was one load of barrage of questions about your childhood, your past life and everything... questions and more questions.

People who had come to England to 'make a better life' did not want to allude to the poverty of a past which they felt they had left behind them and which conflicted with the image of the comfortable life style which they were now attempting to convey. They were similarly reluctant to talk about the different standards of child care which they had experienced in the West Indies which they knew would be unacceptable by current British standards.

---

[17] These conclusions are based on social workers' and applicants' retrospective accounts of the assessment interviews.

Applicants were afraid that the young, white, middle class social workers would not be able to understand and that, by revealing details of their pasts, their chances of acceptance would be jeopardised. As one person explained,

> Life in the West Indies when we was kids was very different from what it is for kids now. A social worker just wouldn't understand.

The white respondents, by comparison, generally found the questions about childhood helpful. One man, for example, commented,

> I didn't really mind. It depends on what sort of childhood you had and mine was pretty good... But I had me ups and downs but I realise now – like I had arguments with me dad and, when I look back now, he was right and I was against him. And I know now that I'm going to have the same trouble with my children because they'll be against me. Then, in ten years' time, they're going to realise...

The black applicants' attitudes were interpreted by social workers simply as consequences of a clash of cultural standards. They were not seen in any way to be possible responses to the assessment procedure itself or to workers' own presentation as white, middle class officials and applicants' consequent attribution to them of white, middle class ideas. Hostility to the asking of personal questions and questions about the past, however, led to the whole issue being raised at a Team Meeting in September 1984 (see Chapter Five) when it was decided to review both the nature of the questions and the manner of asking.

Applicants' ambivalence

A further obstacle to the implementation of a cultural pluralist approach was applicants' own ambivalence. Although there were those who thought that it was important to preserve the child's sense of its cultural heritage, others did not think that it was relevant and some even thought that it would be detrimental to the child. In some cases, their objections were practical: some of the younger respondents, for example, thought that teenagers would object to the older generation's more rigid ideas about discipline, acceptable behaviour and attendance at church. For others, their objections were motivated by an ideological resistance to cultural separatism (cf. Jayaweera, 1991), while others were more concerned with matters of class.

In addition to cultural differences, a number of other factors which might constrain relationships with social workers were identified. These included anticipation of intercultural misunderstandings and/or racist attitudes,

169

antagonism to 'white' authority, ambivalence or hostility to the new policy of 'racial matching' and a rejection of the policy of permanency for children under the age of ten[18] (cf. Ely and Denney, 1987; Payne, 1983; Small, 1982; Brunton and Welch, 1983). In addition, was an awareness of past malpractice, for example, the inappropriate removal of children, together with the knowledge that the main thrust of placement policy in the past had been to remove children from poor homes and to place them in middle class homes. Many applicants perceived the social services as an agency of social control rather than support, with the power, for example, to remove children rather than to restore them (Ely and Denney, 1987: 167) and as a 'white' bureaucracy prejudiced against black people (Arnold, 1982).

Cultural pluralism: a double-edged dilemma?

Current efforts to recruit black foster parents have, thus, confronted social workers with a double-edged dilemma: not only do many black families diverge from the conventional profile of family life on a cultural level but they fall below its material standards. In order to recruit more black foster parents, social workers have been forced to revise their ideas about 'suitability'. This has led to a relaxing of previous standards and the adoption of 'a more flexible approach' and the resultant concern with dual or double standards was justified by a need too take into account cultural differences. The weaknesses of this approach lay in the attempt to separate cultural from economic considerations, the absence of discussion of racism or power relations and treatment of applicants as the passive victims of a discriminatory assessment procedure and of social workers as its unwitting operators.

---

[18] Widespread hostility to the principle of permanency emerged from the interviews with applicants and the issue was also hotly disputed when it was raised on the training and assessment course. Few could accept social workers' objections to long term foster care. Brunton and Welch observed similar attitudes among their black foster parents in Wandsworth:

> Our recently developed belief is that adoption should be the plan for most (younger) children in preference to inclusive fostering and this is not easy for us to accommodate. In our experience, black foster parents often manage inclusive fostering so as not to create tension and confusion for the children, seeing it as a natural arrangement. Adoption poses financial problems and unease when natural parents are in the picture and not in agreement (1983:17).

Payne (1983) has suggested that black families may be deterred by the alien legal ideas of terminating parental rights (cf. Ahmed, 1980).

170

The autonomous conception of culture

Much of the problem lies in the conception of culture as a monolithic steady state (Lewis, 1973) which exists independently of other social and economic influences. Many writers have challenged the independence and autonomy of the cultural sphere by attempting to analyse the interconnections and interdependence between cultural factors and the socio-economic circumstances in which they are grounded (Lal, 1983). Miles, for example, points out that 'the discovery... of culture constitutes an analytical trap if it is divorced, as it has been, from its historical and material context' (1982: 70).

By concentrating on the ways in which the conventional model of family life discriminates against black applicants on cultural grounds, social workers failed to confront the fact that many families are materially disadvantaged in their efforts to build a 'happy family life'. Uncritical acceptance of culturally different patterns without reference to the financial and material circumstances in which they are grounded ignores the stresses and strains which inadequate resources may engender or intensify. As Burgoyne has pointed out,

> although access to the kinds of economic resources enjoyed by the majority of the population is not necessarily any guarantee of happiness, those without it have fewer choices (1987:14).

The 'normal family life' of popular conception is not simply a middle-class 'myth' which can be conveniently swept aside (cf. Barrett and McIntosh, 1982), without first recognising its historical development as the outcome of a complex interaction between social and economic forces. Bill Jordan underlines the dilemma when he points out that

> social workers are increasingly involved in... trying to keep people going under massive economic and environmental stress. As the poverty and disadvantage of social work's clientele increase an almost infinite amount of material resources could be devoted to helping parents to bring up children. Conversely, a large and growing number of children could be made better off just by removing them from unemployed, depressed, ill-housed and impoverished parents, and placing them with comfortably-off middle class foster parents or adopters. (1985:460)

According to Marion Lowe,

171

The precariousness of family life and the social and economic policies that increase the vulnerability of families to poverty, poor housing, ill health and general stress have implications for foster care on two levels. First, in terms of the families requiring substitute and supplementary care for their children and second, in terms of the providers of that service – foster carers who are as likely as other kinds of families to suffer poverty, material stress and unemployment (1989: vii).

A re-evaluation is needed of the impact of fostering not only on a family's cultural life but on its economic base. It is not enough to adopt more flexible criteria of assessment in order to recruit from groups previously under-represented in the foster parent pool, without also recognizing that, for these groups, financial and material considerations are important.

Fostering as employment

Fostering is likely to be one of the few forms of 'employment' open to many families (Rhodes, 1989) and the recruitment of single parents and the unemployed will inevitably lead to a questioning of its status as a charitable service and as something that a woman does for 'pin money', something peripheral or additional to her husband's income and therefore not a challenge to his status as primary breadwinner (Morris, 1987). This is reinforced by developments within fostering as a whole towards a more 'professional' and 'professionalised' service (Rhodes, 1989) and many agencies have now implemented what are termed 'professional fostering schemes' (Shaw and Hipgrave, 1982; Hardy *et al.*, 1986), in recognition of the fact that fostering today involves far more than a mere extension of the motherhood role (*Foster Care* January 1986a; cf. Lowe, 1989)[19]. Placement agencies are finding it necessary to train foster parents not only in the skills required in the care of difficult, disturbed, physically or mentally handicapped children but in the management and organisational skills necessary for report writing, liaising with social workers, attending meetings, case conferences and reviews, dealing with teachers, education officials, health workers and the police, making court appearances and so on. The efforts to recruit substitute carers from black and minority ethnic groups have exposed these conflicting images of female competence at their sharpest (Rhodes, 1989). Changes in the role of foster parents and the increasing demands now made of them, ironically, may mean that, in order to carry out the fostering task adequately, financial stability and

---

[19] There is widespread belief that the new more 'professional' approach to fostering has contributed to greater 'success' measured in terms of fewer breakdowns compared with the traditional approach (London Boroughs Children's Regional Planning Committee 1982), although the evidence from research is patchy (Shaw & Hipgrave, 1982).

172

material circumstances may be becoming more important not less so. The use of a telephone, for example, is now almost a prerequisite and the use of a car extremely useful, if not often a necessity[20].

Lowe has argued that 'playing down the work element of foster care preserves the division between paid employment (outside the home) and unpaid work (within it)' (1989: viii). She draws attention to 'a growing recognition' among women involved in foster care that 'all parents need skills and financial support if they are to raise children successfully'. In demanding that fostering be remunerated as a form of work, carers confront masculine distinctions which define traditional female spheres of domestic labour as non-work, set apart from the 'real work' of paid employment outside the home. Foster carers, she argues,

> will increasingly recognise their commonality of interest with informal carers and with other groups of workers offering care to dependent groups. Women foster carers will begin to think through the issues for them which pose difficult questions about their role as unpaid/underpaid providers of care in a domestic environment. They will identify more closely – as the person in the family charged with maintaining the life of family members in difficult circumstances – with the woman whose children they offer substitute or supplementary care to.

And this development, Lowe suggests, may well be led 'by black women carers whose sense of oppression and experience of racism has given them a head start in finding common ground with the families to whom they offer a service' (1989: viii).

Racism and power

Roger Ballard (1979) has suggested that white people tend to assume that cultural factors lie at the root of most minority problems because such a view is the least disturbing. The model of cultural diversity avoids structural considerations, including racism and class, and reduces tensions in black–white relations to problems of cultural mismatch and failures of intercultural communication (Pearson, 1983; Lawrence, 1982b). The approach ignores the possibility that cultural dominance may be cultural tyranny and mask straight-forward racism. Cultural pluralism is not a simple matter of 'live and let live' and of granting equal respect to different cultural

---

[20] Applicants who do not own a car are handicapped not only in their ability to attain the sort of middle class life-style which has come to be regarded as 'normal family life' but in their ability to fulfil the more professional role now demanded of foster parents (Rhodes, 1989).

173

practices but a complex process of negotiation and compromise and that, where something is valued, compromise will be resisted. Nor is any consideration given to imbalances in relationships of power in the negotiation process. 'Multiculturalism', Sivanandan suggests, 'denies power relations by denying the hierarchical structure of society' (1985: 28). According to the pluralist view, members of different cultural groups are assumed to meet on equal terms which leaves little scope for an appreciation of the impact of racism and its interplay with cultural and economic factors (Pearson, 1983; Lawrence, 1982b).

In the same way that white social workers are not simply the innocent operators of a discriminatory assessment process, black applicants are not simply its passive victims but must be recognised as active participants able both to influence social workers' approach and to adjust their self-presentations according to what they believe to be the most acceptable stance. Developing 'a more ethnically sensitive service' was, thus, not a simple matter of social workers adjusting their ideas and approach to take into account cultural differences but a process of change negotiated within unequal relationships of power. Although the balance was tipped in favour of the social workers by virtue of the assessment relationship and their ethnic identification, class location and employment status as white, middle class professionals, black applicants' new-found power as a scarce and valued resource gave them a new capacity to resist social workers' attempts to fit them to the mould of their own ideas.

As was demonstrated in the previous chapter, in contradiction of social workers' expectations, applicants were often reluctant to mobilise their ethnicity as a resource to consolidate their position. A complex of reasons included an interpretation of their problems in economic or class rather than cultural terms, a suspicion that differential treatment would mean inferior treatment in practice, a fear of eliciting a 'white' racist backlash, and an ideological resistance to cultural separatism. In this reluctance, applicants were able to challenge not only social workers' pluralist approach and its artificial separation of cultural from economic considerations but the traditional conception of fostering as a vocation rather than a job of work. Applicants' reluctance to accept social workers' delineation of the problem of their recruitment in terms of cultural differences shifted the frame of reference towards a more general reappraisal of family assessment skills and, in the following chapter, it will be argued that this proved to be a more fundamental and potentially more damaging challenge to social workers' professional competence than the simple questioning of their intercultural skills.

9 Inter-cultural skills, professionalism and commonsense

In this chapter it will be argued that a cultural pluralist approach which failed to address questions of representation and power sharing both undermined confidence in white social workers' professional competence and was a weak basis from which to argue for the employment of black social workers on the grounds of the possession of 'special' cultural skills. Applicants' mistrust of a cultural diagnosis helped to shift the frame of reference to a more general reappraisal of family assessment skills where personality and commonsense were set against professional training and it was in this area that social workers faced the more serious challenge to their authority as professionals.

The views of the social workers

As noted in the previous chapter, the new developments undermined social workers' confidence in their professional abilities. As one explained,

SW5 It is hard to admit that a black social worker could probably vet black families better than I can, but there's a limit, I think, to what you can do as a white person. I've worked quite a lot with black people and I think I'm quite experienced. But, now, more and more, I've come to question just how experienced I am. I've begun to question a lot more the way we, as white workers, do things.

These abilities could no longer be taken for granted as confidently as they had been in the past. It was no longer enough to explain the under–representation of black people in the foster parent pool with the argument that black people did not possess the necessary qualities and workers were forced to examine their own role in the assessment process.

Opinions in the Fostering Section were divided between the conservative majority, who retained a faith in the adequacy of their professional competence and ability to learn the relevant new skills (cf. BASW, 1982[1]; Stubbs, 1985[2]; Connelly, 1989[3]; Brown, 1986), and the radicals, who believed that, as white workers, they could never acquire the necessary skills (cf. Bernard, 1987). There were three strands to their argument: the first was the contention that only a person brought up in black culture is competent to assess black families; the second referred to mutual empathy and understanding based on common experience of racism and discrimination, and the third to the argument that only another black person can inspire applicants with the confidence necessary for mutual trust. Underlying all three, was the belief that black people and white people inhabit different social worlds (cf. Harris, 1987). No–one was prepared to admit to a belief that intercultural skills were irrelevant. In the absence of black workers, social workers fell back on the conservative position. Their success in recruiting black foster parents seemed to fly in the face of the radicals, whose argument for the recruitment of black workers on the grounds of their 'special' cultural skills was thereby weakened.

---

[1] The qualities required for effective practice with clients from ethnic minorities are no different from those required with any client. Good practice requires sensitivity to the feelings of the client, awareness of cultural influences on behaviour, recognition of informal helping networks and an ability to work with them. (BASW Project Group, 1982: 1)

[2] My review of the positions taken by white workers revealed a widespread belief that general social work 'skill', as exemplified by a professional qualification, especially when combined with actual experience of multi-racial areas, more than adequately equipped workers to work with all clients (Stubbs, 1985: 13).

[3] White social workers who have many years' experience of working with black clients argue that they are managing quite adequately (Connelly, 1989: 9).

176

Applicants' views and perceptions

White social workers' skills

Applicants' opinions about the relevance of cultural factors to the assessment process and about the competence of white workers to assess black families were mixed. Some considered that cultural differences were unimportant or too transient to be worthy of serious attention. As black people became assimilated into mainstream society, cultural differences, they argued, would fade. Others put their faith in social workers' 'professionalism': in their training and experience and in the framework of rules and regulations within which they imagined workers were constrained to work. In answer to the question, 'Would you prefer to see a black social worker or a white social worker?', one person, for example, replied,

I   They (social workers) go by the red tape that they don't forget.

JA   What do you mean 'by the red tape that they don't forget'?

I   Yes, from your government. The red tape, how they are supposed to carry on is set down by the government. Or some of them may do over what they are not told, but they have to go by the red tape.

JA   You mean social workers are all the same, whether they are black or white?

I   Whether black or white, I suppose they do what they are told. No, it doesn't make any difference, I suppose, to any individual whatever category you are.

These people seemed to be appealing to a universalist ideology in which every citizen is treated the same. They emphasised that, with adequate training, social workers should be able to work with any client, irrespective of colour, culture or religion, and that the remedy for present short–comings lay in more and better training. Others believed that the situation would improve if there were more black workers who could 'teach' white workers the necessary knowledge and skills (cf. Brown, 1986). Some people suggested that assessment visits should be carried out by a black and a white social worker conjointly. This strategy, they reasoned, would leave few grounds for complaints about prejudice, 'racial' bias or misunderstandings. Some, however, thought that intercultural understanding could be acquired only through sharing the lives of black people, a route closed to most white workers, and that significant improvements in service delivery could be achieved only through the employment of more black workers.

Opinion was similarly split when respondents were asked whether they would prefer to see a black or a white social worker[4]. A majority (61%) claimed not to care either way; others (29%) expressed a preference for a black worker, and a minority (10%) for a white worker. Those who preferred to see a black social worker and who thought that, on the whole, they were better equipped to work with black clients gave a variety of reasons, most of which referred to cultural affinity. They believed that black workers would be better acquainted with the cultural backgrounds of applicants who had lived in the West Indies, more likely to share similar attitudes about family life and child care, and more likely to appreciate the stresses which migration and the splitting up of families involved, the difficulties of becoming established in a new country, and the day–to–day strain of life as a black person in Britain.

Several people thought that a black worker would approach the assessment interviews in a less formal fashion and that many black applicants, especially older people, would feel more comfortable talking to another black person. Difficulties in communication and language problems were also mentioned. Several people remarked that continuity was important and that, since the campaign was concerned with 'finding black homes for black children', it ought to be run by black workers. Informants often seemed unable (or unwilling) to elaborate and fell back on comments like, 'It just seems right somehow', 'I just feel it would be better to have black people doing it' or 'It's better if we each look after our own'. Very few mentioned racism or prejudice, in this context.

In terms of improving their chances of acceptance, applicants viewed the employment of black workers with mixed feelings. On one hand, it was assumed that a black worker would make applicants feel more at ease and promote better communication and understanding than a white worker. On the other, black workers were thought to be more confident about broaching sensitive subjects and asking personal and searching questions and more skilled at preventing applicants from 'pulling the wool over their eyes'. An increase in the rate of approval of black applicants would not, therefore, necessarily follow from an increase in the employment of black social workers. An improvement in the quality of assessments was thought to be a more likely outcome. The general opinion was that assessments by black workers were

---

[4] Some people disclaimed any preference for themselves but thought that others would prefer to see a black social worker indicated, perhaps, that they were giving a 'public' response rather than the response they might have given, for example, if speaking to a friend. The answers may have been influenced by my colour on some occasions but the fact that the two black interviewers were given similar replies suggests other factors may have been at work.

more likely to be effective because black workers were more skilled at eliciting and evaluating information and at reaching an appropriate decision.

Several people pointed out the danger of assuming that a black worker would be better able to work with black people simply because she or he was black. They referred to examples from their own experience. Some had experience of both black and white social workers and had found that they had got on as well or better with the white, while others, whose experience was limited to white social workers, reported that they had not experienced any problems on account of their colour. Very few seemed to equate colour with better training and ability. Others spoke of island and class differences.

Several people thought that black social workers tended to come from more middle-class backgrounds than many of their clients and tended to be unsympathetic or patronising towards them. There seemed to be a greater sensitivity to differences in status and social background in relation to black social workers than in relation to white. Considerable antagonism was exhibited towards black people who, through social work, had gained access to the professional middle classes and thought themselves superior to their fellows on account of their new-found status. They were regarded as allies of the 'white' establishment and, at worst, as the dupes of white social workers, naïvely allowing themselves to be used to give black people visibility but without the attendant power. Not only had they betrayed, in this way, their social origins but they had achieved their positions on the basis of their blackness and ethnicity. For these reasons, some informants seemed to think that their chances of acceptance would be reduced if they were assessed by a black worker rather than a white.

No-one thought that skin colour alone was a sufficient qualification for work with black applicants. Several thought that upbringing and place of birth were important and that a black worker, born and brought up in England, would be as distanced from black applicants who had spent much of their lives in the West Indies as would a white worker. Many thought that black people who had been brought up in England would have no difficulty relating to a white social worker.

Black representation

There seemed to be much greater awareness among applicants than among social workers of the political implications of increasing the numbers of black social workers employed by the borough. Among those interviewed, issues of representation and incorporation into the power structure, access to decision-making and policy formulation seemed to be of greater concern than the technical debates about cultural skills.

A few black faces don't mean anything for ordinary black people. How many of them is actually taking the decisions at the top? They just have to do what the whites tell them. No, until you get black people as the bosses, you won't find very much that will change.

It won't get any better for black people until you have got more black people up there helping to run the show.

A need to employ more black workers was universally recognised regardless of opinions about the value of 'special' skills and competencies as black people. The obvious disparity between the numbers of black and numbers of white workers employed by the borough was evidence, for some, of the insincerity of the Social Services and, what one person described as, 'the mockery of equal opportunity'.

The borough is prejudiced, anyway. You look around, you might see the odd black in there but, as I say, it's just a face, to have one face in there. It's just a cover-up. Look how many blacks in this borough and you go into the Town Hall and, maybe, see one or two black girls. The Council is the same. It is disgusting.

It is going to take them quite a long while because they are very slow slow worker. They are not really interested in employing black people.

People expressed bitterness and cynicism about the motives of the Social Services Department and its commitment to change.

They say they want all this racial harmony and equality. But where is it? I don't see many black social workers running the thing. This society is hypocritical and the Social Services is part of it.

The employment of more black workers, especially in positions where they would be able to influence policy, however, was not necessarily seen as the 'solution' to the 'problem' of what was perceived by many informants to be a service which was insensitive to the needs of black children and black people. Several people emphasised the importance of 'awareness'. 'Awareness' was not always confined to black social workers. Some people thought that some white social workers were more 'aware' and sensitised to the 'problems' of black people than were many black people, themselves.

It's not just a matter of being black. You have got to want to help your brothers and sisters, you have to want to help black people. There's some blacks would just step on the others and wouldn't care so long as they got the good jobs. Black people like that are worse than some whites. You have to be careful who it is.

It's not all black people who would be any good. There's some white people that know more about black people's problems and is more sympathetic than some black people is themselves.

A further factor which mitigated change was thought to be black social workers' socialization to the ideas and methods of conventional practice during and after training.

You see, I don't know if it will work because it is not the black running an organisation of its own, to say, 'My group'. Who is going to fight against what come out of your (white) group? The black had to take whatsoever practice it be... and they give it out back to the black people. So there will be actually the same problem all the time... Because, if they train you, they train you up to their idea. They don't train you up to the black people culture idea.

Contradictions in people's views

It was clear that many people felt more secure and comfortable in the company of other black people and many mentioned with approval the fact that there had been several black people at the Information Meetings which they had attended and that some of the foster parents (or 'social workers' with whom some people had confused them) there had been black. Yet, when asked about their preferences for a black or white social worker, most said that they had no preference. Many prefaced their replies with disclaimers such as, 'I'm not prejudiced'. Others, who did express a preference, were similarly eager to dispel any impression of prejudice[5],

---

[5] Many of those interviewed did not seem to possess the language of racism and anti-racism which was available to some of those younger and more politically aware with which to communicate a sense of cultural affinity without appearing, in their own eyes, to be prejudiced or 'black-minded'. People, whose attempts to integrate had, in large part, been attempts to counteract the negative stereotyping with which they had been burdened in the past, were wary of allying themselves with a political standpoint which was vulnerable to negative labelling by the white majority.

I'm not Black-minded or anything...

Some people would say I have chip on my shoulder but it isn't true...

It is not that I am prejudiced or anything like that...

All this reinforced the impression that the interviewer was being treated to a 'public' opinion (cf. Cornwell, 1984).

For many people, there seemed to be a conflict between their personal preferences and the belief that all people ought to be treated the same irrespective of colour or life-style. Usually, they appeared to put their ideological (or public) beliefs above their personal (or private) preferences and, for many, it seemed to be not so much differential treatment in itself to which they objected as the fear that different meant inferior. People warned of the dangers of accepting a person as a foster parent merely because he/she was black, of employing black social workers with lower qualifications than white or of restricting black social workers to work with black clients. Many were afraid of being labelled as 'different' and, therefore, as inferior in some way, as trouble-makers or people who presented a 'problem' and they viewed with suspicion attempts by the social services to impose differentiation[6]. They were afraid to assert an identity which set them apart and lacked the confidence to assert their right to be different.

Personality and commonsense

An even greater challenge to white social workers' status as professionals than the undermining of confidence in their intercultural skills was the value applicants placed on personality and commonsense. In view of the conceptual separation of public from private concerns, social work intervention was regarded as an unwarranted intrusion into people's private affairs. The conduct of family life was considered to be a matter of everyday competence and commonsense which was off-limits to professional intervention. No amount of professional training could match the knowledge gained from experience. The skills of motherhood and child-rearing, in particular, constituted an area of contested terrain where social workers' formally acquired professional knowledge was set against applicants' practical experience and commonsense.

---

[6] Although the sample was too small to be able to detect any appreciable age differences in attitude, other studies have found 'huge differences in attitudes to conforming among the over 40s and the under 30s' (Donovan, 1986).

182

The usurpation of motherhood skills by 'experts' has enabled the State to exert a considerable measure of social control (David, 1986). Black families, in particular, have been the victims of past interference from state agencies, through 'expert' interpretation of their patterns and lifestyles in terms of social pathology (Ahmed, 1988; Dominelli, 1988; Brummer, 1988; Solomos, 1988). Black people were, therefore, likely to be particularly hostile to social workers' claims to a professional expertise which had been used against them in the past (cf. Ely and Denney, 1987; Payne, 1983).

Respondents not only rejected social workers' training and dismissed any claims they might have to professional expertise in this field but accused them of incompetence, insensitivity and ignorance. The most often voiced complaint was that social workers lacked 'commonsense'. The following comment was typical:

I felt I could do better than them even though I haven't been to no college. Because, a lot of them things, they are all common sense.

Summed up in the notion of 'commonsense' was not simply a difference of opinion but an open challenge to the status of professional knowledge and to those who professed to hold it. Where the 'professionals' claimed to possess specialised knowledge and skills which were unavailable to the layman, applicants claimed access to a 'commonsense' which was unavailable to the professional. Their appeal to commonsense was, thus, not simply a rejection but an exclusion, a demarcation between 'us' and 'them'. In it could be read an attempt to reject their subordination in relation to the 'professional' status of the middle class social worker and to assert their right to self-determination. Applicants reversed workers' claims to superiority by referring to their own knowledge and skills as 'commonsense' and, therefore, beyond challenge. 'Commonsense' was the possession of 'the people' and, by rejecting 'commonsense', social workers were distancing themselves from 'the people'.

The elevation of 'commonsense' above knowledge derived from formal training was accompanied by an emphasis of the importance of personality as opposed to the attributes of professional status.

It's your personality and the way you approach people, the way you are with people, rather than all those O and A levels. Just because they've got a bit of paper, they think they know it all. They don't.

When asked whether they would prefer to talk to a black rather than a white social worker, most people said that colour did not matter but that personality and manner were more important. Applicants said that they were more likely to respect social workers if they knew that they were, themselves, parents.

183

They appreciated their experience with families and children in care, although some remarked drily that it was not the social workers who were looking after the children but the foster parents. On the other hand, applicants rejected social workers' 'book learning' and claims to professional knowledge based on formal training. Workers were aware of these attitudes and, where they could, tended to stress their experience as parents and mothers in their own right and their experience, as social workers, of dealing with families and children. 'I try not to appear too official', one, for example, explained,

> I try to be as friendly as possible to put them at their ease because a lot of people are suspicious of social workers. I tell them that I have got two children of my own and that I understand the problems of bringing up children.

or another,

> When I am talking with applicants, I use the fact that I am also a mother. I think it gives them more confidence in you when they know that you have got children of your own.

By appealing to social workers' lack of commonsense and to the irrelevance of their professional training, rather than to 'racial' or cultural mismatch, in explanation of their discomfort during social workers' visits, black applicants were united with white applicants. This did not necessarily mean, however, that there was not a 'racial' or cultural dimension: an appeal to social workers' lack of commonsense may simply have been a more comfortable explanation.

Conclusion

Social workers' delineation of the problem of the recruitment of black foster parents in terms of cultural differences resulted in their professionalism being challenged on several counts. Not only was their ability to acquire appropriate intercultural skills questioned but the relevance of the cultural diagnosis itself. Applicants' mistrust of the multi-cultural approach shifted the frame of reference on to a more general plane. Here, the threat to social workers' professional authority came less from a questioning of their intercultural skills than from a rejection of the professionalization of family assessment and consequent revaluation of the lay person's commonsense and practical experience at the expense of the professional's formally acquired knowledge and skills.

184

When asked about their preference for black or white social workers, many applicants were afraid of over-asserting cultural distinctiveness for fear of being seen to be advocating different treatment for black people. They were wary of associating skin colour too closely with cultural affinity and were more concerned with issues of representation, power-sharing and access to decision-making and policy formulation than with technical debates about intercultural skills. Social workers' resort to a cultural analysis and failure to address these issues, however, placed applicants on the horns of a dilemma by making achievement of the political goal conditional upon the assertion of cultural distinctiveness and the possession of 'special' cultural skills. In this way, what was an essentially political stance became transmuted to technical concern about the quality of service.

Confusion between the desire for increased representation and a mistrust of cultural differentiation as the means for achieving it was evident in many people's replies. First, the notion of segregated work loads based on cultural distinctiveness conflicted with an ideological commitment to integration. Second, many people were aware of the risk of creating not only a separate but a marginalised and second rate service hived off from mainstream provision. Because it relied on technical arguments concerned with the possession of specialist cultural skills rather than on political arguments about equal opportunity and access to power-sharing, the case for employing black workers could be overturned if it could be shown that measurable improvements in service delivery could be achieved without them (Schroeder and Lightfoot, 1983). In addition, black workers were not thought likely to be more effective than white where the primary concern was with increasing the rate of approvals rather than improving the quality of assessments.

Applicants' rejection of a cultural interpretation shifted the frame of reference to a more general reappraisal of family assessment skills. The challenge to social workers' professional authority was potentially more damaging than a simple questioning of their intercultural skills. Applicants' rejection of formal training and their distinction between 'us' and 'them' through the possession of commonsense may have been an expression of cultural identity in the sense that different cultural groups may disagree about the components of what each defines as 'commonsense' but it can also be interpreted as an attempt to defend themselves from social workers' authority by rejecting their claims to superior knowledge. Social workers' vulnerability to this challenge lay in their weak position compared with other 'professional' groups such as the medical profession (David, 1986; Stacey, 1988; Timmins, 1989) and in the fact that a large area of their claim to professional competence, 'the family', is popularly considered off-limits to professional interference (Campbell, 1988). Applicants were merely voicing opinions which are supported both popularly and politically.

Paradoxically, social workers' attempts to defend their professional status on the grounds of the possession of 'expert knowledge' were accompanied by the need to persuade applicants that they were acting within the bounds of 'commonsense'. A transformation process occurred whereby workers entered the assessment arena on the basis of their professional status but sought to persuade applicants of the appropriateness of their presence on the basis of non-professional, experiential credentials. Applicants' rejection of the professionalization of parenthood enabled them to constrain both the behaviour and frame of reference of the professionals.

Figure 2
The challenge to social workers' professionalism

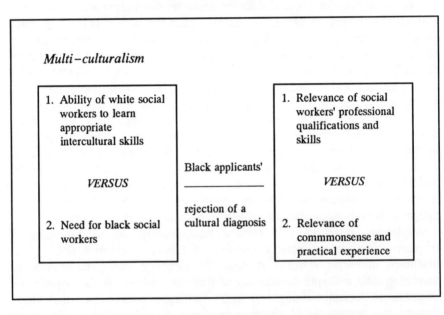

Ironically, social workers' resort to persuasion on the basis of experiential credentials put them at a disadvantage compared with their foster parent co-workers. The engagement of experienced black foster parents as co-workers in order to compensate for white workers' own lack of intercultural skills brought many of these issues into sharp focus. On one hand, it signalled to the black community that the Social Services took the issue of cultural differences seriously. On the other, it made it obvious that social workers lacked confidence in their own intercultural abilities. These issues will be discussed in more depth in Chapter Twelve.

10   Public policy, private space: The inherent conflict in assessment policies

The inadequacy of the portrayal of the family as private space which is separate and distinct from the wider public context has been repeatedly exposed (e.g. Burgoyne, 1987; Barrett and McIntosh, 1982)[1]. As a model which informs practice, the distinction is fraught with contradictions. Foster parent assessment represents a public intrusion into the private domain paradoxically in the context of the family as a model of private space. The social worker purposefully violates this private domain and makes it a matter of public inspection. By engaging in fostering, the foster parent's home becomes the work place and, as such, open to public scrutiny through the agency of the social worker. The significance of this for the applicant is accentuated not only by black–white differences in the understanding of 'public' and 'private' but by the relative structural positions of white, middle class professional and black, working class applicant.

---

[1] It conforms with the conceptual separation of emotional from material life and underlies the persistent fiction that social work practice lies outside the political domain. By focusing on a psycho–dynamic model of family life (Davis *et al.* 1984) and divorcing the assessment procedure from socio–political considerations, such conceptually convenient distinctions reduced not only black applicants' chances of approval as foster parents but the likelihood of any serious structural and political analysis or challenge (c.f. Solomos 1988). Significantly, black applicants began to be seriously recruited as foster parents only when the competition with white applicants had been artificially removed by the changes in ideas about suitable placements for black children received into care.

Differences in black/white understandings of 'public' and 'private'

In the past social workers sought to resolve conflicts between their own and applicants' delineations of public and private by resort to negative labelling and the equation of difference with deficiency[2] (cf. Becker, 1963). As Berger and Luckman have commented, 'He who has the biggest stick has the best chance of imposing his definition of reality' (1972: 127). Black applicants had little power to assert their own opposing interpretations of their way of life.

Concern with form and appearance

An example of such differences in approach was the use of domestic space. Many West Indian applicants kept a 'best front room' which they reserved for visitors and from which children were, on the whole, excluded. Social workers', however, tended to interpret this as evidence of an over-rigid regime of discipline, over-concentration on form and appearance at the expense of warmth and affection, and lack of understanding of the importance of play[3]. As one of them explained,

> We used to think that West Indian mothers didn't really understand about play and were too concerned about appearances. They would show you into the sitting room and you would never see a toy on the floor or anything for the kids to play with. (cf. L.B. Wandsworth, 1986g; Dominelli, 1988).

West Indians' emphasis on the importance of children's behaviour and dress in public was subject to similar interpretations. Applicants were aware of these opinions and complained about white social workers' prejudice and lack of understanding.

Whereas the 'best front room' was interpreted as an indication of over-formality, social workers were often unnerved by the informality with

---

[2] Society generally wishes to see something different about those identified as deviant by the relevant control agencies... social work is influenced by psychoanalysis, with its explanation of present behaviour in terms of the pathology and 'problems' of the past. The tendency is for whatever is or has been the 'story' of the client's life to be perceived and presented as the pathological cause of present difficulties (Ely and Denney, 1987: 146).

[3] These views are supported by a long history of negative interpretations of black and West Indian family patterns and life styles (e.g. Moynihan, 1965; FitzHerbert, 1967; Lepine, 1970; de Lobo, 1978; National Childrens' Bureau, 1973; Bowker, 1968; Hood et al, 1970; Paterson, 1966; Berliner, 1981; Earls et al, 1980a,b; Rutter et al, 1974).

which they were received by applicants. One, for example, described how some friends of the family she was visiting happened to call round while she was there and were immediately invited in rather than being asked to come back at a more convenient time as she believed a white applicant would have done. (cf. Stubbs, 1987; L.B. Wandsworth Study Day tape, 14 February 1986). By contrast, many of the black applicants interviewed complained of social workers' over-formality.

The nature and manner of questioning

Social workers' concern with psycho–dynamic functioning meant that the general thrust of questioning during assessment interviews was likely to antagonise applicants and many found the nature and manner of questioning offensive. They objected, in particular, to the more personal questions. Similar attitudes have been reported elsewhere (e.g. L.B. Wandsworth, 1986e). Many people resented what they considered to be unnecessary intrusion into their private affairs and thought that much of the questioning was inappropriate and even impertinent. Others were torn by a recognition of the need for careful scrutiny of prospective foster parents and a reluctance to discuss their private affairs with strangers, especially an 'official' from a government organisation. Such reticence is characteristic of black people in Britain who have learned, as a matter of survival, not to give too much away (Ben–Tovim and Gabriel, 1979; Ely and Denney, 1987; Donovan, 1986). This sense of vulnerability could be detected in many of the answers which people gave. Some suggested that people were afraid that information would be passed on to the police, immigration officials, or to the Department of Health and Social Security.

Some applicants thought that it was not necessary to interview husband and wife separately nor to interview children.

> They come to interview you once, they come back, they interview you again. They want to come back to interview your kids. They want to come back to interview your husband separate. They want to come back... Oh no, I wouldn't go in for that (laugh). It's an awful lot. I won't go in for that at all. You are going to take somebody in your own house and you have to go through all that. Of course, it put you off!

Several women thought their husbands would be annoyed by having to answer personal questions posed by a white, middle class woman social worker and wanted to shield them from having to do so. Others believed that they would be less patient about answering what they considered to be impertinent or unnecessary questions, that this would turn them against fostering and they would then prevent their wives from pursuing their applications. This appears to have happened in at least two cases. In others, the husbands, themselves, reported that they had been less tolerant than their wives and had found the assessments more frustrating. Differences of class, colour and ethnicity were, thus, complicated by the additional dimension of gender.

It was not only West Indian respondents who had found some of the personal questions embarrassing or inappropriate: some white applicants made similar complaints. One couple, for example, described how they had been 'shocked by some of the questions even though we had been warned to expect them from some friends of ours and we more or less knew from them what to expect'. Their comment underlines the importance of access to informal communication networks with friends and relatives who are foster parents. On the whole, the white applicants were better prepared in terms of what to expect from the assessment process.

Most people were unable or reluctant to be specific about the personal nature of the questions which they had found offensive, although some of the women complained about being asked about previous boyfriends and relationships. By contrast, two of the men (one black, one white) claimed that they had *not* been asked about their sex lives.

> The questions she was asking was nothing to do with looking after foster children. She never asked what I was like with children or about my sexual behaviour – You know, I could be a child molester or a pervert or something – but just went on and on about my childhood and upbringing which is totally unnecessary. What I found was that the scrutiny I had was not necessary.

> They don't know me. I mean, I could be a child molester. They didn't ask about my sex life. They didn't really ask me about how I was as a person. I feel they don't really know me. (White Applicant)

Applicants rejected social workers' concern with details of their past, especially their childhood years and thought that the emphasis should be on how they were currently running their lives. Four men complained that the social workers did not seem to take enough interest in their family lives.

> they weren't really interested in what actual family we had... They never actually sort of asked us what we do with our children, what we like to do for fun. None of that came into it. (White applicant)

> There are better things they could be asking about, like my family, how I bring up my own kids. They hardly asked about that at all.

190

Similarly, applicants found their desire to discuss more immediate financial and material concerns thwarted by the social worker in favour of what many considered to have been an unnecessary interest in their personal lives.

> There was all these questions about when you was a child and about your marriage which was totally unnecessary. Like we didn't get down to talk about how we was going to manage on the money they pay. You know, it's all extra food and clothes and little things, like you take them on the bus and it soon adds up. But she was more interested in what you done as a teenager rather than what you are doing now.

Applicants' inability to fathom the purpose behind many of the questions meant that they were perceived as unnecessary or irrelevant. This caused resentment and undermined their faith in social workers' assessment abilities. The importance of preparing people for the type of questions to expect and the reasons for asking them was, therefore, stressed. The following comment was made by one of the foster parent co-workers.

> With black people, they are very private people. Definitely, they resent (being asked personal questions). They think you are prying. They are very private. They don't want the world to know their business. But, once they get to know you and you have explained what it is all about, I think it is a little bit easier for them.

Several people thought that most of the questions asked had already been adequately answered on their application forms.

> because all the things they asked me or most of them was already written in the form. So I do not see any reason of what's the point of coming. I honestly couldn't see the reason, the personal reason for coming. I just think that (to inspect the accommodation) was why they came.

Further resentment was generated by the style and intensity of the advertising campaign which had not prepared people for the interrogations to which they felt they had been subjected. The urgency of the advertisements had led them to believe that they would be welcomed with open arms. Many were, therefore, unprepared for the reversal of roles from profferer to supplicant which they had experienced during their assessments. They resented being treated as if it was they who were suing the Social Services rather than offering them a valuable service. Three people compared the

191

feelings which they had experienced with being assessed for charity or for Government benefits[4].

In part, this stemmed from applicants' ignorance about the organisation of local authority fostering services and from a failure in communication on the part of the Social Services (see Chapter Seven). A few considered that the fact that they had come forward should be sufficient proof of their honourable intentions and that to be subjected to the scrutiny of an assessment was both unnecessary and insulting. For others, it was not the assessment *per se* to which they objected but the intensity of the scrutiny. Many had clearly been unprepared for the assessment process and had been unaware of what an application to foster for the local authority would involve. Several mentioned that formal fostering in this way was unknown to them in the West Indies (cf. Arnold and James, 1989), although there was a well-established tradition of caring for other people's children, usually by a close friend or relative. They knew of no machinery for formal assessment or 'vetting' and relied on other people's generosity, their good name and their own personal knowledge of them. To question someone's generosity by subjecting them to the sort of scrutiny involved in a formal assessment would have been considered insulting.

Black applicants' hostility may also have been, in part, a consequence of social workers' failure to adapt their new approach to the change in dynamics of supply and demand for black foster parents. Although their assessment role was not obviated[5], it was tempered by that of supplicant: they needed the services which applicants were offering. Many, however, found the new role difficult to accommodate within the framework of their training and experience. As one remarked, 'Our whole approach will have to change'.

There was, for example, a general lack of sensitivity to the structural bases of asymmetry in their relationships with applicants. The asking of questions establishes an alternating sequence of question and response. The question sets the tone of the exchange since people usually feel obliged to answer it. The questioner decides on the topic to be discussed and dictates how the talk will proceed while the respondent depends upon the questioner for the right to ask questions him/herself. This asymmetry of interactional rights, based on the question and answer format which is the defining characteristic of interview talk, lock the roles of interviewer and respondent into a dominant–subordinate

---

[4] This was particularly resented by older applicants, many of whom had a horror of 'going on the welfare' and were too proud to claim many of the benefits to which they were entitled (cf. Donovan, 1986).

[5] We cannot avoid the fact that law and commonsense require some element of inquiry (references, medicals, etc.) to safeguard the child and that ultimately the agency has the final say in the placement (*Parents for Children, First Year's Report 1976/77*).

relationship (Silverman, 1973). In the assessment interview, this was reinforced in the wider social context.

Interviewer	Interviewee
white	black
middle-class	work-class
official	lay person
professional	non-professional
adjudicator	applicant/supplicant
assessor	assessed

Social workers' assumed that, in their official and professional capacities, they had a right and duty to ask personal questions not normally asked of 'strangers' and that applicants had an obligation to answer. Applicants, however, often neither recognised social workers' right to ask such questions nor their own obligation to answer. They resented what they perceived to be a reversal of the proper roles for each party to adopt, regarded themselves as people offering a valuable service, a view encouraged by the campaign advertising, and resented being placed in the position of supplicants. 'It is as if the children were fostering us', one husband remarked.

Despite these reservations, most (60%) of those who had been assessed thought that the social worker had gained an adequate impression of what they and their families were like. A minority (40%), however, thought their assessments had been superficial and that the social worker had not known how to ask the right questions. Eight people, only two of whom had been assessed themselves, thought that workers did not dig deeply enough and that, in one person's words, they should 'leave no stone unturned'. Alternative approaches, including less formal sessions, on-the-spot visits and sharing in family activities, were mentioned. Some people thought that interviews were a waste of time – first, because workers did not know how to ask the right questions and, second, because applicants would not answer honestly – and thought that medical and police records[6] and personal references were all that were necessary.

Inormants described various strategies they had employed to defend themselves from workers' intrusiveness. Some complained that the social

---

[6] Several people expressed hostility towards the requirement of police records, especially when it involved other people living in their homes being investigated. Many observed that a criminal record did not necessarily indicate guilt and this became a repetitive theme. There was a general mistrust of the police and judicial system which underlined their general sense of vulnerability as black people living in Britain.

worker had visited them at inconvenient times and had stayed too long. They explained how they had dealt with this by refusing to sit down with the social worker and, instead, getting on with household tasks and answering questions as briefly as possible. One woman described how she had purposefully not told the social worker facts about her life and had held things back in order to forestall further questions. The withholding of information gave applicants a sense of power in that it was their decision what to reveal and what to withhold. They deliberately retained a part of their history about which the social worker did not know but deluded her into believing that she had obtained the 'full story'. 'I laughed when she was gone', one woman declared,

> because I hadn't told her even half of it. Not that I really had anything to hide. I just didn't want her to know all about me. She irritated me, I suppose, so I just held some things back. It was like a game really. These social workers, they come and they think you are going to tell them everything, just like that. In the end, they only know what you tell them.

Another woman, who had been particularly angered by the social worker's visit, said that the social worker had been made more nervous by these tactics than she had been, herself.

Gender

Within the terms of social workers' uni–dimensional cultural model of client–worker interactions, the impact of gender, like 'race', is reduced to matter of simple cultural difference. The quality of interaction between white, female social worker and black, male client or, alternatively, between black, female social worker and white, male client, however, is likely to be especially strained where the social worker is present in an assessment role or social control function. In the present study, many wives reported that their husbands had been more intolerant of the social worker's questionning than they had themselves. The conception of fostering as 'women's work' may have explained some men's reluctance to be seen to be publicly involved and the belief that the training and assessment groups were predominantly female groups may have deterred some men from attending.

In the assessment encounter, however, the focus was on candidates' parenting skills and, in particular, the woman's skills as the primary carer. Here, the confrontation was primarily between women (there were no male social workers in the Team) and the contested terrain, the conventional female skills of child–rearing and household management. Applicants' consideration of fostering as 'a job of work' rather than a vocation and the desire of many

194

to combine it with paid employment outside the home challenged conventional ideas about the woman as mother and home–maker (Lowe, 1989; Rhodes, 1989). Their rejection of formal qualifications and training and assertion of the value of experience and 'ordinary commonsense' challenged social workers' professional authority in the realm of family assessment. As women, social workers were more vulnerable to this challenge as a consequence of applicants' central location of motherhood in the fulfilment of the female identity, especially where workers lacked the experience of motherhood and child–rearing, themselves.

Public façade and private 'truth'

A crucial distinction for social workers was that between public façade and private 'truth', based on the belief that people lead two lives, one public and one private. They believed that it was their professional duty to delve behind the public façade which people present to the outside world to reveal the 'truth' about their 'real' lives which are conducted in the privacy of their own homes. Investigations were conducted under the assumption that applicants would attempt to present a 'public face' and would try to hide their 'real' or 'true' selves (cf. Parents for Children, 1976/7[7]). As one worker explained, 'It might not be their real reaction that you get at first. You have to wait until they feel more comfortable with you and they put their guard down' (SW4). The value of this approach was related to the general strategy of minimization of risks: rather than asking 'What makes this person likely to be a good foster parent?', workers looked for contra–indications. As one commented, 'What we are really looking for is any reason why this person should not be accepted' (SW6). The main purpose of the interview was to discover possible reasons for disqualification. It was assumed that applicants would attempt to hide information which might damage their applications and that it was the task of the social worker to try to penetrate this deception.

The various strategies employed to persuade, trick or cajole applicants into opening a window on to their private lives ran the risk of backfiring. The lack of explicitness, indirect questioning, circuitous approach or 'beating about the bush', as one woman described it, which often seemed to characterise social workers' approach, aroused suspicion and resentment and jeopardised any fragile trust between applicant and worker.

---

[7] We firmly believe that if people are approached to be 'investigated' they will put on their best front, be defensive, and the aim becomes 'passing the exam' instead of 'let's look at what this entails and see if we want it and have got what it takes to do it' (*Parents for Children, First Year's Report 1976/77*, p3).

195

A few people seemed to regard the covert purpose of some of the questions and the depth of scrutiny to which they were subjected as a disguised means of excluding black people from becoming foster parents.

They put out these advertisements and say they want black foster parents but they aren't really interested. It is just to satisfy the black people, to have a few black faces, but they are not really interested. They take so much time, you give up. And the questions they ask, some of them are weird. There's no need to ask half of them and it puts people off. I can't see that they really want black people: they have enough white and put so many things in your way, you don't bother.

If they is really genuine with this fostering, they will have to change their tactics. If people is complaining of what questions they are asking, that is pushing people away, so they will have to find another way.

Managing self-presentation: black/white profiles of competence in the fostering process

As we have seen in Chapter Eight, applicants seemed to have had some idea of the image which they thought would convey to social workers a sense of their capacity to become good foster parents and were able to adjust their answers accordingly. Where people were unable to fathom the purpose behind the questions, they became unsure about how to present themselves and afraid that their answers might be 'used against them'.

Rees describes how prospective adoptive parents were able to manage their self-presentations because they 'had some prior idea of the probable criteria affecting decisions' (1978: 126-8). In contrast with the black, working-class fostering applicants of the present study, the adoption applicants were articulate, white, middle class people from similar social backgrounds to the social workers who were assessing them and could reasonably expect to share similar ideas about child care and family life. The greater ability of people from middle class compared with people from working class backgrounds to manipulate encounters with officials and professionals and to achieve favourable outcomes in their dealings with them has been reported elsewhere (e.g. Flett, 1979; Lipsky, 1980).

The self-presentations of both the black and the white applicants in the present study were constrained by the context of unequal power: their desire to be approved as foster parents was set against the social workers' power to accept or reject, overlain by differences of class and status in the wider society. The social distance between black applicant and white social worker, however, extended beyond considerations of class to include skin colour and ethnicity. Whereas social and cultural affinity permits learning, black–white differences present blocks or barriers. The differences in attitude towards questions about childhood (Chapter Eight) are but one illustration. Many white applicants, far from resenting this line of questioning, had found it useful and had enjoyed talking about their pasts, whereas the black applicants' reluctance risked being interpreted as 'having something to hide'.

Both workers and applicants conceived of the assessment as a test which had to be passed. To social workers, it was also a contest in which they assumed applicants would attempt to put up a public façade or screen which it was their task to penetrate to reveal the private 'truth' behind. White applicants, being more familiar with the rules of engagement and with the rationale which informed social workers' approach, were better able to present themselves in conformity with expectations than black applicants whose disadvantaged position was further complicated by the addition of a cultural dimension. Unaware of social workers' current more flexible attitudes and wider definitions of the 'good' foster family, older applicants, in particular, tended to stress an affluent, law–abiding, church–going life–style, good behaviour, discipline and morality. On the other hand, attempts to present themselves in conformity with a 'white' model of family life could lead workers to suspect them of insincerity. Furthermore, white social workers' intercultural skills may not always have been adequate to the discernment of what may have been fine cultural distinctions between public and private presentations and they may sometimes have misinterpreted black applicants' responses.

Private shame or public injustice?

A further significance of the distinction between public and private lay in the penalties of rejection. Failure to be approved as a foster parent was often no longer a matter of private shame but of public injustice. Rejection was perceived not so much in personal, individualised terms as in terms of the moral failure of the Social Services. Although some people were philosophical and seemed to accept that they did not fit with Social Services' criteria for selecting foster parents, others were angry about the 'injustice' of a 'system' which excluded them and interpreted their rejection as further evidence of discrimination against black people. Their confidence to speak out was encouraged by public censure in the black press of past discriminatory practices within the social services. The fact that it was now acceptable to interpret rejection in group terms rather than personal failure provided both a

197

means of 'saving face' and a confidence to express dissatisfaction in public. Friends and relatives who were known to have been rejected were rarely 'blamed' for their failure but were treated, instead, as the victims of a hostile assessment procedure implemented by racially prejudiced social workers.

The language and discourse of racism had increasingly provided applicants with an alternative explanation to that provided by social workers, an alternative couched in structural and political terms and sought at the level of group relationships rather than individualised in terms of personal inadequacy and family failings. It pointed to the under–representation of black people in the foster parent pool and the preferential placement of black children outside the black community and interpreted these discrepancies in terms of the structural relationships of power between the two communities, black and white. Its strength lay not simply in the provision of a means of 'saving face' but in its identification of the individual with the group. In one fell swoop, the assessment process was lifted from the private domain of intra–familial relationships into the public arena of political contest between social groups.

Conclusion

The conceptual distinction between public and private had a number of consequences for the assessments of black applicants. The separation of family from society meant that family life was examined in terms of a psycho–dynamic model which divorced it from the economic and political context (cf. Ely and Denney, 1987)[8]. For those whose family lives deviated from the conventional norm, either in structural or material terms, this separation left them vulnerable to the label of deviancy or pathology.

In the context of the family as the private domain, the assessment interview represented a public intrusion into private space. The significance of the intrusion for black applicants lay not simply in different cultural understandings of public and private but in the social distance between themselves and the intruder: the intrusion was not simply that of a social worker but that of a white middle class person into a black working class home. As Hilary Graham has pointed out, '"private" and "public" do not... have an exact and tangible location: places remain constant while definitions of their social space change' (1983: 135). Shirley Ardener (1978) has argued

---

[8] According to Ely and Denney, 'Contradictory West Indian stereotypes emerge: for some it is the absence of a father and the presence of a 'dominating' mother that is the problem; for others, the presence of a forceful, 'authoritarian' father and a weak, anxious mother is the contributory situation. Parents feel it is always they who are held to blame, never the pressures they are under, the discrimination they face or the problems of bringing up children in an inner–city neighbourhood' (1987: 147).

that it is the presence of men which typically defines a space as 'public'. In the context of the assessment interview, however, it was the presence of the social worker which transformed the private domain into a public arena.

The terms of the exchange were largely set by the social worker who initiated the pattern of questions and answers which governed the conduct of the interview. Applicants' refusal to answer the social workers' questions risked prejudicing their chances of acceptance and the ability to ask questions themselves was largely dependent on the social worker granting them the right. The language of the assessment was the language of the social worker who determined both what was relevant and what was inappropriate and the model of family life which the social worker brought to the assessment was that of a psycho–dynamic system which functioned more or less independently of the economic and socio–political context. Discussion of these issues was, therefore, not considered appropriate to the context of the assessment. Edwin Ardener (1975) has suggested that there are 'dominant' and 'muted' modes of expression reflecting, and generated by, the wider power divisions within society and that, since the dominant mode expresses the relation of the dominant group to the social world, it fails to capture the relations through which the experiences of the muted group are mediated.

Discussions of public and private usually refer to the different ways in which men and women's lives are structured and several writers (Ardener, 1975; Rich, 1980; Spender, 1980) have argued that these gender divisions have their equivalent in language. According to Spender, the language of the public sphere is a 'man–made language' in which not only are women's voices unheard but significant aspects of their experience ignored or unrecognised. According to Rich, they become 'not merely unspoken but unspeakable' (1980: 199). A parallel could be drawn between the language of social workers and the language of applicants: not only might the words be different but the ideas and experiences to which they refer. The problem is not simply one of understanding the differences but of expressing and rendering them visible in the first place. The scope of applicants' expression was restricted by the social distance separating them from the social worker along lines of class, colour, ethnicity and, in the case of the men, gender, and by the social worker's control over the terms and language of the encounter and model within which family life was to be presented and analysed. Culture was only one among several relevant dimensions. For a truly ethnically sensitive practice, it is, therefore, not enough simply to try to take into account cultural differences without consideration of the wider context and the relationships of power which under– and overlie them.

The public–private distinction which informed social workers' model of family life was mirrored in their distinction between public and private presentations, between public façade and private truth. The assessment interview was approached as a sort of 'cat and mouse game' in which social workers conceived their role as trying to penetrate the public screen which they assumed applicants would put up to try to hide their 'true' identities. Not only were black applicants handicapped in comparison with white by their lack of familiarity with 'the rules of the game' but the notion of contest conflicts with the theory and language of 'partnership' and 'self-assessment' which is discussed in the following chapter.

Finally, the distinction between public and private had implications in terms of the penalties of rejection. Explanation in the terms of the language and discourse of racism lifted the assessment process out of the private domain of family life into the public arena of political contest and provided an alternative to explanation in terms of individual failure. Ironically, as applicants gained in confidence, social workers' own confidence was undermined. Not only were their attempts to confine the assessment process within the private sphere undermined but their decisions likely to become more visible and open to public scrutiny, both at the level of the individual, when rejected applicants were prepared to publicise their rejection, and at the level of the group, in terms of the numbers of black foster parents recruited.

11   A new departure: Group assessment and training

In Spring 1985, the first training and assessment courses, one 'black' and one 'mixed' were run. The use of group methods was heralded as 'a radical change of policy' (Team Meeting minutes, March 1985) from the previous approach which had relied entirely on home visits. The mixed course comprised eight two–hourly sessions and the 'black' course three sessions. A further three sessions were planned after a break of a few weeks, during which time the home interviews would be carried out, but these sessions were never implemented. The courses were held in a local teacher training centre on a weekday evening and the course content was based on the National Foster Care Association 'Parenting Plus' material. The mixed course was divided into two groups which were held in different rooms in the centre and was, thus, effectively divided into two courses which ran concurrently (Table 8). One of these (course A) was attended by the researcher as a participant observer.

The analysis in this chapter is based on participant observation and informal discussions during the course and post–session adjournments to the pub and more formal interviews with the social workers who ran the courses, the foster parent facilitators who helped, and the applicants who attended. The interviews with applicants were conducted in their own homes soon after the home visits had been completed, although before some had heard the outcome of the final decision. This timing was agreed in order to avoid the researcher's role being confused with that of the social workers.

Table 8

The course participants

	Mixed courses		Black course
	A	B	C
social workers	2	2	2
white foster parent facilitators	2	3	–
black foster parent facilitators	1	–	2
white applicants*	11	17	1
black applicants	6	2	15

* The presence of the white applicant was entirely fortuitous. She had arrived with a friend, uninvited, but had seemed so at east in the group that the social workers had considered that it would have been inappropriate to have asked her to leave, despite the advice of the black foster parents to the contrary.

Group methods have been justified on the grounds that they are a more efficient way of processing a large number of people, with economies of labour and resources, than individual assessments (Davis *et al.*, 1984; Thethi *et al.*, 1988; Light Stanley, 1971) and bring fostering more into line with the 'professional status' demanded by an increasing number of foster parents (e.g. Theze, 1983; Rhodes, 1989). In the borough of the case study, the introduction of group methods was primarily a response to the large volume of applications generated by the recruitment campaigns and to the shortage of social workers available to carry out individual assessments. The 'black' course was also justified on the grounds that black applicants had 'special cultural needs' and would 'feel less isolated' and 'more at ease' in an all black group. Two workers, however, thought that these reasons were secondary to the main purpose of experimenting with the group method of assessment. As one explained,

SW6 Right from the beginning, I didn't think that it was going to be just something specially for the black people. That would be wrong. But I suppose they were guineapigs in a way.

A fourth reason concerned consistency: the setting up of an all black group was thought to be consistent with the advertising campaign to recruit black foster parents for black children.

The courses took place, first, within the context of changing ideas about assessment away from the old concept of 'vetting' towards new ideas about partnership and shared decision–making[1] and, second, within the context of a high profile campaign to recruit black foster parents and professed commitment to 'providing a more ethnically sensitive service' (Team Meeting minutes, January 1984) and 'anti–racist approach' (Meeting of Black Action Group April 1985). On neither count were they notably successful. Despite the language of radicalism and change and of participation and partnership, there were few opportunities for applicants to influence, let alone to challenge, social workers' approach. Even the 'all black' course operated more as a reaffirmation of than a departure from the *status quo*. The opportunities for black applicants to discuss their needs or even to define them for themselves were limited and the potential for change through dialogue or challenge denied. The tactics of consensus management and conflict avoidance noted earlier (Chapters Four and Five) were carried on to the courses and helped to preserve what was essentially a conservative approach.

The 'Mixed Group'

Partnership and shared decision–making

According to the Team, the move to group assessment was inspired by an article which appeared in *Adoption and Fostering* in 1984 (Davis *et al.*, 1984). The authors criticised previous reliance on 'an individual home study' and 'the psycho–dynamic model' of assessment and outlined the advantages of adopting group methods. Throughout, the importance of equality and partnership with applicants was stressed. This theme was expanded in a later article (Theti *et al.*, 1988) which stressed that 'assessment should be an open and shared process' and that 'preparation for fostering must promote equality between applicants and workers'. At no point, however, was the possibility of conflict

---

[1] In theory, social workers considered themselves to be moving away from their traditional judgemental role towards a more facilitative and egalitarian approach. They saw themselves exploring the nature of the fostering task together with the applicant. Their language was that of 'partnership' and 'sharing' as opposed to the old language of 'vetting', 'approval' and 'rejection'. Whereas, previously, the investigation had been of the suitability of the applicant to the fostering task, social workers now spoke of 'the suitability of the fostering task to the applicant's capabilities, needs and wishes' (Team Leader). The group approach was considered fundamental to these new developments. It helped participants to explore together the task of fostering and to assess their own motives and capabilities in relation to it. In theory, the social worker's assessment role would become a mere formality, a rubber–stamping of a decision already taken by the applicant to proceed or not to proceed with the application.

203

between the aims of training and assessment or between those of assessment and partnership acknowledged[2].

The notion of partnership was important to the workers in the Fostering Team as one of the course leaders explained,

SW2 We are trying very much to move away from this idea of 'us' and 'them'. The idea of the groups is partly to develop the idea of partnership and working together as part of a team. It's not easy. It's a big change, really, and I think that not all of my colleagues would agree, but I try to think of the foster parents as equals, as partners in a common task, each doing our different bits.

As another put it,

SW7 It's giving the applicants a chance to express their views and to talk with other applicants, to learn more about what it's all about before they eventually decide. It's giving them more of a say right from the start.

Related to the idea of partnership was that of self–assessment. The same social worker explained,

We try to work with (the applicants) in the group to help them to understand what fostering would mean to them, to recognise their strengths and their weaknesses and to decide for themselves whether or not fostering is really for them.

Theory and the practice, however, did not always mesh for she went on,

It doesn't always work that way, of course. You get some people who don't drop out of their own accord and you have to tell them that they won't be accepted.

Despite their appeal in theory, workers found their ideas about partnership and self–assessment difficult to put into practice. The sources of tension and conflict discussed in the previous chapter were accentuated on the courses where the distinction between 'public' and 'private' was drawn at its sharpest. The distinction had a number of dimensions. Not only did the course participants find themselves on unfamiliar ground and among unfamiliar faces but they felt themselves exposed to the public scrutiny of both social workers

---

[2] Carroll touches on, but does not really explore, these problems in her article, `Using Groups' (1980).

and other applicants. Their insecurity was intensified by the knowledge that their performances were being formally assessed (cf. Carroll, 1980). For the black applicants on the mixed course, there was the additional dimension of their colour and ethnic visibility and its interpretation in the wider society. These factors had a number of implications for the ways in which participants attempted to present themselves. The distinction between public and private presentations which participants felt so acutely was both created and accentuated by the assessment process. Participants' awareness of the public nature of their self-presentations on the course encouraged conscious manipulation and consequently devalued their performance as a guide to behaviour in their own homes. In other words, the process of assessment was obstructed by the public–private distinction which it had helped to engender.

Almost everyone said that they had felt inhibited by not knowing how other participants would react. One person, for example, explained,

> You want to say something completely different but you might shock someone else, you know what I mean? You are thinking of what you are going to say and how the others are going to think as well. (Black participant)

A fear that they were not like the others in the group made people anxious about speaking out and drawing hostile or disapproving reactions. This fear was likely to have been especially acute for the few black participants[3] on the mixed courses as the following comment illustrates,

> I didn't go in much for the role play. I just tend to keep quiet and don't say much. I think the white people seemed to know a bit more about what was expected because, if you notice, not many of us (black people) joined in all that much. I think we were more afraid of saying the wrong thing. (Black participant)

Although they were hostile to the notion of separate treatment and disliked the idea of segregated groups on ideological grounds, at the level of experience, two of the black applicants admitted that they would have

---

[3] People who had constructed their own personal identities and who had tried to live their lives in the belief that they could become assimilated to 'white' culture in such a way as to make themselves 'invisible', people who were committed to the liberal ideology of the 'melting pot', or whose experience of racism had taught them that any attempt to rock the boat of liberal idealism by drawing attention to their cultural difference would expose them to, at best, criticism and, at worst, verbal and even physical abuse, found their vision of the world threatened and its fragility exposed by the new moves.

205

preferred there to have been more black participants. The sense of difference was evident in the following comment from one of the white participants:

> One or two of the older coloured women, they were a bit...well, you didn't like to say too much in front of them.

Impression management: 'playing the game'

Participants also felt constrained by the presence of the social workers and were afraid of saying something which might prejudice their assessment. As one of the white participants explained,

> It put you into a position where you felt very awkward... Because you don't know what is the expected reaction.... It's like a lot of the questions that they throw at you sort of there on the spot, a lot of people don't answer up because they don't know what they're expected to say... You think, 'Oh, maybe I'm saying the wrong thing. Will I get my foster kids?' You know, that sort of thing.

Applicants believed that there were 'right' and 'wrong' answers to the social workers' questions and a 'right' and a 'wrong' way of performing the role play exercises. A few admitted that they had deliberately tailored their answers to what they thought the social workers had wanted to hear, while others confessed that they had withheld information or even lied for fear of offending other participants or of giving a bad impression to the social workers.

> We did one role play and I actually did what they (the social workers) wanted to hear but my views were completely different. (White Participant)

> Like we had one scene about coming in and setting a time (for children to come home at night). I said I'd compromise. That's what I said in the role play. But I wouldn't. No, I would set a time and that's it. I wouldn't compromise... I expect, if they (the social workers) thought that about me, that I wouldn't compromise, then I was no good, as good as useless. (White Participant)

> You are just letting people hear what they want to hear, not what you actually feel deep down inside. (Black Participant)

Participants felt that they were 'playing along' according to 'the rules of the game' or, as one man put it, 'just playing a part'.

People didn't enjoy it (role play). I suppose that everybody felt the same in the group but had to sort of play along. (Black Participant)

Applicants made more or less informed guesses about the standards or model of good parenting according to which the social workers were operating and were able to modify their judgements as they learned more about the social workers' approach as the course proceeded. Many admitted to having had preconceptions about the qualities which they thought social workers would be looking for and confessed that these had influenced their behaviour and that they had been able to modify their ideas as the course proceeded. This process of incremental learning and gains in competence, that is the ability to recognise and interpret correctly the various signals and clues dropped by the social workers and to adjust one's self-presentation accordingly was, perhaps, what was meant by 'playing the game'. The black applicants were doubly disadvantaged: not only were the social workers' standards likely to have been based on a 'white' profile of family life, but the white applicants were likely to have been more familiar with the 'rules of the game' and more proficient at playing it. One, for example, commented,

I had a fair idea of what they (the social workers) were after. You do at times, you want something so you play the game.

In the context of assessment, applicants did not have the confidence to challenge the social workers' approach and their standard or model was, therefore, not open to negotiation or challenge. A presentation which did not conform ran the risk of jeopardising the non-conformist's chances of approval. Where the majority of participants were white, it would have been difficult to introduce an alternative black perspective.

The emphasis on assessment[4] set the agenda as one of potential conflict. It not only constrained or distorted participants' behaviour but hindered the process of learning:

I was too nervous to learn. I don't think I learnt anything from it. (White participant)
I was playing a part. I didn't know what I was doing most of the time because I felt so nervous and embarrassed. I was virtually talking for the sake of it. (Black participant)

---

[4] Despite the theory of 'partnership', workers continued to conceive their primary role as that of assessor rather than facilitator and to refer to the courses as 'group assessments'. The assessment element was formally built into the structure: after each session, workers and foster parents met in a pub to discuss their observations of participants and to compare notes.

but constrained the social workers' own behaviour, conflicted with their training role and prevented the formation of relationships with applicants of mutual trust. The course leaders reported that they had found it difficult to carry out the dual roles of trainer/facilitator and assessor and had been unable to give sufficient attention to the assessment aspects of their role.

Differential treatment?

These tensions were especially significant for the black applicants who were in a minority and for whom the need to 'put on a show' had the additional complication of colour and ethnic visibility. The desire to 'belong' and fear of antagonising the white members of the group constrained them to play down cultural and ethnic differences. The course leaders were also wary of treating them differently for fear of making them feel uncomfortable or of antagonising the white majority. As one explained, 'It wouldn't have been right to have treated them differently'.

Their minority position on the course combined with its social significance in terms of black–white relations generally meant that, in the context of the course as in the wider society, the black participants formed a muted group whose ability to express themselves seemed to exist only in so far as it conformed with the dominant majority perspective. Not only was it difficult to express experiences and opinions which diverged, but opportunities for negotiating change on the basis of challenge were closed. Racism, for example, was neither discussed on an experiential level nor in terms of possible changes in practice and approach. Where differences did surface they were resolved in favour of the white majority. The divergent responses to the public discussion of participants' own childhoods are an example:

> I don't think it was really necessary to go into all that stuff about childhood. ...It's not really necessary, is it? I couldn't say about my childhood in Barbados. They wouldn't understand. (Black participant)

> What I liked about it was when we split up into small groups and were able to look back on our own youth and have frank and honest discussions. That was one of the good points. (White participant)

Husbands' attendance at meetings

Another example of possible cultural misunderstanding and/or insensitivity was the issue of husbands' attendance. Several people complained about workers' insistence that husbands attend the course and thought that non–attendance would affect the success of their applications. Although most thought that it

208

was important for husbands to attend, black participants argued that, among black people, men often leave their wives to take on the public role but retain their authority as heads of household in the private sphere.

> I think men always push women in the front of this kind of thing, especially the West Indian men. They give their opinion and their orders from the back but the women have to get on with it. The husband is interested but doesn't really come along to meetings and things like that. They leave that to the women. So, it doesn't really matter (that husbands don't go to meetings) because, as a matter of fact, it is the woman that is really doing it (the fostering) unless it is a one–parent man that is doing it.

One of the black facilitators took up the same theme,

> I don't think that it really matters (if husbands do not attend) because men, really, they don't like to go ahead and take the initiative. But they will stay behind and say what they think and give advice and their opinions. My husband is a tower of strength with the teenagers but he hates going to the meetings and things like that. He hates going so it is nearly always me that goes.

Others, who attended the 'black' course, argued that many men would find it difficult to attend because the time was inconvenient, especially if they worked nights. Their complaints had, thus, both a cultural and a practical dimension. The potential for 'racial' antagonism should the non–attendance of black husbands be more readily tolerated by the social workers than that of white husbands, however, was demonstrated by the following comments from a white couple:

Husb Well, I said (to my wife), 'Can't you go on your own and then tell me afterwards?' But she (social worker) said both of us have to go. Yes, but one of the black ladies, her husband didn't go, you see.
Wife Yes, because on our report there, it's got the number of attendances what we made.
Husb Yeh, you see.
Wife But we did miss one and it's down there that we missed one.
Husb But, the other lady, we never saw her husband.
Wife Yes, and I did think that, you know, it ought to be the same for all of us. But, perhaps, he was working. He must've been.

When asked about the issue, one of the course leaders explained,

> I don't think we could have introduced different rules. It wouldn't have been fair, although we did consider it.

As a consequence of majority position, the democratic resolution of any disputes which might arise with a cultural component would always be in the white applicants' favour.

Discussion of 'racial' and cultural issues

There was little or no discussion of 'racial' or cultural questions nor of the new placement policy of 'racial matching'. But, when asked whether there were any topics which they would like to have covered in greater depth, several applicants in both the mixed and black groups mentioned 'racial' and cultural issues in relation to the new policy. The course leaders on the mixed course and several of the white participants suggested that the presence of the black applicants may have inhibited discussions of 'racial' and cultural issues. The following comments, for example, were from a white applicant and a social worker, respectively.

> That was really missed out. I think it would have been embarrassing because we was a mixed group. Perhaps, the social workers didn't want to really bring it up too much in front of the coloured ladies because it would have been embarrassing. But we should have definitely had more on it. We could have had a whole session on those sorts of things at the group.

> I think, perhaps, the black people in the group might have inhibited them (participants) a bit from bringing up sort of racial issues.

Coverage of the more conventional aspects of fostering seems to have been considered more important and to have taken precedence over 'racial' and cultural issues. 'We had so much to cover in the time', one of the course leaders commented, 'that those sorts of questions rather got left to one side'. This may have been, in part, a reflection of the low prominence given to such topics in the source material but a more important reason was probably the fear of exciting conflict within the group by raising controversial and possibly painful issues. The course leaders admitted that they had not only found such

210

subjects difficult to broach but had not felt competent to raise them[5]. One of them, for example, commented,

> Personally, I don't feel all that confident about talking about issues to do with race and culture. That's where, really, you need a black social worker.

The initiative seems to have been left to the applicants, themselves, for the same social worker went on,

> No, we didn't really get around to talking about those issues but the applicants didn't raise it either. I suppose we were sort of waiting for them to raise it, really.

The emphasis on consensus and avoidance of conflict, however, meant that it was difficult for applicants to raise potentially controversial issues. The sense of 'belonging' which seemed necessary for the functioning of the group, especially for exercises like role play, encouraged conformity and meant that the black participants were anxious to avoid drawing attention to their difference from the rest of the group. As one explained,

> Those sorts of things just weren't really discussed. I mean, I think it would have been a bit uncomfortable, really. You didn't want to cause trouble.

The topic of racism may have been too sensitive and painful for them to feel confident enough to raise it in the potentially unsympathetic context of the group. The failure to discuss the issue of appropriate placement was similarly the result of tacit collusion between both leaders and participants to avoid raising potentially contentious subjects. Not only was it controversial among participants but among the leaders and facilitators themselves. None of the white foster parent facilitators who were interviewed supported the new approach and even the social workers and black facilitators were ambivalent.

---

[5] Others have reported that white workers are frightened to confront issues of racism directly (Rooney, 1982; Fletchman–Smith, 1984; Stubbs, 1985; Dominelli, 1988, 1989) and have suggested that this is partly due to ignorance about racism as a social force and lack of understanding of black people's life experiences as they are mediated by and through racism (Kadushin, 1972; Dominelli, 1989).

The 'All Black Group'

Even in the 'black' group there seems to have been no discussion of these issues, although the virtual absence of white participants meant a comparatively 'safe' environment in which to have raised them. Although such discussions might have been expected to have been built into the structure of the course, they were consciously avoided and the three main areas – 'racial' and cultural issues, placement policy and segregated assessment procedures – where the encouragement of discussion and dialogue might have been expected were, in practice, played down.

'Racial' and cultural issues

The course leaders' discomfort about their visibility as white outsiders may have encouraged them to play down issues which would have emphasised their difference and increased their sense of exposure. Both admitted that they would have found ethnic and 'racial' subjects difficult to broach but gave shortage of time and a belief that the issues were too sensitive to bring up in the early sessions as reasons for their failure to raise them on the course. A more plausible explanation was a certain tacit reluctance to raise what were known to be controversial and sensitive issues. As this was their first training course for black applicants, the leaders were unsure about how they would be received by an all black group and nervous about introducing a potentially controversial subject which risked upsetting the tenuous and hard–won rapport which had developed by the third session.

Another factor may have been applicants' own reticence. When asked whether there were any topics which they would have liked to have covered in greater depth, only two mentioned 'racial' and cultural issues unprompted. Others thought that they were only relevant to the white applicants. As one person explained, 'those things certainly should have been discussed but, with us, it was different. I mean the advertisement was for black foster parents so that was the intention.'

'Racial matching'

The second area where discussion might have been expected was the new approach of 'racial matching'. The presence of the single white applicant may have had an inhibitory effect but the discrepancy in views between the social workers and foster parent facilitators was also a contributory factor. Although both social workers supported the new moves, the foster parents were ambivalent. When asked about the desirability of running an all black group, one, for example, replied,

212

I think, if you are going to have a mixed group of foster parents, they should take any child not just black or white. If you are going to have a mixed group, they should take both. Because I see myself as a foster parent and, if I'm going to foster a child, it doesn't matter to me: a child is a child, be it black or white.

Her views, however, were not clear-cut for she continued,

But, if they are recruiting black foster parents for black children, then I think it is better all black (training groups). I think that one has to look at what is in the best interests of the child, actually. I wouldn't be rigid but I would rather to see a black child go to a black family if the black family was available. It's a big question ... (nervous laugh) It's very tricky. You have to look at what is in the best interests of the child, really. I would go for a black family first and then, if one wasn't available, I'd go for a white.

The other foster parent's views on the subject were more coherent but even less in tune with Team policy.

The only thing that I always criticise the social workers for is that they don't give black families white kids. I asked them once and the answer I got was that, if you give a white kid to a black family, then the place is wasted because they don't have enough black families for the black kids. That is the reason they told me. When I was fostering for (another borough), I fostered any nationality. You would get a phone call and you wouldn't know what you would get until the child arrived on your doorstep. It could be black, white or any colour or nationality. You wouldn't know 'till the kid came to your doorstep. As far as I am concerned, a child is a child and all children need families. It doesn't matter what colour or race or nationality that child is, it's still a child. I'm not a racialist. As far as I am concerned, a child is a child. I didn't say to them, 'I don't want a white child'. I am a foster parent and every child is a child to me.

As in the mixed group, support for the new approach was not whole-hearted, even among the workers, who were far from presenting a united and coherent stance. The subject seems to have been skirted by unspoken agreement to avoid risking conflict, both within the group and between themselves. It was not an issue which was open to public debate or challenge. The new policy was, thus, imposed as a *fait accompli* which was open neither to discussion nor to negotiation.

213

The exclusiveness of the 'all black' group made social workers uneasy and they were at pains to play down its segregated nature and to deny that it had been a matter of intended policy as opposed to pragmatic convenience. Despite these views, all those interviewed agreed that black applicants would probably 'feel more at ease' and 'more prepared to "open up" in an all black group'.

The social workers' ambivalence about differential treatment for black people was matched by that of the black foster parent facilitators. Both agreed that the distinction between public and private was stronger for black applicants than for white.

They are very private: they don't want the world to know their business.

Well, it was slow to start... I think you go into a room – of course, it is all strange people so you wait for someone to speak first. I think a lot of them, they want to say something but they think that, it they say something, it might be the wrong thing so they wait for someone else to speak first.

But, whereas one thought that 'racial' and ethnic affinity would help to break down the public–private divide and promote free expression,

They were more relaxed because it was mainly other black people than if it had been mainly white. They feel more comfortable with their own than if they had been the only black there. You know, how to bring up kids and thing like that, they more likely to speak out their mind because white people sometimes have different ideas.

the other thought that the lead of the white applicants in a mixed group helped to reduce the black applicants' inhibitions,

It's mixed so people start talking and so picking up from each other. They're more open. The black people pick up from the whites.

In other words, the sense of affinity based on ethnicity and skin colour was thought to strengthen adherence to a culturally determined interpretation of appropriate behaviour in public which served to confound the aims of both group training and of assessment. Both foster parents, however, agreed that most black people would feel uncomfortable in a predominantly white group. Significantly, neither mentioned political considerations concerned with self–determination, power–sharing or measures to counteract the effects of racism such as positive discrimination or affirmative action when discussing the pros and cons of running an ethnically exclusive group.

A further explanation for the black applicants' reticence may have been the presence of the white social workers and the role distance and cultural and status differences which set them apart. The black applicants seem to have been more concerned about the impressions which they gave to the audience of white social workers than they were to the audience of their fellow applicants. Several mentioned that they had felt constrained by the presence of the social workers.

Both course leaders were surprised that none of the participants had commented on the fact and that it was an 'all black' group. The participants, however, were not invited to comment, and the presence of the single white applicant, together with the fact the course had not been advertised as an 'all black' course meant that none of those who were interviewed had been aware of the intention to run it as an all black affair. Some were obviously uncomfortable with the idea that, as black applicants, they were being treated differently from white. When it was put to them, they vehemently denied the possibility that the course was being run specifically for black applicants and pointed to presence of the single white applicant as proof.

The presence of the white applicant was initially entirely fortuitous. As one of the social workers explained,

> She was a friend of one of the black applicants so she just came along. She'd heard about the group although she hadn't been invited... But she'd been married to an African and actually had been quite used to the mixed–race children and she seemed so comfortable in the group. She didn't really stand out. She seemed to sort of chat away with them. We felt it would be wrong to just say, 'Sorry, you can't come because you are white'.

Implied in her words was the idea that it is one thing to only invite black people but another to actually exclude people because of their skin colour. In addition, asking the white person to leave would have made it obvious that the group was being run specifically for black applicants which might have excited hostility from participants and antagonised white applicants who felt excluded. By allowing the white person to stay potential confrontation was avoided[6]. The presence of the white applicant was, therefore, in part, engineered by the

---

[6] The decision to allow the white applicant to stay was taken against the advice of the black foster parents.

social workers and was indicative of the weakness of their commitment to separate groups from the start[7].

A third reason for playing down the group's particularity and for emphasising the common elements which united it with other non–segregated groups was the leaders' own sense of the inauthenticity of their position as white workers running an all black group. Ironically, it was the white workers running the group who seem to have felt most exposed and 'on show'. As one explained,

> It felt odd to begin with. I felt very nervous, being the only two white people and wondering if they were going to accept us.

Both thought that they had been accepted by the group and one commented that her initial sense of strangeness probably arose from her own insecurity rather than from any uneasiness or hostility from the rest of the group. That the social workers were so easily accepted may have stemmed, in part, from the fact that the group was not perceived by participants to be an ethnically exclusive affair and cultural and 'racial' issues did not have a high prominence.

The role of the black foster parents

The presence of the black foster parents was undoubtedly an influential mediating factor and their presence was conceived by the course leaders as a bridge which could span the social and cultural distance between themselves and applicants.

> They were a great help and made it much easier and more relaxed.

> I think, perhaps, the group members were reassured by there being black foster parents there.

No–one mentioned the fact that the group reflected, in microcosm, the social relations existing between white people and black people in the wider society. The fact that the course leaders were white and the rest of the group black mirrored a more general power and status differential and underlined the unequal relationship between a predominantly white social services department and its black clientele. The presence of the black foster parents, although it may have softened it, could hardly disguise the sharpness of the division.

---

[7] Unfortunately, it was not possible to interview the single white applicant to discover her own views about her position in the group because she was admitted to hospital and had to withdraw her application.

Before the course was implemented, a group of black foster parents had been invited to a consultation meeting. The decision to run the course had already been taken and discussion seems to have been restricted to technical matters of implementation. Neither of the social workers, however, thought that the meeting had been as productive as it might have been. As one explained,

> We didn't get a lot of feedback from our black foster parents that we need to do things differently, which is surprising. They did tell us about one or two things... but they didn't say much. We kept saying, 'Is the material relevant? Do you think we should alter it?'. But we didn't get a lot of feedback. Whether we would have done if we had had another group (of black foster parents), I don't know... Perhaps they would have been more in touch with the community and more critical.

The implication was that the foster parents were not necessarily representative of community feeling and opinion. The social workers had expected them to be more critical of their approach and more politically aware. On the other hand, the foster parents, themselves, may have lacked the confidence to be openly critical.

The only black foster parent on the mixed course did not seem to make any distinctively ethnic contribution which would have marked her out as different from the other foster parent facilitators. She adopted a low profile both during the course sessions and in the post–session discussions in the pub. One of the white participants commented, 'She didn't say much but you could see she would be a good foster mum'. The foster parents on the 'black' course seem to have been equally reluctant to raise cultural or 'racial' topics and one suggested that discussion of such issues was more appropriate for white applicants. The significance of the black foster parents' presence, thus, seems to have lain less in their potential role as cultural interpreters or challengers to the prevailing ethnocentric approach than in their visibility as foster parent role models. Significantly, although they were engaged on the basis of their presumed cultural knowledge, it was their skills and experience as foster parents which were stressed rather than any specifically ethnic or cultural knowledge or skills. These issues will be discussed in more detail in the following chapter.

Conclusion

The sources of tension between public and private were accentuated in the group training and assessment sessions where applicants' sense of public exposure was intensified by the knowledge that their performances were being continuously assessed. This had consequences for the way in which they presented themselves in a number of ways. For the black applicants on the mixed course, who were in a minority, the distinction between public and private was complicated by the additional dimension of colour and ethnic visibility and their social significance in the wider society. Possible tension within the group was avoided, at least superficially, by the failure to publicly acknowledge colour and ethnicity as sources of differentiation and all parties – social workers, foster parents and applicants, both black and white – colluded in the attempt to render colour and ethnicity invisible. Despite the Fostering Team's professed commitment to providing 'a more ethnically sensitive service', the emphasis on group consensus meant that the courses were not suitable forums for the raising of potentially controversial cultural and 'racial' issues, nor for the achievement of change through negotiation and challenge. Applicants' dependent position in terms of the assessment relationship meant that they were unlikely to risk jeopardising their chances by raising issues which were likely to be contentious.

The radical nature of the course specifically for black applicants was more apparent than real. First, the rationale for a segregated course on the grounds of differential treatment for differential needs was the most weakly argued. Second, the course's ethnic composition was portrayed as an outcome of pragmatic convenience rather than policy design. Despite the appearance of radicalism, the course was not seriously regarded as a prototype for differential service provision except, perhaps, in the early stages by the few more radical members of the Team. Both social workers and foster parents considered it to have been primarily a learning experience with lessons not just for the assessment of black people but more general application. The illusory appearance of radicalism was soon dispelled by the Team decision not to pursue the 'experiment' and to run only mixed groups in the future. The following comment from a course leader reflected the general opinion:

SW3 I think that it is good to have groups that are mixed racially and that it is good to have both black and white... I think that it is a shame that we separate off entirely from each other. I and other people in the group have learnt from being with black foster parents and *vice versa* and that seems very valuable to me. Everyone has learned from each other.

218

The potentially controversial nature of the 'all black' course was played down and potential challenge effectively diffused. In this way, issues which would have emphasised the distinctiveness of the group's ethnic composition were avoided, although an all black group might have seemed the most appropriate forum for them to have been raised.

It could be argued that the courses were not appropriate forums for the discussion of these issues were it not for the fact that they had been set up in the context of the changes in rationale and approach which the 'mixing/matching' debate had set in train. The language in which these developments were discussed was that of 'radical change' and 'new initiatives' to provide 'a more ethnically sensitive service', 'more in line with the needs of black people themselves', and the new language of assessment was constructed around the concept of 'partnership with the applicants' (Extracts from Team Meeting minutes). Opportunities for course participants to discuss their needs and to define them for themselves, however, were severely limited and the potential for change through challenge denied. The approach was defined by the social workers with little or no dialogue with those who were its subjects and little room for negotiation or compromise. Although the way in which the courses were conceived and constructed limited the potential for challenge and therefore for change, both participants and foster parent facilitators acquiesced with the social workers' approach.

The social construction of ethnic and 'racial' differentiation was as significant in its absence as in open acknowledgement and the failure to confront it more a reaffirmation of its importance than a negation. The tactics of consensus management and conflict avoidance were in unspoken recognition of the inadequacy of the courses and inability of the leaders to handle issues of such deep-rooted and potent nature. Not only were they handicapped by the social distance between themselves and the applicants in terms of colour and ethnicity but, together with the foster parents and applicants, they brought with them experiences, beliefs and opinions shaped over a life time. The courses could not provide the safe environment cocooned from the outside world where discussion of such potentially explosive issues could take place without cost to both sides.

12 An ambivalent station: The contradictory position of the black co-worker

One of the most innovative changes introduced during the course of the study was the engagement of experienced black foster parents to work with social workers in the assessments of black applicants. The suggestion, first mooted in March 1984, was put to the Team for discussion in July when it was agreed to run the experiment for a trial period of six months. Although their inclusion in joint visits was held to be 'a very important and necessary development' (Team Meeting minutes, January 1985), it was regarded as a second best option in lieu of qualified black social workers[1]. The initiative was heralded as 'a radical new departure' and achieved a degree of black representation and visibility but without significantly disturbing the existing power structure or assessment rationale. In other words, the engagement of the foster parents was less of a departure than a legitimation of existing processes by providing a limited degree of participation. First, the foster parents' position as co-workers was achieved within a framework of consensus-management which effectively prevented the adoption of a challenging role; second, the lack of a clearly defined role weakened the policy base on which it was grounded; third, although engaged on the basis of their ethnicity, it was the co-workers' skills

---

[1] 'As there seems to be very few black social workers who can be involved, the involvement will have to be primarily with foster parents' (Team Meeting, July 1985). It was assumed that their role would become obsolete as more black social workers became employed and/or white workers learned the necessary cross-cultural skills.

and experience as parents and foster parents which assumed greater relevance during assessments and which enabled them to consolidate their positions and to challenge the conception of their role as a temporary expedient[2].

A challenging role?

The potential for a challenging role was not considered. The foster parents were engaged, first, to compensate for white workers' lack of understanding of black culture and to teach them intercultural skills. It was 'accepted that some joint sessions when interviewing black families would be invaluable in helping social workers understand the cultural aspects of their family life.' Second, it was thought that 'black applicants would feel more comfortable with another black person present' (Team Meeting minutes, July 1984). These were pragmatic considerations aimed at increasing black foster parent recruitment as opposed to ideological or political considerations. There was little or no discussion of the ways in which racism or socio-economic disadvantage might structure black applicants' chances of approval, nor of questions of black representation[3] and power-sharing, for example, participation in decision-making and policy formulation.

The co-workers were recruited from the small pool of black foster parents whom the social workers knew personally and whom they considered 'suitable' to undertake the work. The importance of 'being able to work with the department' meant that those thought likely to challenge social workers' and/or departmental policy and approach on any other than minor cultural grounds

---

[2] As a consequence of their marginal status, it might have been expected that the foster parents would have been less influenced by a need for acceptance by social worker colleagues and loyalty to the Team and, therefore, less afraid of adopting a challenging stance than black social workers who, through their training, had been socialised and conditioned to conventional rationale and practice. The foster parents' lack of formal training and non-professional status allied them more closely with the working class black community from which most of the applicants were drawn and they might, therefore, have been expected to have been more likely to share the concerns of 'ordinary' black people and less likely to have been motivated by 'professional' concerns. The conditions of the foster parents' engagement, however, were not generally conducive to the adoption of a challenging stance.

[3]The employment of black workers to reflect the racial mix in the community was mentioned only in passing in the paper presented to the Black Home Finding Unit Working Party ('The Needs of Black Children') but the concern was with black visibility rather than the political issue of access to the power structure. Again, the main consideration was pragmatic and involved the desire to change the image of the service as a predominantly white organisation in order to gain the trust and confidence of the black community.

would be unlikely to be considered[4]. The main reason why the black co-workers were welcomed by social workers was to reduce their feelings of insecurity in cross-cultural work and not as people who would challenge them or act as trouble-shooters to initiate change.

Not only was the potential for a challenging role not envisaged in the initial codification of their role but the necessary institutional support was lacking. As foster parents, the co-workers lacked the status and security of salaried employees and their lack of formal training was set against the professional qualifications of the social workers. They were not members of professional bodies or unions and there were no support groups of black foster parents in a similar position either within the borough or without. Their structurally weak position in the organisational hierarchy was further weakened by the social distance of colour and class between them and the social workers with whom they worked. There were no colleagues in comparable positions in other boroughs whom they could consult and draw on for mutual support, no role models to follow nor pre-defined framework within which to operate and the foster parents found themselves having to break new ground and to forge their role for themselves.

If more black foster parents are recruited as co-workers and the experiment is repeated in other boroughs, the potential for forming a mutual support group and potential power base will increase, giving them greater confidence to adopt a challenging role. On the other hand, as more black foster parents are recruited and the pool of potential co-workers becomes larger, the opportunities for social workers to select conformist candidates will be correspondingly greater.

The foster parents' failure to adopt a more challenging role was partly attributable to their lack of a group identity. They had been recruited on an individual basis and did not meet together as a group independently of the social workers. Most of their work as co-workers was carried out and discussed with the social workers whom they partnered and opportunities for discussions between themselves were limited. This meant that they were more likely to ally themselves and to identify with their social worker partners than with each other.

They failed to present a coherent and united stance as to the relevance of their own ethnicity which had been largely predefined by the social workers who had recruited them. When later, both white and black foster parents were engaged as facilitators on the training and assessment course, the foster parents formed a 'natural' group *vis à vis* the social workers and applicants. The strength of common experience as foster parents to unite proved to be greater

---

[4] Rooney (1982) and Stubbs (1985) make similar points in reference to the recruitment of black social workers.

than the strength of skin colour and culture to divide. The tendency was to play down the latter in favour of the former in order not to antagonise their white colleagues who had fostered black children in the past and were resistant to the new policy of 'racial matching'.

On the whole, the black foster parents did not share a common ideological or political stance except for the common desire to maintain a low profile in terms of 'racial' and cultural difference. The potential for a group identity and affinity with black applicants based on shared opposition to the cultural hegemony of 'white' society and to the authority of its institutions and a common belief in the importance of taking an active challenging role was not acknowledged. The foster parents differed in their views about 'racial matching' and in their conception of their own role as black co-workers, and the interviews revealed considerable personal confusion about the issues. As a group, the co-workers lacked a sense of political purpose. All were keen to stress that they were 'not really very interested in politics' and none could be described as particularly 'conscious' or politically 'aware'[5].

Ambiguous role definition

Failure to clarify the co-workers' status and role contributed to the insecurity of their position and deprived them of the confidence necessary for effective challenge. Although satisfactory working relationships seemed to have been worked out within each pair of social worker and foster parent, this was with little recourse to guidelines from the Team. This opened the way for discrepancies in practice and inequalities both within and between pairs. In addition, the Team's consensual approach and fear of conflict masked a number of potential sources of discord.

Remuneration

The foster parents' confused status was highlighted by the issue of remuneration. How much should an unqualified foster parent receive compared with a qualified and experienced social worker? To what extent can experience as a foster parent count as the equivalent of social work training? To what extent can 'knowledge of black culture and lifestyles' be

---

[5] The foster parents may, perhaps, have denied an interest in politics in order to prevent discussion of political topics during the interview and to avoid confrontation. In other words, they may have tried to avoid potentially controversial subjects for the same reasons that they tried to avoid them avoid them in assessment interviews with applicants. The fact that political issues were brought up spontaneously in relation to other issues, however, suggests that this was not the case.

considered specialist knowledge? And how should life experience be rewarded? The issue of payments was complicated by the fact that the foster parents had no formal training. White foster parents who had been trained to work on the National Foster Care Association's 'Parenting Plus' and 'Added to Adolescence' courses were paid per session but it was thought that the black foster parents, who were untrained, could not be paid at the same rate. Later, it was agreed that an hourly rate, based on the unqualified social worker scale, should be worked out which would apply to 'foster parents helping out at initial meetings, black foster parents involved in assessments etc.' (Team Meeting minutes, August 1984).

Differences of opinion

Another issue of potential conflict was the resolution of differences of opinion between social worker and foster parent. Those differences which had arisen had so far been satisfactorily resolved within pairs but the potential for discord remained. It was decided that 'the view of the social worker would not automatically be accepted' (Team Meeting minutes, November 1984) and that the Team Leader would take advice from the only black social worker in the Team or from the Ethnic Relations Adviser. Recourse to a third party, however, was considered to be an option of last resort and the strong ethos of conflict avoidance together with the foster parents' accommodating stance meant that the situation had thus far been avoided.

Confidentiality and access to social work files

The issue of confidentiality was, perhaps, the most thorny since it highlighted more than anything else the limits of the foster parents' role. The first problem was 'where applicants find they have a mutual friend of the visiting foster parent' but, more important, was the 'issue of sharing the content of District Office files' on applicants who were past or current clients of the Social Services. The Team had to try to reconcile a number of conflicting positions:

a. The foster parent could not be responsible for a decision if she was not fully informed;
b. The foster parents are paid and should be fully part of the process;
c. Sharing District files (with foster parents) is a breach of clients' confidence' (Team Meeting minutes, November 1984).

The issue of confidentiality split the Team and, although the question of the foster parents' access to District files was finally removed from the Team agenda when workers in the District Offices refused to give their permission, the issue of confidentiality and clear definition of the social workers' and foster parents' respective roles remained unresolved. Confrontation and conflict rarely erupted between individuals but the placid surface masked a smouldering discontent.

The issue of the files undermined the foster parents' image of themselves as 'professionals' engaged to perform a skilled and responsible task. There was a certain ambiguity in their position: if they were considered responsible enough to be trusted with the highly personal information given in the individual interviews, why not also the information contained in the files? The ambiguity of their position and hollowness of their status as equals in a partnership was underlined. It was social workers who had control over the flow of information and who decided what was and what was not relevant to the assessment task. Despite social workers' attempts to circumvent the problem by relaying any relevant information,

> I always try to tell the foster parent anything that I think she ought to know so we get round it that way and, so far, there haven't been any problems. (Social Worker)

> I work it out with my social worker what I should know and we never disagree up to now. The social worker that I work with, she always tell me, 'What do you think?' and 'This is so and that is so' and so on. And we get on alright. (Co-worker)

the foster parents' exclusion caused anger and frustration. 'How can you possibly carry out an assessment,' one declared,

> if you do not know half the relevant information? It's ridiculous! Because, even though they have white social workers and black foster parents, they still haven't got that far (in terms of equality) because there is this thing that the black foster parents should not see the files.

Not all the foster parents, however, thought that they should have access to the files, as the following exchange between a foster parent and her husband makes clear:

Wife Well, it would be O.K. if you have got nothing to hide. But I wouldn't like everyone to read it. I don't think it is fair. Because it is a personal thing and, even if you have got nothing much to hide, you don't want other people to see it. I don't think it would be right.

Husb There is foster parents whose mouth is as wide as the door that would go blabbing it around to all the world. You have got to protect people's privacy. There could be nothing bad in it (the file) but you must have some privacy. I think they (the social workers) should tell the foster parent a little bit but not the basic, not everything.

Wife No, it's better that the foster parent don't see them because you have to respect people's privacy and a lot of it, probably, wouldn't be relevant anyway. And the social worker can tell you what you need to know. She tell me what I ought to know.

Husb Because if people get to find out, it would wreck the whole system because people don't want the world to know their business. You couldn't have it.

As would be expected, a lot seemed to depend on how well individual social workers and foster parents worked out their relationship and method of working between them, and this seemed to vary between pairs. Most seem to have reached an amicable agreement. The husband's point – that the applicants would be less likely to co-operate if they knew the foster parent had access to their files – is, perhaps, the most pertinent to this debate. As the foster parents were drawn from the local community, it is likely that, even if they did not know the applicants personally, they would be tied in to overlapping social networks. The risk of public disclosure was, therfore, much greater than with the soical workers who either did not live in the local area or whose social networks did not coincide with those of the black community.

Report writing

Similar confusion about respective roles surfaced in discussions with social workers about report writing. Most said that the main reason why they took it upon themselves to write the reports was that the foster parents did not have the time. One mentioned that her co-worker had seemed reluctant to contribute, and that she, herself, had much greater experience of report writing. Two referred to report–writing in delineation of their own professional territory as distinct from the foster parents' role. As one of them explained, 'We have to draft the report as part of our responsibility as employees and agents of the Local Authority'.

'Partnership' and 'working together'

Underlying these issues was the fundamental question of the sharing of power. A division of opinion existed within the Team between those members who wanted to regard the foster parents simply as 'helpers' and to restrict their role to a purely advisory and mediatory capacity and those who wanted to consider them as equals in a working partnership. 'She is a co-worker as far as I am

226

concerned, there is no question', one declared. What was meant by 'equal', however, was not always clear – 'equal' as a person, perhaps, but not necessarily 'equal' in a professional sense.

When workers were asked how they tried to accommodate the different roles of social worker and foster parent on a joint home visit, all agreed that 'it is important to be able to get on and work together'. The emphasis was on consensus as opposed to challenge which, by implication, was considered detrimental to a 'good working relationship'. A foster parent who initiated confrontation risked being labelled as a 'bad' co-worker, someone with whom it would be 'difficult to work'[6]. As Becker (1963) has pointed out, the initiation of confrontation was likely to be regarded as evidence of personal inadequacy and something to be avoided and condemned rather than encouraged as a positive strategy for change. 'Working together' seemed to mean avoiding conflict. 'It would be no good if you couldn't get on together, for example, if there was a personality clash or if you were always disagreeing about things,' one social worker explained. 'You need to be able to work together... It has to be someone you can work with'. The foster parents were equally keen to stress the partnership qualities of their relationship and seemed to lack the confidence to be critical, fearing that criticism would reflect on their own abilities rather than those of the social workers. In other words, their compliance can be interpreted as a strategy for avoiding, to use Knights and Wilmot's phrase, 'identity–damaging disciplinary controls' (Knights and Wilmot, 1985:25).

The relationship between social worker and foster parent, however, was not simply an exploitative relationship between the powerful and her subordinate determined by strategies of control and resistance (cf. Lukes, 1974) but a relationship of interdependence (Knights and Wilmot, 1985). For both, their immediate existential concerns were 'to create and sustain a sense of order in which 'identity' is secure' (*op cit.*:33). Mutual support was important to both social workers and foster parents as neither felt entirely secure in their new roles[7]. In addition, for the social workers, responsibility for the difficult decision of whether to recommend acceptance or rejection was now shared. Most important, the decision to reject was shared and, thus, the applicant's potential anger, resentment and disappointment. Joint decision–making

---

[6] Cf. Liverpool, who notes that 'the good black social worker' is 'expected not to be assertive or self–conscious' and that assertiveness is punished by negative labelling 'as pushy, aggressive and over–sensitive ... anti–social, unfriendly and even anti–white' (1982: 225; cf Thomas, 1984).

[7] One social worker, for example, described how much easier she had felt being able to share her disquiet about a particular applicant with her black co–worker and the reassurance she had felt when the co–worker expressed similar reservations to her own.

reduced social workers' sense of individual isolation and added a dimension of potential power to the foster parents' role. The mutual support which they gave to each other engendered a feeling of partnership. This sense of having been accepted was especially important to the foster parents in view of the insecurity and ambiguity of the co-worker role. The social workers clearly regarded the foster parents as potential allies and the pre-visit meeting with the foster parent was as much about the presentation of a united front as it was about the adoption of an appropriate strategy. As one of the social workers explained, the purpose of the meeting was 'to anticipate possible problem areas and how we will approach them. We talk about (the applicants) beforehand and about *the need to back each other up*'. In Knights and Wilmot's terms, what, their relationship was maintained by 'a set of self-interested reciprocal exchanges' (1985:25).

Both parties were motivated to believe in the 'equality' of their relationship and there was a tendency to ignore and repress, by tacit agreement, sources of inequality and potential discord. Social workers interspersed their talk with words like 'equal', 'agreement', 'consultation', 'partnership' and 'sharing' and the same language had been picked up by the foster parents. But the language of equality, viewed from the perspective of the structural imbalances in power in the relationship, masked sources of tension and potential discord. Even where workers were willing to grant equal respect for the skills and experience of the foster parents compared with their own, the professional/ non-professional distinction remained and was reinforced by their relative positions in the organisational hierarchy. Using the language of 'partnership', social workers were able to transmit the illusion of an equal working relationship and to disguise the fact that the balance of control was strongly tipped in their favour. Social workers' language of 'equality' revealed a subtle paradox in view of the hierarchical organisation of staff and management which was in marked contrast to the egalitarian model projected.

In attempting to create and protect a sense of 'professional' identity by maintaining a compliant stance towards the social workers on whom that identity was perceived to depend, the foster parents were unwittingly contributing to the conditions of their subordination. Their collusion in perpetuating the myth of equality in their relationship meant that the inequalities in their relative structural positions and in the inter-personal dynamics of the assessment encounter remained unchallenged. By accepting or complying with the social workers' definition of professionalism, the foster parents were implicitly accepting their inferior status.

Although individual workers tried to implement a degree of equality in their working relationships with their black co-workers, their organisationally distinctive roles meant inevitable inequality. These different roles weremost clearly marked in the domain of management and administration. It was the social worker who made arrangements for the home visits, gave the initial information about fostering to the applicants and explained about the assessment procedure and purpose of the visit. It was the social worker who introduced the foster parent and 'explained' her role and who, thus, set the scene for the visit and controlled the terms of the interaction. The clearest demarcation of roles was, thus, not in the practice domain of skills, aptitudes and qualities relevant to the task of assessment but in the administrative domain. It was here that the official/non-official distinction was underlined. Inevitably, applicants regarded the social worker as the senior in the partnership, the person with authority by virtue of official status.

An additional factor was time. All were active foster parents as well as co-workers and had neither the time to accompany social workers on every home visit nor to attend meetings and discussions. The bulk of the assessment was, therefore, managed and carried out by the social worker. Some would have liked to have involved the foster parents in more of the process but were reluctant to ask them to give up more of their time. As one explained,

> It's not that we don't want to ask them to come to everything. We do ask if they want to come. But, sometimes they've given so much of their time to the critical bit of the work, that we can't really ask them to do more.

At the Team level, the commitment to 'partnership' and 'equality' extended little beyond simple rhetoric. The foster parents were not considered part of the Team or invited to Team Meetings and were, thus, denied access to the main forum of discussion and policy formulation.

Joint decision-making and the assessment role

Despite the co-workers' active participation in the decision-making process, their role as joint assessors was played down on both home visits and training and assessment courses. Social workers reported that applicants saw them as having different roles.

> They see the foster parent as a helpful 'expert' while the social worker is there to 'judge' them .

> They relax more with foster parents as they can identify with them more easily. Social workers, with the best intention, are seen as judgemental.

In other words, social workers were aware of applicants' misperceptions and, by their silence, colluded to maintain an illusion which was reinforced by the expected power differential between black people and white people generally (cf. Liverpool, 1982). When asked about the benefits of joint visits, workers said that the interviews were more relaxed and that, because applicants could identify more easily with the foster parents, they felt more comfortable with the social workers. The foster parents' 'less professional approach' was thought to make it easier for the applicants to relate to them[8]. As one worker explained, 'I see the foster parent as someone who is able to act as a bridge between the applicant and the social worker'.

The problem lay in the contradiction between the different expectations of the foster parents' role as joint assessors and as mediators. The foster parents' assessment capacity simultaneously aligned them with the social workers and distanced them from the applicants. It was easier, however, to manage the face-to-face interaction with the applicant by playing down aspects of their role which were likely to increase the social distance between them and, therefore, to suppress their role as joint assessors. Applicants seemed to want to relate to them differently from the social workers and to regard them as having a different and, more importantly, non-judgemental and, therefore, non-threatening role. They related to them as people who were 'more on our level', who possessed a practical experience and commonsense knowledge which distinguished them from the professionally trained social workers, thus preserving the non-official/ official, non-professional/ professional, black/ white distinction which united them in an alliance of the non-powerful versus the powerful. Applicants' different perceptions of the foster parent as adviser and social worker as judge seemed to be a necessary counter-balance[9]. Although the degree of conscious action differed, all three parties colluded in playing down the foster parent's assessment role. Although they were party to the decision-making process, the foster parents' presence was without the understanding of power on the part of the applicants, thus, reinforcing rather than challenging the power differential existing between black people and white people generally. This will be discussed more fully in the next chapter.

---

[8] By 'less professional' they seemed to mean less formal and to equate the black/West Indian approach and manner with a non-professional approach and manner. Implied is the equation of professionalism with 'the way white social workers do things'.

[9] Some applicants even maintained that foster parents were better equipped to conduct assessments than social workers. It is likely, however, that were they to take over the entire role of assessment, they would lose, in the applicants' eyes, the very attributes of homely friendliness and sense that they are 'one of us' which applicants seemed to prize so highly. By refusing to acknowledge the possibility that the foster parents had an assessment function, applicants were able to reduce the threat of the assessment encounter but, in the absence of an accompanying social worker, the foster parent assessor would probably assume or be attributed with many of the qualities currently associated with social workers.

The relevance of ethnicity

Social workers identified the co-workers' most important attributes as their mediatory skills as cultural interpreters and their ability to empathise with black applicants. Their skills and experience as foster parents, which later came to overshadow their ethnically-grounded skills, were initially considered to be of only secondary or incidental importance. Skin colour was considered to be an essential, if not sufficient, qualification for the co-worker role. It was, for the social workers, the banner which signalled the rest. 'Colour', as one pointed out, 'is something you can't do anything about. You can't go and have training can you?' By contrast, none of the applicants thought that skin colour alone was a sufficient qualification for the co-worker role and many rejected it as irrelevant.

The inclusion of the black foster parents in joint assessments made social workers feel more secure in an area where they had come to doubt their own competence[10] and there may have been a tendency to rely too heavily on their advice and opinion in 'racial' or cultural matters. This had several possible consequences. For the social workers, it meant avoiding having to confront the issues themselves and shifting the responsibility for decisions made on the basis of applicants' ethnicity on to the shoulders of the foster parents. The danger for the foster parents was that of assuming an expertise which they did not possess[11], a problem mentioned in passing by only one social worker and one foster parent. By contrast, applicants were sensitive to the prejudices which shape other black people's attitudes and feared that social workers would place too great a reliance on the opinions of the foster parents merely because they were black[12].

---

[10] New developments in the domain of work with black and minority ethnic group clients had shaken many white social workers' confidence in their professional abilities. First, new ideas had led many social workers to recognise deficiencies in their past practice in relation to the assessment of black applicants and second, the drive to recruit more black foster parents meant that they found themselves confronted with an area of work of which they had little previous experience. Their professional self-confidence was further undermined by the threat of public censure (cf Parker, 1988; Roys, 1988; Blythe and Milner, 1987; Ely and Denney, 1987).

[11] Similar dangers in relation to black social workers have been noted elsewhere (eg Rooney, 1982; Ely and Denney, 1987: 114; *Community Care* 13 July 1989; Owusu-Bempah, 1989).

[12] In their study of 'the out-group homogeneity principle', Park and Rothbart (1982) found that members of the in-group tended to see their own fellow members as dissimilar to one another more than did out-group judges, while out-group members tended to see these people in more homogeneous, stereotypical terms.

231

Among the social workers, there was a split between those who regarded the foster parents primarily as advisers who could teach them the necessary cross-cultural skills and the 'hardliners' (the social workers' own term) who thought that white social workers could never become fully competent in the assessment of black families. Workers' perceptions of the foster parents' relevant skills depended, first, on their view of their own 'professionalism': their confidence in generic, trans-cultural skills and whether or not they perceived the foster parents as a threat to their own professional competence and, second, on their ideological outlook and 'race relations' goal (cf. Denney, 1983): their commitment to the ideology of the 'melting pot' or to cultural pluralism and the maintenance of distinctive 'racial' and cultural identities. There was resistance to a policy of treating black applicants differently from white and some workers were reluctant to acknowledge the role of cultural factors and racism in shaping black peoples' lives or that their own training and experience might not be adequate for work with black people (cf. Stubbs, 1985). The Team Meeting at which the engagement of the foster parents was first discussed was recalled as a scene of heated debate. Any potential challenge to social workers' claims to professionalism, however, was effectively neutralised by defining the foster parents' skills and experience as complementary rather than competing. Both sides were motivated to stress complementarity by the desire to avoid confrontation but, although this promoted more harmonious working relationships, it had the effect of both devaluing and restricting the foster parents' role.

The way in which social workers' presented the co-worker role was influenced not only by their attitudes and beliefs but by the context and the likely reactions of their audience. In the management of face-to-face interactions they may have been tempted to put pragmatic above other considerations in the hope of avoiding confrontation. The following is an example of how one worker introduced her partner and her hesitance is indicative of the difficulty of the task.

> I always say, 'I'm taking along a black foster parent.' I've always... I've never had any fears about phoning up and saying, you know, 'I'm white but, to make it easier, I'm going to bring along a black foster parent,' because, well, I feel... OK it seems to me as straight as possible. They usually say they don't mind, anyway.

Others were more circumspect and simply introduced their co-worker as 'an experienced foster parent'. Both social workers and foster parents were careful to avoid alienating applicants which meant that they were more likely to play up foster parenting skills and experience than the role of cultural interpreter which might have raised the potentially contentious issue of discriminatory

232

treatment and have undermined confidence in the social workers' own skills. Applicants were motivated to collude with this designation of the foster parents' role for fear of jeopardising their chances of approval by raising potentially contentious issues and it was easier to handle the face-to-face interaction by preserving an atmosphere of consensus, albeit an illusionary one.

Some of the confusion and ambivalence regarding the black foster parents' relevant qualities and skills is evident in the following extract from a conversation with a social worker who thought of herself as more aware of the difficulties of cross-cultural work than many of her colleagues, though she added, 'I wouldn't say I'd got it all right.'

SW4   Personally, I feel that the foster parents probably know far more about fostering than I do. They know about it from the foster parent's point of view which is half of what it's about and, therefore, I feel that they can give as much as I can, probably... I mean, I wouldn't feel that I had particular skill. I mean, I have some skills that, perhaps, the man in the street won't have, obviously – perhaps, the skills in being non-judgemental as much as anything, and taking people as they are and not putting one's own opinion and not putting oneself in to the situation, not putting oneself across and one's own feelings. These are all the bits that, perhaps, as a social worker, one can do. But on the other hand, I suppose the foster mother can still judge the person as a foster parent, if you like, and the way their life has affected them, particularly for the black applicants, if you like, and the relevance of all that and whether it's normal or not, you know, whether one might expect this or that or whether one should be concerned about it.

It is significant that she thought that much of her own 'professionalism' as a social worker lay in her ability to be 'non-judgemental' and to avoid putting herself into the situation, although it was to counteract this very danger of white social workers imposing their own ethnocentric judgements that the black foster parents were initially engaged. It was the foster parent's knowledge and experience of foster parenting which was stressed while her ethnically-based skills as a black person were mentioned almost as an afterthought in a rather vague and ill-defined manner. No specific mention was made of racism or discrimination as being part of 'the way their life has affected them' nor of possible cultural factors. If the black foster parent is better equipped to assess black applicants, both as black people, on the basis of cultural and ethnic affinity, and as potential foster parents, on the basis of experience of fostering, the social worker is forced to retreat into the myth of professional objectivity and neutrality in order to retain a separate area of competence which leaves her identity as a 'professional' intact. Ironically, it was the exposure of this myth which led to the need to introduce a 'black perspective'[13].

The views of the co-workers

The black co-workers saw themselves in an essentially advisory capacity *vis à vis* the social workers and believed that they possessed special culturally-derived knowledge and skills and empathy with black applicants which white workers did not share.

> A white person doesn't really know how a black person is thinking. A white person wouldn't know a black person's ways or understand a black family properly because you have been brought up differently.

> I don't think a white person can assess a black person because – how should I say? – because you don't really know black people.

They saw themselves in the role of 'watchdog', guarding against misperceptions and misunderstandings, picking up things which a white person would probably miss, asking the more penetrating questions and generally making it more difficult for the applicant to dissemble[14].

> With the white social worker and black foster parent, that is very good. I don't think white people do understand black people. You get straight forward black foster parents to go round with the social worker and they'll pick up what the social worker might miss. They'll be prepared to ask more searching questions and not let the black person get away with not saying some things, just putting on a show. They'll notice when things are not quite right in a family which a white person wouldn't.

---

[13] It is, perhaps, worthy of note that, despite the new thinking underpinning the language of 'partnership' and 'sharing' which supposedly informs the new approach to assessment, she slips unwittingly but tellingly back into the old language of 'vetting' when applicants were still 'judged' by the social workers.

[14] Such arguments are based on the belief that whites and blacks inhabit essentially different social worlds and that cultural misunderstanding is uni-directional. In other words, it is whites who misunderstand blacks, not the other way round. The implication is of cultural disadvantage of black people. Where membership of both cultures enables black people to move with relative ease between both, white people's experience is only of the dominant culture. They are therefore liable to misinterpret the behaviour of members of the subordinate culture which puts the latter at a disadvantage.

234

Because, just the same as you think the white will take the bribe, doing it for money, the black will do it as well.

In common with the social workers, the foster parents rested their case on technical arguments, on white social workers' misunderstanding of black culture, in other words, on errors made rather than on arguments about social identity. Common culture was regarded as a basis for correct decision–making as opposed to concern with wider issues of black representation, power–sharing and the construction of esteem within the black community. None mentioned a potential trouble–shooting role or saw themselves as representatives of a beleaguered community struggling to assert its distinctive cultural and political identity and right to social and political equality by challenging the structures of power of the dominant culture. Like the social workers, the foster parents stressed that they were 'not really interested in politics'. They talked in terms of possible cultural misunderstandings rather than racism and prejudice and saw themselves primarily as assisting and supporting the social workers in their assessment role rather than the applicants. They were aware of social workers' worries about introducing lower standards and approving applicants merely because they were black and their concern was, therefore, with assessment rigour as an indication of profesionalism.

Besides cultural affinity, however, the foster parents believed that they could relate to the applicants on a number of other levels – common social class, as a woman, wife and mother and as a non–professional and non–official. They viewed their role in an essentially mediatory capacity *vis a vis* applicants, as the following conversation between a black foster parent and her husband illustrates:

Wife It gives the person that is being assessed that moral support. They relate better to the social worker with the foster parent being there. Because some of them, they only have to hear the word, 'social worker', and they clam up and feel very rigid about it. Some of them would just clam up without that the foster parent was there.
Husb At least, then, you have someone who is at your own level.
Wife Yes, someone who is at your level who you can relate to. It helps them to relate better to the social worker. It gives them more confidence because some of them think a social worker is like high up, an official to them, so they just clam up. I could see with taking foster parents for black people it would help them to open up, one of *them*, so to speak.

There was no consensus, however, as to which of the possible dimensions of affinity was most important and the foster parents were no less likely than either the social workers or applicants to have resolved the debate about the relative importance of skin colour, culture or class in determining a person's structural position and lot in British society.

As with the social workers, the way in which they perceived their role depended partly on their philosophical and political outlook. Most were integrationist in their aspirations, although pleased that their cultural heritage was no longer to be regarded a source of weakness. Although they were aware of structural inequalities (at a local level, the conspicuous absence of black faces in the upper echelons of the council services was mentioned), because of the way in which their role had been conceived by the Team, as co-workers, they seemed to be more concerned with cultural matters. Similarly, racism was down-graded as a force which shaped black people's lives and, although the theme emerged in their accounts of personal experiences, in their public accounts, social class and culture were the dominant themes. Their reluctance to raise the issue in the context of their role as co-workers may have been partly explained by a desire to avoid antagonising or upsetting their white colleagues. As one explained,

I don't think that it would really be appropriate to bring up all that sort of thing. I think it would put people off.

The conditions under which power can be achieved will inevitably shape people's self-identifications and, thus, the extent to which ethnicity becomes important in any encounter. As Sandra Wallman (1979) has pointed out, mere differences between groups, objective to the extent that they are discernible to an outsider, are merely 'potential identity markers' until they are incorporated into the subjective consciousness of members and endowed with meaning. The process is neither static nor immutable but dynamic and reactive and 'the potential is taken up and mobilised only where it suits the purposes of a particular encounter' (*op cit.*6). 'Ethnicity', she explains, 'is the recognition of significant difference between "them" and "us". Neither the difference nor its significance is set' (*op cit.*3). 'Depending on the perceptions of the actors, and the constraints and opportunities of the context in which they act, ethnicity may be an essential resource, an utter irrelevance or a crippling liability' (*op cit.*4–5).

A self-identification as the possessors of non-transmissible cultural knowledge and skills gave the black foster parents a niche within the decision-making structure but other pressures meant that a self-identification as the possessors of generic fostering skills was often more appropriate. The assertion of a 'special' cultural expertise runs counter to the universalist philosophy underpinning the conventional definition of 'professionalism' as the ability to work with any client regardless of colour, culture, creed or class (cf.

236

Stubbs, 1985). It compromised the foster parents' wish to be accepted as 'professionals' with the ability to consolidate their position by expanding their area of competence to assessments of white applicants as well as black and meant the risk of marginalisation from mainstream fostering. By playing down the specificity of their cultural skills, they colluded with the social workers in managing the face-to-face encounter with the applicant and were able to reduce the threat to social workers' conception of their own professionalism.

The lack of a clearly defined status and role not only engendered feelings of insecurity among the co-workers but weakened the policy base in which their role was initially grounded. As the demands of the context changed and the relevance of their generic fostering skills was accentuated at the expense of their specific cultural skills, so too did the foster parents' self-identifications. The conditions of their engagement encouraged the foster parents, when talking about their role, to emphasise affinities of colour and culture at the expense of other possible common ground, whereas the actual conditions of the assessment visits resulted in other aspects being stressed. There was, thus, a clear disjunction between the theory and the practice.

The following exchange between a black co-worker and her husband illustrates many of these contradictions. It reveals the wife's ambivalence. Her belief that, as a black person, she had something special to offer which was unavailable to white social workers conflicted with her desire to be regarded as a professional who could perform equally well in the assessment of a white as a black applicant. There was similar conflict between her knowledge, gained from experience, that some white social workers allow their prejudice to affect their practice and her desire to believe that they are capable of understanding and of moving professionally between both worlds. In loyalty to the rationale to which she owed her recruitment, she felt constrained to defend her cultural affinity with applicants and her cross-cultural skills against her husband's view that social class was the more significant dimension.

PR   What do you make of John Small's comment to a group of white social workers, 'I can assess a black family but you can't'.

Husb It's fifty-fifty. You could say it was the other way round as well, a black social worker can't assess a white family.

PR   I think John Small's argument was that black social workers have to live in both worlds, black and white. They have to mix every day with white people so they know how to assess a white family, whereas white workers might not really mix with black people at all.

Husb That is very true... But I don't think it is just because they are white. It is also their class. You have some very middle class white social workers that come into your home and they are very high in their ideas and they won't come down to your level. You have some very middle class social workers, with the plum in their voice and everything, who wouldn't know anything about how ordinary people live. So, it's not just colour. It's class more than colour.

Wife I don't think a white person going into a black home could straight away know about the culture.

Husb This word 'culture'. I don't understand what is meant by it. What is this 'culture'? I think it is just a lot of talk. Some of the social workers come from middle class backgrounds. They are not interested in knowing anything about anyone else, and not just white social workers but black as well.

Wife I think it is better now. You get quite a few who is not so middle class now, and some middle class ones who learn about how black people live, who are just as good as the others.

Husb Yes, but they are still very middle class. They are so high and mighty, some of them, they don't want to know about the rest of us. You get a middle class social worker like that going into a black person's home, they wouldn't know how to assess that black family.

Wife Well, for me, you see, the question is very difficult to answer. You see, in my job (in a children's home), I work with both black and white, so it is difficult for me to answer. I probably could assess a white person just as easily as a black person. It is how you relate to people, really. If you try to be interested in them, then you will have a better knowledge of them. But these social workers, how could they know if they are not in touch with black people? They wouldn't know at all. You may say you have a black friend but it is probably a black friend who is just as white as you are. Because there are some black people who are just like the white in everything except the colour of their skin. You have to be really in touch with black people, mix with them all the time, really mix to know.

Husb But there is some black people who is not in touch with their own kind. I think that class have a lot to do with it.

Wife Then again, I know a white social worker who could assess a black family just as well as a white family. But it is difficult for me to answer because I remember a white worker where I work who came back one day from going to vet a black family. 'A typical West Indian family' is what she said. But, I think to myself, 'That is not so!' Because all black families are not the same. All are different. I don't know what is 'a typical West Indian family'. And I was really angry.

Husb But there you have it! Most white people see black people as all the same, end of story. I mean, how ridiculous! Of course black people are not all the same, any more than white people. So what do you expect?

Wife   And that was a social worker, a white social worker who said that all
West Indians are the same. I don't know what she meant, 'Typical West
Indian family'. If someone came to you and said 'typical West Indian
family', you wouldn't know what she meant by it because there is no
such thing. They are all different...[15] It is fairer with a black foster
parent as well as a white social worker. I think it's very important to
have the foster parent because we meet on the same level. Although we
may be different education and so on, we are all foster parents so we
can relate better to each other, to them. Years ago the social worker
was the middle class (right hand raised high to indicate high status,
uppity manners and so on). It's still there but it is dying out.

The views of the applicants

Confusion about the foster parent's role was evident in the differing
perceptions of applicants. Among people who had not progressed as far as an
assessment, opinion was divided about the desirability of joint visits. Many
expressed no preference. Some thought that a black foster parent might make
black applicants feel more at ease but the possibility of an interpretive role in
cases of inter-cultural misunderstanding was less frequently raised. Others
were openly hostile and rejected the notion of differential treatment on the
grounds of colour or culture. Some even thought that the foster parent's
presence would be detrimental to the success of their applications. Four, for
example, believed that older foster parents would not be able to understand the
way that younger people organised their lives and would condemn them
unfairly[16]. On the whole, however, respondents referred to the foster parents'

---

[15] The point about treating black people as if they were all the same was made repeatedly.
They following comment, for example, was from a black applicant:

> Some white people judge black families with other black families but it isn't really so.
> Because they don't know about black people. They meet one black family and then they
> think that all black families are like that.

[16] Some of the younger applicants, in particular, held stereotypical views about the rigidity
and old fashioned ways and outlook of older black women. They thought they would not
understand the attitudes and life style of members of the younger generation and that they
would be prejudiced against them in an assessment. When this was put to some of the social
workers, they responded with the reassurance that the black foster parents with whom they
worked were very flexible and open-minded and did not conform with the popular image of
the 'typical older black woman'.

(continued...)

239

fostering skills and experience rather than to their colour or cultural skills. Those who had undergone joint assessment rarely objected to it in practice, although at least two had been annoyed that the social worker had brought along a black foster parent merely because they were black. Some explicitly denied the relevance of a cultural component and most either did not or did not want to associate their own colour or culture with the decision to bring along a black foster parent.

From comments made at other points in the interviews, however, it was apparent that, for many, ethnic identity was not as unimportant as had at first seemed. There seemed to be a conflict between their feelings at the experiential level and their beliefs at the ideological level. They seemed to feel more comfortable in the company of other black people but were reluctant to admit this for fear of endorsing a political standpoint which advocated 'racial' and cultural separatism. Many were afraid that differential treatment would mean inferior treatment and that it would undermine their capacity to compete on equal terms with white people. Among those who had not received a joint visit, many more were suspicious of the social worker's motives for including a black foster parent and hostile to the implication that black people were being treated differently from white. This suggests that, although many were opposed to the inclusion of black foster parents in the assessment process on an ideological–political level, at the level of experience, they reacted differently and the conflict was neutralised by denying the relevance of ethnicity.

Wallman (1979) has pointed out that the relevance of ethnicity may not be the same for all parties to an interaction. The problem for the foster parents was that the relevance of their ethnicity to the assessment process had been asserted by the social workers and not by the two parties for whom it was assumed to be relevant. In any encounter where ethnicity is deemed to be relevant, it is both the difference and the sense of difference that count or, alternatively, the similarity and the sense of similarity. It was the sense of difference between themselves and the visiting social worker and similarity

---

[16](...continued)
SW5 Probably, if we do take along older ones, they are not representative of the, er, stereotype that the ones people are talking about have, a black mama, a big black mama sort of vision, yes. But I think they (the foster parents) are much more aware than that. Otherwise, I don't think they would be able to foster the difficult teenagers that they do. And I'm not saying, 'them all', because I do think that one or two of them do have the black mama image, the typical, you know, strict and very religious.

No–one chose to deny or to reject the popular stereotype. Clearly, it was a stereotype or ideal type which social workers still had available to them in their repertoires of knowledge for categorising and, thus, 'understanding' black people.

between themselves and the foster parent co–worker which social workers assumed on the part of applicants. The dimensions of affinity, however, were often misconceived. For many applicants, who were hostile to differential treatment on the grounds of colour, it was easier to interact with the foster parent as a mother and foster mother and to ignore the possibility of an alternative role by maintaining that colour and ethnicity were irrelevant to the interaction. Faced with a choice, applicants chose the role with which they felt most comfortable and, in so doing, tended to deny or suppress the existence of the other. Discussion of racism is missed out from Wallman's account but, in the context of the assessment encounter, it was the consciousness of actual and potential racism which both reinforced and constrained applicants' promotion of their own ethnicity. Fear of prejudice and hostility from white people reinforced a preference for their own company but fear of being treated as second class citizens caused them to reject notions of differential treatment.

Conclusion

Although heralded as a 'radical new departure', the innovation of the black foster parent co–workers was originally conceived as little more than a stop–gap measure. The co–worker role was circumscribed by the narrow boundaries of the 'ethnic sensitivity' model of service provision (cf. Stubbs, 1985) and restricted to that of cultural mediator or interpreter and teacher of inter–cultural skills. Although enhanced 'service relevance' was assumed to be a straightforward consequence of the co–workers' recruitment (cf. Stubbs, 1985[17]), the ability to make a difference to the way in which service was provided was limited to filling a cultural gap. The way in which the assessment was conducted and the relationship between the social worker and foster parent was structured restricted opportunities to question or challenge and ensured minimum disturbance to the *status quo*.

The language of 'partnership' merely served to disguise the inequalities in the relationship. The participation of the foster parents was restricted to the assessment visit and access to the policy forum of the Team Meeting was denied. Participation in the decision–making process was limited to the assessment outcome for individual applicants. But, even here, although the foster parents possessed a limited degree of power, it was without the understanding of power on the part of the applicants. Professional/ non–professional distinctions were reinforced by wider black/white status

---

[17] Black workers are seen to have an incremental effect whereby they are able to induce a shift in service provision to make it more relevant and accessible to ethnic minorities – in short, 'ethnically sensitive' (Stubbs, 1985: 15).

differences in society at large and, far from challenging, served to perpetuate the prevailing discriminatory climate.

The co-workers' role was limited to advice on technical details of implementation of policy already formulated. Reliance on technical arguments was encouraged by insecurity about their status and their need to be accepted by social workers as having a valuable contribution to make. This generated concern about their own 'professionalism'. By using technical arguments, the co-workers were adopting the conceptual framework and language of the social workers, i.e. ostensibly ideologically neutral and apolitical. In this way, they become socialised to the *status quo* and lose their capacity to question or to initiate anything more than superficial change (cf. Rooney, 1981; Liverpool, 1982; *Community Care*, 13 July 1989; Owusu–Bempah, 1989,; Ely and Denney, 1987).

In order to avoid the political implications of what Stubbs (1985) has termed 'class autonomy' and 'race autonomy' models of the structural dimensions of state social work, social workers resorted to cultural explanations of social inequality which downgraded economic, material and political considerations. The co-workers were constrained to accept these interpretations by their dependence for their position on others' (white social workers') definition of their skills, qualifications and competencies, the elements of which had been pre-defined, leaving little scope for self-expression and negotiation. Their role was circumscribed by absolutist notions of 'race', ethnicity and culture (cf. Gilroy, 1987a[18]) which divorced them from the economic and political sphere and left no room for notions of adaptation and change (cf. Dex, 1983). Culture was conceived as a static and impermeable phenomenon rather than a dynamic and interactive complex of elements which can be utilized, adapted or discarded, dismantled or reconstructed according to circumstance and context. To the social workers in the Fostering Team, West Indian culture was a brittle and fragile anachronism rather than a plastic resource which could be adapted to changing conditions.

'Race' was treated as a fixed social category rather than an identity which has to be socially and politically constructed. The notion of a 'Black identity' was reduced to an ethnic and cultural identity which effectively severed it from the economic and political context. Although they spoke in terms of 'racial matching', in practice, social workers tackled the problem of recruiting black

---

[18] The absolutist view of black and white cultures, as fixed, mutually impermeable expressions of racial and national identity, is a ubiquitous theme in racial 'common sense' (Lawrence, 1982a), but it is far from secure. It is constantly under challenge from the activities of blacks who pass through the cultural and ideological net which is supposed to screen Englishness from them, and from the complex organic process which renders black Britons partially soluble in the national culture which their presence helps transform (Gilroy, 1987a: 61).

foster parents from a cultural perspective. A 'Black identity' was reduced to a West Indian cultural identity and racism was reduced to ethnocentricism and ignorance about other cultures. Like ethnicity, however, 'race' is a resource or handicap which can be constructed or deconstructed, negotiated, denied or imposed in different situations and different historical periods. It need not have a single meaning or significance but a number of meanings and different significance depending on the situation (Gilroy, 1987a). By assuming a single black identity and simplifying it to a West Indian cultural identity, social workers effectively undermined the possibility of alternative, more forceful and politically–motivated assertions of what it means to be black[19].

The conflation of 'race' with ethnicity and culture and its artificial separation from class prevented workers from recognising the possibility of 'reciprocal determination' (Gilroy, 1987a: 16) and they found themselves having to choose between rival mono–causal explanations of social inequality. Groups were distinguished in terms of cultural differences which obscured the inter–relationships and common ground between them. The cultural focus gave social workers a technical model for practice which meshed with their conception of 'professionalism' as apolitical. But, for the foster parents and applicants, the artificial separation of 'race', culture and class pulled apart the different elements of their identity as black, West Indian and working class.

Although the conditions of the foster parents' engagement encouraged a view of themselves as the possessors of 'special' cultural knowledge and skills, other factors meant that an emphasis on their generic skills as mothers and foster parents was often more appropriate. The claim to possession of 'special' cultural knowledge was reliant on the argument for differential treatment on the grounds that black people and white people inhabit different cultural worlds. This conflicts with a commitment to assimilation and runs counter to the philosophy of universal provision and the same treatment for all. The presence of the black co–workers was, thus, a political statement which threatened the personal philosophies and social aspirations of many of the applicants. In order to avoid direct confrontation, all three parties to the interaction, – social workers, foster parents and applicants – colluded by tacit consent to avoid politically contentious areas. Despite the rationale underpinning their recruitment, it was the exigencies of the context in which the assessments were undertaken which governed the relevance of the black foster parents' ethnicity and it was frequently suppressed in favour of their generic fostering skills.

The lack of a clear role definition meant vulnerability to reinterpretation and change which explains how quickly the specifically ethnic component was

---

[19] The fact that the bulk of the 'black' population in the borough was of Afro–Caribbean origin encouraged workers in this assumption.

243

usurped and eroded by more general concerns. It was suggested that foster parents could also be used in assessments of white applicants. This did, in fact, happen on the mixed course and was subsequently introduced more generally. Thus, what had begun as a form of differential treatment, became generalised to all applicants, black and white, and the specifically black component was eroded.

Without structural issues of representation, power–sharing and the construction of esteem within the black population having been tackled, the situation is liable to revert to its previous state without the achievement of anything more than superficial or cosmetic changes which leave the structural relations of power intact. The irony lies in the fact that it was their competence as foster parents which gave the co–workers the more secure basis on which to ground their position but, without the initial 'boost' from their ethnicity, that position may never have been achieved. Ironically, as more black foster parents are successfully recruited, the urgency of the recruitment drive is lessened and concern with specifically black issues declines.

Black representation and power–sharing was achieved, albeit on a limited basis, only by the black foster parents 'selling' their ethnicity. This is not to suggest that ethnicity was irrelevant to the selection process or that the foster parents were cynically manipulating their role but to point out that the emphasis on practical issues concerned with increasing foster parent recruitment was at the expense of political and structural considerations. Because they were not argued independently, black representation and power sharing were achieved, as it were, 'on the back of' cultural considerations and when the arguments about culture were compromised, they too were threatened.

The importance of the black co–workers' engagement seemed to lie not so much in cultural practice as in their visibility as role models to the black community and in the challenge to social workers' claims to professional expertise in matters of family assessment. Negotiation over the demarcation of roles revolved as much around the foster parents' skills in child care and foster parenting as around issues of cultural competence. Similarly, the contested value of life experience as opposed to formal training was potentially more threatening to social workers in the domain of parenting skills and family assessment than in the domain of cross–cultural competence.

Figure 3
Family assessment skills

BLACK FOSTER PARENTS		SOCIAL WORKERS
as black people	*as parents and foster parents*	
Claim based on affinity of:	Claim based on affinity of:	Claims not based on affinity but on distance from applicants as qualified professionals but, in order to gain acceptance, stress affinity of:
1. race 2. ethnicity	1. class 2. gender 3. parenthood 4. non-professional status	1. gender 2. parenthood
Skills:	Skills:	Skills:
1. as cultural interpreters 2. as cultural 'watchdogs'	1. practical parenting skills 2. practical fostering skills Practical experience and commonsense set against social workers 'book learning' and 'pieces of paper'	1. professional skills acquired through training 2. professional skills acquired through experience of social work

13 A discriminatory dilemma: Examining the inter-personal dynamics of black co-worker presence

Although enhanced 'service relevance' (Stubbs, 1985) was assumed to be an inevitable consequence of the black foster parents' engagement, the precise definition of 'relevance' was unclear: there was confusion between the twin, but not necessarily complementary, aims of increasing both the quantity and the quality of applicants recruited. The 'commonsense' view, upheld by both social workers and foster parents, was that the presence of another black person would make the assessments easier for black applicants and that more black applicants would be encouraged to apply. Both social workers and foster parents, however, also believed that the involvement of a black person would result in more rigorous assessments and, thus, in an improvement in the quality of applicants recruited. Ethnic and cultural affinity was, thus, thought to serve both an *enabling* and a *screening* function. The potential for conflict between the two, however, does not seem to have been recognised. In this chapter, it will argued that the inclusion of the black foster parents in the assessment procedure served less as an *anti-discriminatory* than as an *extra-discriminatory* measure by introducing an additional dimension of screening and the possibility of alternative frames of reference.

The optimum strategy for the applicant

The applicant had to work out whether his or her chances of approval would be improved by forming an alliance with the social worker, foster parent or neither; whom it was more profitable to try to please or impress; to what extent it was possible to please or impress both; whether impressing one would risk alienating the other and, if so, which one's alienation was the most to be feared. None of the actors walked into the assessment as in to an historical vacuum in completely neutral garb but entered a complex, historically–determined situation with all its social and emotional accoutrements. The interaction was structured not only by the social, political and institutional context (the fact of assessment and the interactors' relative positions in the Social Services hierarchy) but by their personal biographies. How the foster parent or social worker related to the applicant was not simply a one–way process dependent on the applicant's self-presentation but depended, in turn, on the applicant's own perceptions.

Second, relationships within the triad were not ones of equality between the actors. An imbalance of power existed between social worker and foster parent as a consequence of their respective positions in the Social Services hierarchy but an even greater imbalance existed, by virtue of the context of assessment, between social worker and applicant and foster parent and applicant. As a 'working partnership', the social worker and foster parent had opportunity to form an alliance more powerful and potentially more threatening to the applicant than the social worker working alone. The shared role of joint assessment gave both a power which was strengthened by the fact that their relationship persisted outside and beyond the face–to–face encounter with the applicant. They could discuss strategy and exchange opinions about the applicant before and after each home visit. No such opportunity was available to the applicant whose contact with either social worker or foster parent did not extend beyond the immediate face–to–face encounter, except, perhaps, for the odd telephone call to the social worker. Even where additional contacts were possible, the nature of the relationship precluded much, if any, discussion about the absent member of the triad.

The fact that the social worker and foster parent continued their relationship beyond the face–to–face meeting with the applicant enabled them to formulate a 'hidden agenda' which meant an inequality of access to the information necessary for devising an optimum strategy for managing the encounter. The foster parent's role as cultural interpreter, for example, tended to be played down during an interview in favour of her generic knowledge and experience of fostering and this may have encouraged applicants to play down their own ethnicity and to present themselves in accordance with a 'white' model of family life and good parenting. In the post–visit discussions between social workers and foster parents, however, ethnic issues might well have resurfaced[1].

Not only were applicants disadvantaged in terms of relative power, but found themselves having to persuade two parties of their suitability where, previously, there would only have been one. Neither could they be sure that both social worker and foster parent held the same opinions about what makes a 'good' foster parent. Black/ white, working class/ middle class, non–professional/ professional, foster parent/ social worker dichotomies were now built into the assessment representing different and possibly conflicting frames of reference. At best, the applicant was presented with a wider field of potential relevance giving greater 'room' for a positive self–presentation and, at worst, with a stark choice between conflicting approaches.

These difficulties were compounded by the ambiguities of the foster parent's role. It was not clear to applicants whether the foster parent was present as an assessor or adviser and, if an adviser, whether to the social worker or to the applicant, as an experienced foster parent or cultural representative, nor whether these roles were mutually exclusive or, if not, which were primary and which were secondary. Different social workers and different foster parents held different views and, even within a partnership, social worker and foster parent were likely to have differing conceptions of the foster parent's role. Most applicants seem to have been unaware of the foster parents' role as joint assessors and this affected their perceptions of the foster parents and the way in which they reacted to them. The nature of the situation encouraged them to relate to the foster parents on the basis of a sympathetic, though illusory, alliance of the non–powerful versus the powerful (i.e. assessor and decision–maker).

Both social workers and foster parents worked on the assumption that applicants led two lives, a public and a private, and that the public façade which they presented to the world masked what they were 'really like'. Maintaining an aura of ambiguity around the foster parent's role gave applicants less opportunity to 'stage–manage' their answers and encouraged them to relate to the foster parents as non–officials and non–decision–makers and, thus, to reveal aspects of their private lives which they might otherwise have attempted to conceal.

---

[1] Although there was no opportunity to observe these discussions directly, reports from both social workers and foster parents, however, suggested that ethnic issues were not high on the agenda.

The foster parent as an ally?

As expected, applicants felt more in common with the foster parents than with the social workers and related to them as potential allies. Their task was to work out how best to enlist their support and, of the various possible dimensions of affinity, to decide which was the most appropriate.

Ethnicity

It was assumed that the primary basis of affinity would be shared culture and ethnicity. The commonsense assumption was that it must be better for the applicant to have a black person present but, in practice, the choice of an appropriate strategy was complicated by the inclusion of the black foster parent which introduced an ethnic and cultural dimension and the possibility of a specifically 'black' profile of family life in place of or in addition to that of the conventional bourgeois family. The problem for applicants was to determine whether either or both was represented and, if social worker and foster parent were operating according to different frames of reference, which of them was likely to have most influence on the final assessment decision.

If both foster parent and social worker remained true to their different understandings of family life within distinct cultural frames, impressing both became problematic. That the foster parents remained 'true', of course, was fundamental to the rationale which underlay their recruitment. Alternatively, both social worker and foster parent may have become sufficiently similar in outlook for it to be possible to please both but, if so, had they moved towards a 'black' or a 'white' cultural profile? In many ways, it may have been easier for applicants if both social worker and foster parent had been either black or white and presented a common cultural profile. With both black and white profiles potentially represented, it was not always clear to the applicant which frame of reference was most appropriate. To black applicants, who have to move between the 'black' and the 'white' social worlds (cf. Harris, 1987), both profiles were potentially available. The different options which were open to the applicants are presented in Figure 3. The simple case where all three parties operate according to a common profile are represented by C and H. D and G are clearly inappropriate strategies for the applicant to adopt, whereas B and E would only be appropriate where the social worker has greatest influence over the assessment decision and A and F only were the foster parent has greatest influence.

The simple dichotomy between 'black' and 'white' profiles of family life, however, is misleading since it is complicated by the fact that there are at least two elements to 'white' cultural determination of the 'appropriate' image of family life. The first is largely constructed from messages passed down from

Figure 4
The assessment triad

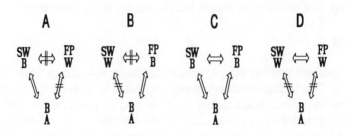

Legend:

FP = foster parent   **B** = black profile of family life

SW = social worker   **W** = white profile of family life

A = applicant

⟺ = potential alliances   ⫡ = potential cleavages

the dominant 'white' culture in Britain – through the media, advertising, politicians and so on. The second is based in the values of the 'Victorian English family' which older applicants have brought with them from the West Indies. The new commitment to the maintenance of a 'black' cultural identity, however, may mean that neither is appropriate. A simple dichotomy, moreover, implies adherence to one of two distinct and coherent models, whereas people's actual views and practices may be constructed from an amalgam of elements combined in any number of different ways. A social worker may, for example, tolerate different methods of child-rearing on most counts, but refuse to compromise on matters of discipline. The applicant's decision about which is the most appropriate stance to adopt has, therefore, to be taken anew as each new issue is raised.

In line with the 'old-fashioned' model of family life, older applicants, in particular, may stress religion, good behaviour, discipline and outward appearances (e.g. tidiness and dress), while playing down family problems, experience of hardship and warm, affectionate relationships with children. This may conflict with social workers' emphasis on freedom and self-expression as opposed to discipline and conforming behaviour. The West Indian parents often lacked the appropriate language with which to communicate with the social workers and their respective frames of reference may not only have been different but mutually conflicting (cf. L.B. Wandsworth, 1986g).

The alternative 'white', middle class version of family life presented in the media may be similarly inappropriate with its emphasis on affluence and family harmony in contrast to the new approach to family assessment which seeks to re-evaluate experience of hardship as a possible source of strength rather than evidence of inadequacy. Applicants' attempts to present themselves in accordance with conventional notions may be difficult to sustain and may lead social workers to suspect that they are not being entirely honest or, worse, have 'something to hide'. They may, additionally, be encouraged to play down their ethnicity and, in so doing, to be out of step with the new emphasis on the importance of cultural identity. Many of those interviewed seemed to lack the language of racism and anti-racism with which to communicate a sense of cultural affinity without appearing, in their own eyes, to be prejudiced or 'black-minded'. Elsewhere, it has been noted that social workers are often negatively disposed towards applicants who profess a strong political 'black identity' and express anger about racism (Stubbs, 1987). The importance attached to the maintenance of a 'black' cultural identity will depend on social workers' and foster parents' political and ideological outlook and their commitment to an assimilationist or pluralist perspective. The applicant had not only to try to gauge the views of both social worker and foster parent but to determine whether or not they were complementary or conflicting.

In the context of assessment, the official/ non-official, professional/ non-professional distinctions seemed to assume greater significance for the applicants than ties of ethnicity or common culture and they were able to influence both social workers' and foster parents' frame of reference by implicitly rejecting a cultural dimension. It was on the basis of common class and as parents and foster parents rather than as cultural representatives that the applicants related to the co-workers and it was their 'commonsense' and experience of foster parenting rather than any cultural knowledge and skills which were set against the professional training and lack of practical experience of the social workers and which united them in an alliance of the non-powerful versus the powerful[2]. Ironically, this alliance was built on an illusion which it was in the interests of both foster parent and social worker to maintain.

The foster parents, on the other hand, were more likely to ally themselves with the social workers than with the applicants. First, the emphasis was on consensus and the presentation of a united front. Second, the co-workers were dependent for their position on forming a 'good working relationship' with their social worker partners. Third, they seemed to take their cue from social workers' own conception of 'professionalism' and to think of their primary role in terms of assessment rather than mediation and as a screen of applicants' attitudes and behaviour rather than of social workers'. 'Toughness' was considered a mark of 'professionalism' and they reported that they had been able to ask more penetrating questions and to pick up things which the social worker might have missed. Few instances of cultural monitoring where the foster parent was able to act as a brake or control on the behaviour and attitudes of the social worker were reported but, on one occasion, the foster parent was able to challenge the opinion of another professional where the social worker alone would not have felt confident to do so[3].

---

[2]   Applicants' expression of affinity with the foster parents in terms of a professional/non-professional distinction may, to some extent, have been a proxy for a sense of ethnic and cultural affinity which they were reluctant to admit publicly for fear of appearing to endorse a separatist stance. The fact that many suggested that other people would have felt more comfortable with a black social worker and black foster parent supports this possibility.

[3]   The social worker described an instance when her black co-worker was able to challenge a white doctor's judgement where she, herself, would not have had the confidence to do so.   The decision to go against the doctor's recommendation was joint and the responsibility for it shared, whereas, on her own, the social worker would have been more hesitant.

(continued...)

Conclusion

There is no simple answer to the question of whether or not the foster parents' presence was perceived and/or experienced as extra- or anti-discriminatory and the answer depends, in part, on the role which culture and ethnicity plays in the process. A problem arises where there are discrepancies between the views and of the different interactors, where the social worker, for example, is operating according to one profile of family life and the applicant according to another. In instances of conflict, the foster parent can either support or challenge the social worker's frame of reference or can act as a mediator and/or cultural interpreter.

Colour and ethnicity, however, were not the only dimensions of affinity between applicant and foster parent and, in practice, were relegated to second place behind social class, non-professional status and common experience of parenthood. A potential alliance between foster parent and applicant, however, was weakened by the way in which the assessment encounter was structured which encouraged the foster parents to ally with the social workers. Applicants, by contrast, were more likely to perceive an affinity between themselves and the foster parents, albeit along lines not envisaged or given prominence in the original conception of the foster parents' role and based, at least in part, on a misrepresentation of its nature.

The presence of the foster parent shifted the assessment from the 'public' towards the 'private' domain. This raises the question of the extent to which this blurring of the boundary between public and private makes the assessment easier or more difficult for the applicant. Is it easier for a black applicant to put on a 'public face' and to hide certain aspects of his/her 'private life' from a white social worker than from a black foster parent? Does the foster parent's greater ability to assess an applicant's private life make him or her feel more or less secure? In part, this depended on the relative prominence of the foster parents' mediatory and assessment functions and whether or not they considered their primary role to be a screen of applicants' or of social workers' attitudes and behaviour.

---

[3](...continued)
for instance, the applicant I was telling you about, whose G.P. obviously thinks that her life is very traumatic and channelled and insecure, whereas I think that Y (foster parent) certainly felt that, you know, there was none of that and that it was very much to be expected given the sort of marriage she'd made and not necessarily her fault in any way, whatsoever.

The woman's application was subsequently approved despite the doctor's recommendation against approval.

The answer to the question posed at the beginning of the chapter will depend, to a large extent, on the relative importance attached to the pursuit of quality or quantity in the recruitment of black foster parents. Despite the Team's pre-occupation with the dangers of 'lower standards', the shortage of black foster parents meant that quantity was the primary objective during the course of the research. As the pool of black foster parents becomes larger and/or ideas about appropriate placements change, quality may re-emerge as the dominant concern. Quality, however, is a more complex notion. Ideas about 'suitability', for example, may differ between social worker and foster parent and may have differing implications for the applicant's chances of acceptance. Whose ideas come to hold sway will be largely dependent on the balance of power between social worker and foster parent.

14 Conclusion: Cultural politics and fostering practice

The focus of this study has been one London borough's response to the changing ideas about family placement for black children away from a colour blind approach towards an acceptance of the principle of 'racial matching'. This change had two consequences: a need to recruit black families and, in order to achieve this, a commitment to providing a more 'ethnically sensitive service'. Although the findings relate to the response of a single social services department to a particular policy issue, they have general implications for the problem of appropriate minority representation within a system and structure dominated by white people.

Black people's hostility to the social services (cf. Connelly, 1989) has been shaped by their experience as victims of its punitive functions in, what many considered to be, the unnecessary removal of children from their natural families and their placement outside the black community. A policy of 'racial matching' helped to redress past injustice. Advantage for black children was redefined as placement in a black rather than a white family and the door opened to black people to entry into the 'market' for fostering jobs. By defining the problem of black foster parent recruitment in terms of cultural differences, the new policy also provided a niche in the service structure to black social workers who could claim 'special' cultural knowledge and skills. The emphasis on cultural identity, however, meant that black people's participation in the provision of fostering services, either as foster parents or as social workers, was based on the possession of culturally distinctive

255

attributes and skills rather than concern with equal opportunities and power sharing.

Responses to the challenge of 'racial matching': 'patchy, piecemeal and lacking in strategy'[1]

Within London, the impetus for change germinated among black social workers and gathered momentum with their collective organisation under the aegis of ABSWAP. In order to gain general acceptance for their ideas, those advocating change had to employ different strategies to appeal to different audiences. They managed to command the attention of both social workers and the population at large and were successful in claiming legitimacy among many black people, especially social workers. They were less successful among the white population where their ideas were introduced into a climate of ideological hostility and presented a challenge to professional social work norms. In consequence, the implementation of changes was initially patchy, tempered by ambivalence and timidity in the face of public opposition. The pattern of responses varied from borough to borough, dependent on local conditions and personnel. A number of common features emerged, however, which were replicated in the case study of the single borough.

Fear of a 'white' backlash, in terms of the possible electoral consequences and the alienation of existing white foster parents, provoked a cautious response. It encouraged the adoption of a low profile and confinement of the debate to professional concern among social workers. Second, lack of consultation or dialogue with the local community meant that the changes occurred more or less independently of community influence reinforcing the popular image of the Social Services Department as 'the castle on the hill'. The weaknesses of this 'top-down' approach were evident in the lack of adequate diffusion structures to disseminate information about the changes to local black communities (cf. Kaniuk, 1991) and a failure to engage in public debate to gain the confidence and support necessary for effective implementation. Third, the 'problem' of recruiting black foster parents was interpreted in terms of cultural differences rather than economic circumstances or the structural relations of power.

---

[1] ADSS/CRE (1978), Association of Directors of Social Services and Commission for Racial Equality, *Multi-Racial Britain: The Social Services Response*, London, Commission for Racial Equality.

Responses to the challenge in the borough of the case study: radical talk, conservative practice

Within the borough of the case study, the apparent radicalism and rapid pace of change belied an inherent conservatism which began to reassert itself as the immediate pressure to recruit black foster parents declined. The emphasis on team consensus and strategies of conflict avoidance prevented serious challenge to the *status quo*. The fragility of the new moves rapidly became obvious as the more radical initiatives, one by one, were dropped and the Fostering Team reverted to its old practices and approach. Differential assessment criteria were initially justified by a need to accommodate cultural differences. Ideological resistance to the operation of dual standards and fear of arousing white applicants' hostility by seeming to give preferential treatment meant that the changes were later generalised to all applicants. The holding of segregated meetings and groups was discontinued for similar reasons. Experienced black foster parents were originally engaged as co–workers only in the assessments of black applicants. Later, joint assessments were introduced for all applicants and the original justification for their role, in terms of colour and ethnicity, was superseded by an emphasis on skills and experience as parents and foster parents. But it was the disbanding of the 'Black Action Group' which revealed most clearly the weakness of the Team's pluralist commitment. What had, only weeks earlier, been declared 'top priority' was overtaken by 'more pressing needs' – a shortage of white foster parents. The excuse of resource constraints allowed the Team to continue to pay lip service to the goal of same race placement whilst withdrawing from any practical commitment.

Ironically, in the very success of 'the black campaign' lay the seeds of its demise as an ethnically exclusive venture. First, the success of the recruitment drive had been achieved without the aid of black social workers and, second, the alleviation of the acute shortage of black foster parents removed the campaign's main stimulus. The specifically 'black' concerns which had provided the initial impetus became muted and dispersed amid more general concerns.

Despite the failure to sustain a 'black' perspective, significant changes in policy and practice were accomplished during the course of the study. The review of assessment criteria in order to accommodate black applicants led to a review of the fostering task, itself, and of the qualities necessary and/or desirable to accomplish it. It not only drew into the fostering net more black applicants but a significant number of white applicants who would previously have been excluded. The assessment process was streamlined for all applicants and, from being 'social worker orientated', became more 'applicant orientated'. Where, previously, there had been little difficulty in attracting applications, procedures had evolved to suit social workers' convenience. The language of 'vetting', 'approval', 'passing' and 'failing' indicated the nature of the process as a test or trial. The new language of 'partnership' and 'sharing' and replacement of the term, 'rejection', by the concept of 'counselling out', indicated a change in emphasis away from judgement towards mutual exploration of the suitability of the fostering task to the applicant's aptitudes and needs. Two important innovations, initially conceived in response to the pressure of applications from black people and later generalised to all applicants, were group training and assessment and the use of foster parents in joint visits[2].

Collective organisation and the influence of the Association of Black Social Workers and Allied Professions

The founding of ABSWAP and confidence which it gave to black social workers as a group was a crucial development. For individual workers, isolated in predominantly white departments, the costs of trying to initiate change, in terms of the range of social and organisational punishments which could be brought to bear (Liverpool, 1982; Bernard, 1987; Thomas, 1984), outweighed the benefits of conformity. Collective organisation gave collective power. The Association provided a central forum for the development and co-ordination of ideas and an organisational base for their outward diffusion to local agencies through their black employees.

For many black activists, transracial placement became a symbol for all that was racist not just in social work but in white society in general:

> Transracial placement as an aspect of current child care policy is in essence a microcosm of the oppression of black people in this society (ABSWAP, 1983a: 12)

The speed with which the controversy hit the headlines has to be seen in the context of the prevailing 'race relations' climate of the time. With the lead of the Greater London Council's Ethnic Minorities Unit and the campaign for 'Black Sections' in the Labour Party, 'race' issues acquired a prominence which they had not enjoyed to the same extent in the previous decade (Solomos, 1989).

---

[2] In many ways, this undermined social workers' professional claims to family assessment skills in ways far more radical than had joint assessments been confined to black applicants. The foster parents' role had initially been conceived in terms of adviser and teacher on cultural matters, with the implicit assumption that cultural knowledge and skills were transmissible. By contrast, their practical parenting and fostering skills could only be learned through experience and were, thus, beyond the reach of the social workers.

ABSWAP's first conference manifesto (December 1983) set the agenda for subsequent debate. Past failure to approve black families was attributed to the assessment of 'suitability' according to the standards of white, middle-class family life and 'institutionalised racism within local authority structures'. The solution was seen to lie in

1. the adoption of a more 'ethnically sensitive' approach,
2. the employment of black workers to compensate for white workers' lack of appropriate cultural skills and
3. greater consultation and dialogue with the black communities.

An ethnically sensitive service?

For white social workers, a cultural focus conformed with the organisational logic by which clients were divided into groups differentiated by their differing service needs (cf. Biehal and Sainsbury, 1991). 'Minority fostering' became a convenient package which could be separated off from mainstream fostering and the 'problem' of black foster parent recruitment, interpreted in terms of cultural mismatch, could be reduced to a technical matter of cross-cultural competence. The model of ethnic diversity elided 'race' with ethnicity, reduced racism to ignorance about other cultures and conveniently side-stepped class and economic considerations (Gilroy, 1987b).

Arguments for multi-culturalism tend to portray cultures as rigid *structures* of rules and meanings which imprison their members rather than dynamic, interactive and adaptive *processes* (Gilroy, 1987a, b), and to confuse ideas about the rigidity or adaptability of culture and ethnicity as group phenomena with the abilities of members as individuals to change their cultural identities, behaviours, attitudes and aspirations (Archer, 1985). Pinder attempts to capture this notion when he writes of 'ethnic diversity' as referring 'not to a taxonomy of groups and individuals who are different but to a process built around encounters between people who differ' (1980: 1). Culture is, thus, not simply 'an intrinsic property of ethnic particularity' (Gilroy, 1987a: 16) but a negotiated product of social interaction.

Lal introduces the notion of *ethnicity by consent* and *compulsory ethnicity* to distinguish between individuals' differing abilities to reject or adopt a specific ethnic identity. Compulsory ethnicity, she explains, refers to 'the institutionalization of ethnic identification as a basis for the assertion of collective claims concerning the distribution of scarce resources[3].

---

[3]Sivanandan, for example, writes of 'Labour councils who, lacking the race-class perspective which would have allowed them to dismantle the institutional racism of their own structures, institutionalised ethnicity instead' (1985: 13).

In the current study, many applicants interpreted the cultural pluralist approach of the Social Services as an attempt to impose a form of compulsory ethnicity and their efforts to provide 'a more ethnically sensitive service' as a means of further oppression rather than of redressing the balance of past injustice. 'Power', according to Ni'am Akbar, 'is the ability to define who and what you are and have that definition respected by others. Oppression is the taking away of that right of self–determination...' Culture, in Akbar's terms, is not simply a set of ascribed characteristics but a positively constructed identity. 'Culture', he maintains, 'is the maintenance of that right to define who we are and should be' (cited in Divine, 20 May 1983).

Although appealing in theory, a plural approach proved difficult to implement in practice. The model of cultural diversity raised the prospect of dual or double standards which challenged social workers' dominant organisational identity as impartial service providers (cf. Rooney, 1982; Lipsky, 1980). The assertion of a black cultural identity to rival the dominant white British identity challenged liberal notions of assimilation and led to fears about a 'racially' divided society. Many applicants, moreover, were suspicious of the cultural label. They foresaw the dangers of creating a second class service marginalised from mainstream provision and regarded separate provision as a retrograde step which would increase their marginality and further reduce their ability to participate in the mainstream.

The problem lay partly in workers' confused notions about what constituted 'culture' or the 'cultural'. 'At the descriptive level', Archer observes, 'the notion of 'culture' remains inordinately vague despite little dispute that it is a core concept' (1985: 333). Workers in the Fostering Team equated 'Black culture' with West Indian culture and tended to talk of it as a single coherent structure of rules and meanings rather than a series of more or less distinct and overlapping systems. Their notion of 'Black culture' ignored the many strands running through it. One strand is the culture acquired in the West Indies, itself an amalgam of African, European and Asian imports. This, in turn, is interwoven with a reactive 'Black culture' characterised as an adaptive response to the hostility or indifference of white society. According to this view, specifically 'Black' aspirations and values are of recent origin; Sivanandan, for example, describes ethnicity as 'the creation of a new reactive culture on the part of British–born Asians and West Indians'[4] (1985: 11). A further strand,

---

[4] `Neither Asian /Afro–Caribbean nor British but afflicted by both, the second generation was adrift of its moorings and rudderless, caught in a cross–current of emotion in its search for identity – not least, to fight racism with. And, in that search, it kept returning to its ethnicity and, redefining it, found refuge therein' (Sivanandan, 1985: 11; cf Ballard and Ballard, 1977 and Naipaul, 1982).

260

which incorporates notions of 'Black Power' and 'Pan–Africanism', is influenced by developments in North America and Africa (Gilroy, 1987a).

A related, but similarly confused, notion was that of 'Black identity'. For most workers in the Team, it meant little more than a West Indian cultural identity and, as such, devoid of political content. In the pronouncements of ABSWAP, however, it was both an ascribed and a voluntarily elected identity: in other words, a matter of skin colour *and* political consciousness. In its ascriptive sense, it is a label imposed by white society and associated with (an inferior) black culture. A 'positive Black identity', by contrast, implies not simply a different cultural identity but pride in that identity and, beyond this, a supra–ethnic political identity constructed around a common colonial past and experience of racism (ABSWAP Conference 1983)[5]. Although sometimes portrayed as a 'natural' outgrowth of these experiences, it is more of an ideological and aspirational construct by 'politically conscious people... to proclaim and forge a political unity' (Ahmed, 1988: 9).

The emergence of 'Black' politics is a recent dimension to the British political scene and the primary importance attributed to 'race' beyond considerations of culture and class (Stubbs, 1985) sparked off one of the most heated of contemporary debates. In a misguided attempt to counteract the racialisation of political debate, a Conservative Party 1981 election poster offered the black electorate the stark choice: 'To Labour you are black, to the Conservatives you are British'. That the two might not be mutually exclusive or that some people might choose to identify themselves as Black British does not seem to have occurred to the Tories. The Labour Party has been equally keen to deny the primacy of 'race' over class and has used 'class–based politics to undermine and deny the specificity of the black experience of racism' (Gabriel, 1989: 157). The dominant response has been to deny legitimacy, as illustrated by the de–selection of Sharon Aitkin after having accused the Labour Party of racism (*The Guardian*, 1 May 1987), and to marginalise, as

---

[5] Modood has criticised this use of the term, `black', in respect of Asians, as `the means of effecting a unity between very diverse, powerless minorities that is necessary for an effective anti–racist movement' (1988a: 4).

... when Asians are encouraged to think of themselves as black, (they)... have to define themselves in a framework, that is historically and internationally developed, by people in search of African roots ... The adoption of the term 'black' here usually means by implication, and certainly as a matter of fact, the acceptance by Asians of an Afro–political leadership (op cit: 5).

261

demonstrated by the relegation of the Labour Party Black Section to the 'extremes' of Party opinion (Gabriel, 1989:169; *The Guardian*, 1 May 1987[6]). The thrust of many local authority equal opportunities policies, by contrast, has been to promote an emphasis on 'racial' and cultural differences (Cain and Yuval–Davies, 1990). Although the aim of identifying specific groups in need of positive action was to draw them into the embrace of the rest of the 'community', groups previously excluded were drawn into mutual competition for resources. The result, paradoxically, was a hardening of divisions. Groups with easiest access to funds were those organising around cultural or ethnic differences. Equal opportunities policies assume that it is only discriminatory practices that produce disadvantage (*op cit.*) and, therefore, do little to tackle the endemic structural disadvantage recognised in traditional class politics. In consequence, local authorities' model of cultural diversity has been criticised as a divisive strategy which leads to the fractionating of both the working class and the black population into competing, inward–looking cultural groups[7].

Gilroy (1987b) has shown how 'the new racism' of the right, identified by Barker (1981), has borrowed the terms of multi–culturalism to reclothe its old biological determinism. 'Apart from the way that racial meanings are inferred rather than stated openly', he suggests,

> these new forms are distinguished by the extent to which they identify race with the terms culture and identity..., (the 'new racism') seeks to present an imaginary definition of the nation as a unified cultural community. It constructs and defends an image of national culture – homogenous in its whiteness yet precarious and perpetually vulnerable to attack from enemies within and without (Gilroy, 1987b: 5).

---

[6] In a blatant appeal to traditional Labour prejudices, Roy Hattersley, for example, commented

As far as I can make out the black sections are more imaginary than real. They are southern professionals rather than manual workers – a rather inbred and small group of people (Roy Hattersley, Deputy Leader of the Labour Party, quoted in *The Guardian*, 1 May 1987).

[7] To Sivanandan, for example, `Multiculturalism deflected the political concerns of the black community into the cultural concerns of different communities, the struggle against racism to the struggle for culture' (1985: 6). `A culture of ethnicity', he suggests, `unlike a culture of resistance, has no community and has no class' (*op cit.*: 15). Sivanandan goes further and suggests that it was a deliberate state strategy motivated by class interests to weaken both the black population and the working class. `Underlying the whole of the state's project was a divisive culturalism that turned the living, dynamic, progressive aspects of black people's culture into artefact and habit and custom – and began to break up community' (*op cit*: 7).

262

In the current study, as previously noted, some white foster parents were able to mimic social workers' language of 'racial matching' as a veil for their own ingrained racist attitudes[8].

To the multi-culturalists, the autonomy and impermeability of the cultural sphere separates it from the world of politics and class. The interaction or, in Gilroy's phrase, 'reciprocal determination' (1987a: 16) of cultural, political and economic considerations, however, can be seen in 'white' opposition to 'racial matching'. This can be interpreted, in political terms, as a defence of 'white' cultural hegemony and opposition to cultural separatism and, in economic terms, as the protection of fostering 'jobs'. The material benefits endowed by superior class position gave middle class candidates an advantage over those less well off. Black applicants were triply disadvantaged by virtue of class location reinforced by 'racial' prejudice and the equation of cultural difference with 'cultural deficit' (cf. Keddie, 1973) and, more recently, as Barker and Gilroy point out, with cultural threat. The pluralist approach was a simple inversion of past pathology, deficit or 'victim blaming' (Ryan, 1976) models. The analysis remained confined within a cultural frame without reference to the wider operation of racism and the structural and institutional inequalities of British society.

'Culture' has been wielded with effect by social workers, as representatives of white middle class society, against the working class, to justify family intervention on the grounds of 'a culture of poverty' or 'cycle of deprivation'; and against minority groups, on the grounds of 'cultural deficit', 'culture clash', 'culture conflict' or 'identity confusion'. But, in Bill Jordan's view, the common underlying cause, is not so much individual family pathology or cultural inadequacy as poverty (Jordan, 1985). The multi-cultural approach does little to address the reasons why black families are disproportionately represented among the urban poor.

Although it challenges reliance on the conventional bourgeois two-parent family as the template for substitute family care (cf. Bebbington and Miles, 1990), the conventional model is increasingly challenged by both demographic trends (one in three marriages now ends in divorce and 57% involve dependent children) and straitened economic circumstances, not just for black families but more generally (Lowe, 1989, 1991; cf. Bebbington and Miles, 1990). Marion

---

[8] The following comments are an illustration:

I agree with the new policy of black children going with only black families and white with only white. You can't mix the races, however hard you try.

I think that it is right that each should look after its own. They are different from us. The boys mature sexually earlier than our boys do. I wouldn't trust a black teenager with my daughter.

Lowe suggests that foster carers will increasingly identify with the women to whose children they offer substitute or supplementary care. This process is likely to be enhanced by attempts to recruit substitute carers from the same communities as the children's families of origin and by the practice of inclusive fostering which encourages the participation of the children's natural families (Holman, 1975b). As Lowe points out, 'society's reluctance to commit resources to families, particularly single parent families, means an increased role for foster families in coping with the child casualties. Many of these carers are aware, from their own personal experience, of the harshness of this process' (1989: viii). The impracticality of trying to separate cultural from economic considerations meant that, in attempting to maintain sensitivity to cultural differences, social workers were forced to confront the economic realities of black people's lives. What had begun as a focus on difference became refocussed on concerns which affected the working class and the position of women as a whole.

In the current study, it was black women's propensity to seek paid employment outside the home, albeit explained within the Fostering Team in terms of cultural preference rather than economic necessity, which posed the greatest challenge to the notion of fostering as a vocation rather than a job of work. An increasing number of foster parents, especially among the black communities, are themselves single parents (Bebbington and Miles, 1990) and know at first hand the problems of raising a family on a limited income in a hostile society. 'It is a paradox, but also potentially a positive factor for the future of inclusive, partnership–based models of foster care,' Lowe notes, 'that such single parent foster carers seek from their work as carers the financial rewards which enable them to keep their own vulnerable families intact!' (1989: viii).

The changing care population, in particular the boarding out of children previously considered 'hard to place', has meant that many foster parents are now asked to care for children with a multitude of problems. Few arrive without a history of disrupted family life, difficulties at school or with the police, emotional and/or behavioral problems, physical or mental disability (National Children's Bureau, October 1978). Caring for such children is recognised as a skilled, time consuming, physically and emotionally demanding job and a number of agencies have set up so–called 'professional fostering schemes' to cater for children with specific needs (Shaw and Hipgrave, 1982; Hardy et al, 1986). Most pay an additional fee in addition to the regular boarding–out allowance and require the foster parents to undergo compulsory training. Many agencies, however, are now finding it necessary to train all their foster carers.

These developments have led foster carers to call for the recognition of fostering as a proper job and the introduction of payment and conditions in accordance with other forms of paid employment.

The future of foster care lies in obligatory training and education for all those involved in foster care. Future courses should be designed to merit a qualification on completion. Such a qualification would, as in any other sphere, merit a salary plus a boarding–out allowance (Correspondent to *Foster Care*, March 1983)

The eruption of 'the Cleveland affair' (Campbell, 1988) in 1987 highlighted the need for foster carers to be adequately trained to deal with the child casualties of sexual abuse and enhanced demands for **all** fostering to be considered a 'professional' service (Robinson, 1991; Pringle, 1991). By 1991, 'the trend to professionalise foster care (had) become well established' (Robinson, 1991: 47) and 'the boundaries between professional and non-professional foster care (were) crumbling' (Pringle, 1991: 20). The full financial implications of these trends, however, have yet to be confronted (*op cit.*).

The employment of black social workers

A second string to ABSWAP's argument was a call for the appointment of more black social workers. Although it was argued that 'the social work staff of each authority should not only reflect the composition of its population but be proportionate to its client group', the main thrust was in terms of the possession of relevant cultural skills. Arguments for the employment of black workers were driven by the need to recruit black foster parents. They revolved around technical debates about the importance of intercultural knowledge and skills rather than political questions concerning the employment of black social workers to represent the black community in positions of power. The problem of contact between white service structure and black clientele was, thus, reduced to a simple question of cultural mismatch which could be resolved by employing black workers with the appropriate cultural skills. It is here argued that neither the diagnosis nor the solution was sufficient.

The divergence of interests between agency and community are evoked in Verol Liverpool's description of 'the black (social worker) ... walking a tightrope between allegiance to his organisation and to the black community' (1982: 227; cf. Divine, 1 April 1983; Nixon, 1983; Stubbs, 1985). The conflicting pressures have been vividly described in a number of personal accounts by black social workers (e.g. Bernard, 1987; Thomas, 1984; Liverpool, 1982; Rooney, 1982). Second, in the 'them' and 'us' attitude between worker and client which Liverpool describes, 'racial' and cultural differences are complicated by those of social class, gender and professional status. Third, black people have been conditioned to accept the professional authority and competence of white people (Phoenix, 1990; Liverpool, 1982: 226).

Black people who entered social work through the politics of cultural matching were doubly disadvantaged: at the prior level, through an education system which left them less well qualified than white students[9] and, subsequently, at the level of entry to the profession[10]. As few black applicants possessed suitable educational credentials, black entry tended to rely on the politics of culture. Many black social workers, therefore, joined without the same professional credentials as their white colleagues (Cheetham, 1981b; Rooney, 1982; Liverpool, 1982; Dominelli, 1988).

Even where they were able to claim equivalent credentials, the emphasis on distinctive cultural skills tended to confine the domain of their competence within areas with a specific cultural content. These were usually specified in job descriptions or defined by white colleagues. This restricted opportunities for long term incorporation into mainstream work and prevented recognition or acceptance of full professional authority by colleagues and clients. The need for cross-cultural skills in social work was seen as a temporary measure or prior stage in the process of full integration into mainstream society. As Hugman observes,

> Recruitment to specially funded posts, as specialists in work with black people .... reinforces the view that where the knowledge and skills exercised by black social workers is not accompanied by a formal qualification then it is less professional. As possession of a qualification has been built into the promotion process, then the racial divisions created at the practice level are reproduced in the hierarchy (1991: 210).

In the borough of the case study, the engagement of the foster parent co-workers was the most significant move to include black people in the structure of service provision. Far from indicating a commitment to change, it may actually have operated as a means of suppressing it. By incorporating black

---

[9] A variety of theories have been constructed in explanation (see Carby, 1982 for a review).

[10] Even the few who possessed the necessary educational credentials were discouraged from applying to social work courses, since social work was widely regarded as a white, middle class preserve and as an agency of social control in black communities (Dominelli, 1988; Divine, 1 April, 15 July 1983).

people into the service structure, albeit in a limited capacity, it helped to head off the call for more radical change. The foster parents were, in effect, incorporated as agents of social control in the containment of potential challenge or resistance by socialization to the dominant ethos and approach of the Social Services. As a consequence, they conceived their primary function in terms of a screen of applicants' attitudes and behaviour rather than of social workers'.

Their engagement in joint assessments was less a departure than a legitimation of existing processes by providing a limited degree of participation. Although party to the decision–making process in relation to individual assessments, they were denied access, except on one or two limited occasions, to the main forum of group decision–making and policy formulation, the Team Meeting. Their presence was without the understanding of power on the part of applicants and, therefore, without public visibility. This reinforced rather than challenged conventional authority relations between black and white people generally.

In deference to the new 'ethnically sensitive' approach, 'culture' and ethnicity were treated, at least in theory, as the predominant, if not the only, dimensions relevant to the client–worker encounter. 'Race' was elided with 'culture', 'race consciousness' transmuted to the politically less threatening question of cultural differences and disparities of professional status, social class and gender masked or ignored. For applicants, however, 'culture' was only one of a set of intricately related and interactive dimensions which structure the relationship between practitioner and client.

Although engaged on the basis of their ethnicity and presumed cultural knowledge, the foster parents' practical knowledge of fostering had greater legitimacy in applicants' eyes than social workers' formal qualifications. Applicants' mistrust of the multi–cultural approach shifted the frame of reference on to a more general plane. The engagement of non–professional workers enabled them to reject social workers' authority by appeal to shared 'commonsense' and rejection of 'professional' assessment skills. Paradoxically, the employment of unqualified workers and resort to 'commonsense' capabilities *in lieu* of professional skills may, thus, present a more fundamental and potentially more damaging challenge to white social workers' professional competence than the simple questioning of their inter–cultural skills.

Social control was a forceful theme in applicants' arguments. Social work was regarded as a middle class profession and entry into it as entry into the middle classes. But it was also a 'white' profession and black social workers risked being seen as the perpetrators of a double betrayal of both 'race' *and* class, achieving middle class status through entry into a 'white' agency of social control in the black community. Applicants argued that, in order to maintain professional credibility, black social workers would align themselves, both politically and economically, with their white colleagues. They pointed out that a black skin did not guarantee either cultural competence or a more relevant service (cf. Divine, 1 April 1983; Stubbs, 1985).

Many people seemed to regard the employment of black social workers as an opportunity for the few to succeed at the expense of their fellows rather than as a secure route for change in the provision of services to black people. Some even suggested that black social workers were likely to act as more effective agents of social control than white workers. It was thought that black workers (and, in the case study, black co-workers) would not only adopt the standards of their white colleagues but be tougher and more effective at screening out black applicants in order to 'prove' their professionalism to white colleagues.

Increasing the recruitment of black people into the ranks of an organisation which is perceived as an agency of social control in the service of particular 'racial' and class interests was considered, by many, to be a means of actually widening divisions within the black community. Divisions in the white community between social workers and their clients are both replicated and deepened in the black community.

The rejection of black professional authority by other black people helps to maintain the political stranglehold of a 'white' service structure in which black people have historically been denied positions of authority. This is reinforced by black entry into the social work profession justified by appeal to the politics of culture rather than to the politics of power–sharing. Although black visibility may go some way towards improving the image of the Social Services Department as a 'white' organisation, it will not necessarily alter the configurations of power and authority within the structure nor the relevance of service provision to the black community. Visibility is achieved without change to the underlying structural relations of relative power.

'Grass roots' support and consultation with the black community

The third strand to ABSWAP's argument was a recognition of the need for grassroots support and for consultation with 'the black community'. One of its 'Aims and Objectives' was, therefore,

(t)o design and develop communication techniques and procedures which will create avenues for the expression and articulation of the ideas, values and sentiments of the black community as they relate to service delivery, thereby enabling recognition and absorption of social issues as defined by the black community (ABSWAP, 1983b: 1).

268

The campaign for 'racial matching' was 'grassroots' in the sense that it was instigated by a small group of black activists within the social work profession and rapidly gained support among black workers. Although they claimed to represent the interests of the black community as a whole, these interests were professionally defined. The ideas and arguments were imported from America and support among the black population was achieved as a result of a campaign of 'consciousness–raising'. For many, the issue became a symbol for all that was racist not just in social work but in white society in general. It acquired a political significance which extended beyond the boundaries of social work and the issue was taken up by black councillors in many boroughs. The campaign was successful in large part because it claimed the support of black social workers and because, as in the United States a decade earlier, it grew out of the upsurge of 'Black politics' on to the political scene.

The founding of the Association of Black Social Workers and Allied Professions gave black social workers a collective professional base. The aim was to create a black power base within social work agencies which would enable black professionals to interpret and mediate the needs of black clients, in other words, to develop a 'black professionalism'.

Richard Hugman (1991) has identified two competing strands in social work professionalism: specialization and localization. Both have been criticised by radical theorists (e.g. Simpkin, 1979): specialization for following orthodox professionalism; localization for failing to address the ideological subordination of social work to the interests of the state. Both were 'directed... at the level of technical autonomy (and) ...allowed for the continued development of social work within existing structures of control' (Hugman, 1991: 205). ABSWAP attempted to combine both strands through the promotion of culturally specific competencies and local knowledge and networking skills. The approach was, therefore, grounded in essentially orthodox notions of social work 'professionalism'. As Hugman observes, 'both specialization and localization have, in different ways, tended to exclude service users from the process of professional and organizational formation' (*op cit.* 1991: 211).

> While professions are constructed in relation to service users, they are based around an exclusion of the latter in a way which reinforces both the professional self–image as 'competent' and the image of the service user as 'needy'.... Specialization, grounded as it is in a focus on categories of need as an organizing principle ... reinforces the division between professionals and service users. (L)ocalization ... creates 'the local' as an object of social work theory and practice (1991: 211–212).

ABSWAP retained the image of the client as 'needy', although explained in terms of specific 'racial' and cultural needs. The black population was presented as an homogeneous 'moral community' and 'professional' representation of 'community' interests as an uncomplicated and straightforward process. Sources of tension in the professional–client relationship were underplayed. Although the moral obligation of the black professional to the black community was stressed, ABSWAP failed to specify adequately the mechanisms through which accountability was to be achieved.

The creation of a black power base within social work may enhance community esteem within the black communities but does little to guarantee improved service delivery to the bulk of social work's black clientele without an overhaul of the mechanisms for sharing power at the grassroots. The campaign for 'racial matching' in child care was essentially the promotion of a professional and political view of 'the best interests' of the black child and of the black community. The aim was not so much to promote dialogue with the black communities as to raise a Black political consciousness.

Within social work as a whole, the mechanisms for consultation with local communities and service users are poorly developed. Professional self-confidence in their ability to define and assess client needs and a 'seige mentality' developed in response to a long history of public scapegoating have meant that social workers have rarely seen public accountability as a high priority.

The changes in fostering practice discussed in the study seem to have taken place with little, if any, consultation or dialogue with local communities. In the borough of the case study, failure to publicise or to engage in public debate resulted in misunderstandings and suspicions about social workers' motives and a failure to gain the support and confidence of the local population. Workers were afraid of invoking the hostility of the white population and, as a virtually all–white team, were timid about presenting a high profile within the black community. Dilemmas and contradictions inherent in the new approach remained unresolved and opposition was never fully confronted. Lack of public debate also meant a weakening of the policy base in which the new approach was grounded which helps to explain the ease with which new initiatives were discarded in favour of a reversion to previous practice.

The new approach was predicated on the possession of a distinctive ethnic and cultural identity which workers assumed on the part of applicants. In other words, the relevance of culture and ethnicity was defined by the social workers and not by those for whom it was presumed to be relevant. Workers believed that, by adopting a model of cultural diversity, they were 'doing something special for a particularly disadvantaged group' (cf. Stone, 1981: 100 referring to multi–cultural education) and that black people would automatically welcome their efforts. Reactions among those interviewed, however, ranged from tepid endorsement, through ambivalence to open hostility. Although ethnicity may have been the initial organising principle for the recruitment campaign, in the face of applicants' ambivalence and social workers' reluctance to operate a differentiating approach, the pluralist perspective was not sustained.

Moving into the 1990s

By the end of the decade, most local authorities had adopted the principle of 'racial matching' (*File on Four*, Radio Four, 23 April 1991; Johnson, 1991) and many white social workers had come to see 'same race' placement as a concrete and positive means of combatting racism (Jane Aldridge of Children First, speaking on *File on Four*, Radio Four, 23 April 1991; Johnson, 1991). In an area where 'success' is difficult to define, let alone measure, it promised relatively quick, measurable and, most important, visible results. Individual boroughs became swept up in the general climate of change and fear of being branded as a racist muted the potential for opposition (Dale, 1987) and encouraged conformity with policy intentions[11] (Brown, quoted in Toynbee 1986; Dale, 1987: 4; Pearson, 1989: 112)[12]. As Grieco (1989) points out, 'change is a threshold dynamic' which develops its own momentum. As more people are recruited to a cause, more are likely to join, until a point is reached when what was once characterised as dangerous radicalism becomes the new orthodoxy. 'Once the process has begun, the social bases for dissent expand and, eventually, not to dissent from the traditional pattern is the odd or negatively characterised behaviour'.

Changes in public attitudes, however, have not kept pace with the changes in professional thinking. The new policy was developed and implemented as a professional in-house affair with little, if any, consultation with local communities. It was this professional chauvinism which helped to stimulate

---

[11] Jane Aldridge of Children First, for example, reports that,

Social workers have said to me that they wouldn't dare suggest making a transracial placement because they would be thought to be racist if they did so even if they, individually, have thought that it is in the best interests of the child (speaking on *File on Four*, Radio Four, 23 April 1991).

[12] Policy changes, however, do not always reflect concurrent changes in practice. In a recent article, Jeanne Kaniuk observed,

Despite the apparent consensus in social work circles about the importance of recruiting black adopters, this does not seem to be reflected in much current practice. It is not uncommon for black prospective adopters to approach us after having approached three or more agencies from whom they received either no reply; an unhelpful reply, or were left on an interminably long waiting list (Kaniuk, 1991: 40).

271

the backlash in public opinion. Endorsement of the new approach by British Agencies for Adoption and Fostering (BAAF, 1987a,b; Hammond, 1991) gave it official legitimacy within the social work profession but failed to carry the bulk of the white population.

With the re-election of a Conservative government, the demise of the Greater London Council and failure of the bid to establish 'Black Sections' in the Labour Party, the heady 'race relations' climate of the early eighties cooled. There was an upsurge of antagonism to the 'race policies' of the 'loony left' among rightwing politicians and the 'white' mainstream press which took up the causes of various so-called 'victims' of leftwing anti-racist policies[13]. One of the left's main weapons against racism, RAT, has been largely discredited (Gurnah, 1983; Sivanandan, 1985; Jervis, 1986; Alibhai, 1988b; Banton, 1985; Lee, 1987; Owusu-Bempah, 1989; Roberts, 1988) and the absolutist construction of 'black identity' which underpinned many of the arguments of the pro-matching lobby has been superseded in many quarters. A more complex understanding has emerged which recognises 'race' as both shaping and shaped by the many other components which contribute to the construction of a personal identity (Gilroy, 1987a, b). As Paul Gilroy observed, there are many different ways of being 'black' in Britain today. According to Gilroy, ABSWAP's voice was that of

> a black nationalism which, though it may have political pertinence in other social formations, is sadly misplaced in this country where the black population is too small, too diverse and too fragmented to be conceptualised as a single cohesive nation... The theory of 'race' and culture which they espouse... reduces the complexity of self-image and personality formation in the black child to the single issue of 'race'/culture. (1987a: 66)

Opposition to the new policy of 'racial matching' mobilised with the setting up of an opposition group, 'Children First', which drew support from both ends of the political spectrum (Toynbee, 23 June 1986; *The Observer*, 10 September 1989; *Phone Kate Aidie*, Radio Four, 5 Aug.1989). In its very name could be read a re-establishment of the conservative article of faith in the separation of politics from child care. The conflict between lay and professional thinking was played out in a series of court cases, which received hostile front page coverage in the press, in which the white foster parents of 'mixed race' children were refused permission to adopt (Johnson, 1991; Hadfield, 1989a,b; Ferriman, 1989; Mills, 1989; Birrell, 1990; Fenton, 1989.

---

[13] The cases of Ray Honeyford and Maureen McGoldrick were two of the most prominent examples (Gabriel, 1989).

These decisions prompted at least one commentator to suggest that social workers have naïvely followed 'whatever theory is fashionable at the time' (Black, 1990). Dora Black dismisses the promotion of same race placement as 'a political ideology' which lacks 'scientific evidence'. 'One cannot help thinking', she suggests patronisingly,

> that the adverse experiences in care of a few articulate and vociferous black people (the Association of Black Social Workers and Allied Professions, 1983) have influenced unduly those who have perhaps lacked the training to consider the *scientific* evidence dispassionately and apply these findings in each case with compassion, discretion and judgement (*op cit.* 1990: 45).

Her condemnation of the arguments for matching:

> The research evidence is either flimsy or entirely lacking for the presence of 'institutionalised racism' in British Society, for the inability of white parents to help equip a black child to deal with racism, and for the extent and permanence of the damage to such children (*op cit.* 44)

however, is somewhat belated (Johnson, 1991). Although the press chose to focus on the 'racial' aspect of the cases, the point at issue was not so much the desirability or otherwise of 'racial matching' as whether or not these could be considered to outweigh the damage of severing bonds formed in an existing transracial placement. The controversy drew ministerial intervention and, in September 1989, David Mellor, the then Minister for Health, threatened to withdraw BAAF's (British Agencies for Adoption and Fostering) funding (Gaffaney, 1989) and declared, 'Love knows no racial barriers nor should seek to erect any' (Mellor, quoted in Mills, 1989).

Recognition of the importance of racial, cultural and linguistic factors in the placement of children, however, had already gained official ratification in the 1989 Children Act (Section 22 (5)):

> For the first time in child legislation, the local authorities will be under duty to consider not only religion, which has been part of child care law for many years, but three other important factors – a child's racial origin and ethnic and linguistic background (Ahmed, 1991).

This was reinforced in policy guidelines issued in a Circular from the Department of Health (Utting, 1990: 3 para.9). Although the primacy of 'race' is explicitly denied:

None of the separate factors involved should be abstracted and converted into a general pre-condition which overrides the others (*op cit.* para.9),

and the option of transracial placement is specifically left open:

There may be circumstances in which placement with a family of different ethnic origin is the best choice for a particular child. In other cases such a placement may be the best available choice (*op cit.* para.3),

the letter makes clear that,

in the great majority of cases, placement with a family of similar ethnic origin and religion is most likely to meet a child's needs (*op cit.* 3 para.9).

Ten years on, the controversy is as fierce as ever: Virginia Bottomly, the current Minister for Health, speaking on Radio Four, was recently described as 'trying to hold the ring between the battling dogmatists' (Paul Barker, *File on Four*, Radio Four 23 April 1991). The issue of contention, however, is no longer the principle of same race placement for black children but the viability of transracial placement as an alternative. In many agencies, black children are now routinely placed in black families: the legitimacy of same race placement for black children is no longer in question.

Appendix 1
Postal questionnaire to the London boroughs

THE FOSTERING AND ADOPTION OF BLACK AND MINORITY ETHNIC GROUP CHILDREN

Questionnaire to Principal Fostering Officers

1. Please give a brief outline of the way in which fostering and adoption services are organised in your borough

2. Does your department have an official policy or practice guidelines in relation to the placement of black and minority ethnic group children in substitute family care?

Yes		1
No		2

If yes would you send me a copy, please.

3. If no, do you have any unofficial policy or guidelines which people try to follow?

Yes	1
No	2

If yes, could you give brief details, please.

4. To what extent has policy in this area changed in your department in recent years?

A great deal		1
Quite a lot		2
A little		3
Not very much		4
Not at all		5

5. To what extent has practice in this area changed in your department in recent years?

A great deal		1
Quite a lot		2
A little		3
Not very much		4
Not at all		5

6. What have been the main changes?

a.

b.

c.

d.

276

7. Has your department been under pressure to change its policy?

Yes		1
No		2

If so, what have the main sources of pressure been?

a.

b.

c.

d.

8. If policy has changed, would you say that it was a political decision?

Yes		1
No		2
Don't know		3

What are the reasons for thinking this?

a.

b.

c.

d.

9. How closely do you think policy (official and unofficial) in this area is followed in practice in your department

Not at all		1
Not very closely		2
Quite closely		3
Very closely		4

10. What, in your opinion, have been the main difficulties in putting the new policies and ideas in this area into practice?

   a.

   b.

   c.

   d.

11. Does your department record the numbers of black and minority ethnic group children received into care in your borough?

Yes		1
No		2

12. Does your council have an ETHNIC MONITORING POLICY? For example, are records kept of the numbers of black and minority ethnic group people employed by the council?

Yes		1
No		2
Don't know		3

13. Does your council have an EQUAL OPPORTUNITIES POLICY?

Yes		1
No		2
Don't know		3

14. Are there any black or Asian councillors who are members of the borough council?

Yes		1
No		2
Don't know		3

15. Are any black or minority ethnic group workers employed in the Fostering and Adoption Section?

Yes		1
No		2
Don't know		3

Please give their job titles or job description.

a.

b

c.

d.

16. Have any members of the Fostering and Adoption Section attended training courses on racial and cultural issues within the last two years?

Yes		1
No		2
Don't know		3

Are there any plans for sending people on race awareness or race training courses in the future?

Yes		1
No		2
Don't know		3

17. Has there been any specific effort within your department to recruit black and minority ethnic group foster and adoptive parents?

Yes		1
No		2
Don't know		3

If yes, what were the methods used?

a.

b.

c.

d.

What were the main difficulties and problems encountered?

a.

b.

c.

d.

18. Do you wish to make any further comments or mention other important issues which have not been covered by the questionnaire?

Thank you for your help and co-operation.

Appendix 2
Organisations consulted during the study

Organisations consulted prior to commencement of the fieldwork

British Agencies for Adoption and Fostering
National Foster Care Association
London Boroughs Regional Children's Planning Committee
National Children's Bureau
Dr. Barnardo's
National Children's Home
Parent to Parent Information and Adoption Service
Parents for Children
New Black Families Unit
Greater London Council Ethnic Minorities Committee
Commission for Racial Equality

Visits were also made to fostering and adoption teams in a number of London boroughs.

Exploratory interviews and discussions were conducted with black foster parents and white foster and adoptive parents who were caring for black children. These were contacted via: the NFCA, PPIAS and the Fostering and Adoption Section of one London borough.

281

Bibliography

ABAFA (1977), Association of British Agencies for Fostering and Adoption, *Soul Kids Campaign. Report of Steering Group*, London, ABAFA.

Abercrombie, N., Hill, S. & Turner, B. (1988), *The Penguin Dictionary of Sociology*, Second Edition, Harmondsworth, Penguin Books.

ABSWAP (1983a), Association of Black Social Workers and Allied Professions, *Black Children in Care, Evidence to the House of Commons Social Services Committee*, London, ABSWAP.

ABSWAP (1983b), Association of Black Social Workers and Allied Professions, *Give the Black Child a Chance*, First national conference on black children in care, Friends Meeting House, London, 15 Nov.1983.

ABSWAP (1982), Association of Black Social Workers and Allied Professions, *Constitution of ABSWAP*, ABSWAP, Dec..

Adams, N. (1981), *Black Children in Care*, Lambeth Social Sevices Department, Research Section.

ADSS/CRE (1978), Association of Directors of Social Services and Commission for Racial Equality, *Multi–Racial Britain: The Social Sersvices Response*, London, Commission for Racial Equality.

ADSS/CRE (1983), Association of Directors of Social Services and Commission for Racial Equality, *Multi–Racial Britain: The Social Services Response*, London, Commission for Racial Eqality.

Agar, M. H. (1980), *The Professional Stranger: An Informal Introduction to Ethnography*, New York, Academic Press Inc..

Ahmad, B. (1988), 'The development of social work practice and policies on race', *Social Work Today* 19,19:9.

Ahmed, S.(1980) `Selling Fostering to the Black Community', *Community Care*, 6 March 1980, pp.20–22.

Ahmed, S. (1981a), `Children in care: the racial dimension in social work assessment', in Cheetham, J. *et al.* (eds.), *Community Work in a Multi-Racial Society: A Reader*, London, Harper & Row.

Ahmed, S. (1981b), `Asian girls and culture conflict', in Cheetham, J. *et al.* (eds.), *Community Work in a Multi-Racial Society: A Reader*, London, Harper & Row.

Ahmed, S. (1982) `Some approaches to recruitment and in-service training for multi-racial social work' in Cheetham, J. (ed.), *Social Work and Ethnicity*, London, George Allen and Unwin, pp.197–207.

Ahmed, S. (1988), `Defining and assessing black families' in Family Rights Group *Planning for Children*, London, F.R.G..

Ahmed, S. (1991), 'Routing out racism', *Community Care*, 869:17–19, 27.

Ahmed, S., CHEETHAM, J. and SMALL, J. (eds.) (1986), *Social Work with Black Children and their Families*, London, Batsford Ltd. in association with British Agencies for Adoption and Fostering.

Alibhai, Y. (1988a), `White mums, black kids', *New Society*, 8 Jan..

Alibhai, Y. (1988b), `The reality of race training', *New Society*, 21 Jan. pp.17–19.

Archer, M.S. (1985), `The myth of cultural integration', *British Journal of Sociology*, 36,3:333–353.

Ardener, E. (1975), `Belief and the Problem of Women' in Ardener, S. (ed.) *Perceiving Women*, Letchworth, Aldine, J.M.Dent & Sons Ltd..

Ardener, S. (1978), *Defining Females: the Nature of Women in Society*, Croom Helm.

Arnold, E.(1982), `Finding Black Families for Black Children in Britain' in Cheetham, J. (ed.), *Social Work and Ethnicity*, London, George Allen and Unwin, pp.98–111.

Arnold, E. & JAMES, M. (1989), `Finding black families for black children in care: a case study', *New Community*, 15,3:417–425, April.

Atkin, K. & Rollings, J. (1991), *Informal Care and Black Communities: A Literature Review*, London, DHSS.

BAAF (1987a), British Agencies for Adoption and Fostering, *The Placement of Black Children. Practice Note 13 Sept.*.

BAAF (1987b), British Association of Social Workers, `Guidelines for the placement of black children', *Social Work Today*, 14 Dec..

Bachrach, P. & Baratz, M. (1970), *Power and Poverty*, Oxford University Press.

Bagley, C. & Young, L. (1979), 'The Identity, Adjustment and Achievement of Transracially Adopted Children: A Review and Empirical Report' in Verma, G.K. & Bagley, C. (eds.), *Race, Identity and Education*, Macmillan Press, Chap.12 pp.192–219.

Bagley, C. & Young, L. (1982), 'Policy dilemmas and the adoption of black children' in CHEETHAM, J. (ed.), *Social Work and Ethnicity*, London, George Allen & Unwin, pp.83–97.

Ballard, C. (1979), 'Conflict, Continuity and Change. Second Generation South Asians', in V.S. Khan (ed.), *Minority Families in Britain*, London, Macmillan.

Ballard, R. (1979), 'Ethnic Minorities and the Social Services. What type of service?' in Sulaifah Khan (ed.), *Minority Families in Britain*, London, Macmillan Press.

Ballard, R. & Ballard, C. (1977), 'The Sikhs: the development of South Asian settlements in Britain' in Watson J.L. (ed.), *Between two cultures: migrants and minorities in Britain*, Oxford, Blackwell.

Banton, M. (1985), 'RAT: back to the drawing board', *New Community*, 12,2:295, Summer.

Banton, M. (1987), 'The battle of the name', *New Community*, 14,1/2:170–5.

Barker, M. (1981), *The New Racism*, London, Junction Books.

Barrett, M. & McIntosh, M. (1982), *The Anti-Social Family*, London, Verso Editions/NLB.

BASW (1982) British Association of Social Workers, *Social Work in Multi-Cultural Britain: Guidelines for Preparation and Practice*, Birmingham, B.A.S.W. Dec..

Beattie, J. (1964), *Other Cultures*, London, Routledge & Kegan Paul.

Bebbington, A. & Miles, J. (1990), 'The Supply of Foster Families for Children in Care', *British Journal of Social Work*, 20:283–307.

Becker, H. (1963), *Outsiders*, New York, Free Press.

Ben-Tovim, G. & Gabriel, J. (1979), 'The Politics of Race in Britain 1962 –79', *Sage Race Relations Abstracts*, 4,4:1–56. Reprinted in Husband, C. (ed.) (1982), *'Race' in Britain*, London, Hutchinson.

Ben-Tovim, G. & Gabriel, J. , Law, I. & Stredder, K. (1986), *The Local Politics of Race*, Basingstoke, Macmillan.

Benyon, J. (1984), 'The riots, Lord Scarman and the political agenda' in Benyon, J. (ed.) (1984), *Essays reflecting on Lord Scarman's Report, the riots and their aftermath*, Oxford, Pergamon Press, pp.3–9.

Berger, B. & Berger, P. (1984), *The War Over the Family, Capturing the Middle Ground*, Harmondsworth, Penguin Books.

Berger, P.L. & Luckmann, T. (1972), *The Social Construction of Reality: A Treatise in the Sociology of Knowledge*, Harmondsworth, Penguin Books.

Berk, S.F.(1980), *Women and Household Labour*, London, Sage Books.

Berliner, W. (1981), `Schools and parents at root of West Indians' failure', *The Guardian*, 18 June, p.3.

Bernard, J. (1987), `White diplomacy is at the heart of racism', *Social Work Today*, 2 Feb. pp.10–11.

Biehal, N. & Sainsbury, E. (1991), 'From Values of Rights in Social Work. Some issues in practice development and research' *British Journal of Social Work* 21:245–257.

Bhatia, S. (1983), `Happy family', *The Observer*, 25 Sept..

Billingsley, A. & Giovannoni, J.M. (1972), *Children of the Storm – Black Children and American Child Welfare*, Harcourt Brace Jovanovich inc.USA.

Birrell, I. (1990), `Minister orders inquiry on `mixed race' adoption', *The Sunday Times*, 18 Mar..

Black, D. (1990) 'What do children need from parents', *Adoption and Fostering* 14,1:43–51.

Black and In Care Steering Group (1986), *Black and in Care: conference report*, London, Black and In Care Steering Group, National Association for Young People in Care (NAYPIC).

Blom–Cooper, L. (1986), *A Child in Trust. The Report of the Panel of Inquiry into the Circumstances Surrounding the Death of Jasmine Beckford 1985*, London Borough of Brent, Kingswood Press.

Bloor, M. (1983), `Notes on member validation' in Emerson, R.M. (ed.), *Contemporary Field Research: A Collection of Readings*, Boston, Little, Brown, pp.156–172.

Blunden, G. (1988), `Becoming a single foster parent' *Adoption and Fostering* 12:44–7.

Blythe, E. & Milner, J. (1987), `Reaching potential', *Social Services Insight*, 14 Aug. pp.20–21.

Boateng, J. (1989), `Black families offer pride and identity', *The Independent*, 28 Oct..

Bowker, G. (1968), *Education of Coloured Immigrants*, London, Longman's Sociology of Education.

Brewer, J.D. (1984), `Competing understandings of common sense understanding: a brief comment on `common sense racism", *British Journal of Sociology*, Mar. pp.66–73.

BSA (1990), British Sociology Association, *Anti–Racist Language: Guidance for Good Practice*, London, BSA.

Brown, B. (1984), `Policy placed above needs?', *Social Work Today*, 12 Nov. p.11.

Brown, B. (1986), `Educating the Whites', *Foster Care*, 21 July, p.6.

Brummer, N. (1988), `White Social workers: Black Children – Issues of Identitiy' in Aldgate, J. & Simmonds, J. (eds.), *Direct Work with Children*, Chap.6.

Brunton, L. & Welch, M. (1983), `White agency, Black Community', *Adoption and Fostering*, 7,2:16-18.

Bulmer, M. (1982), *The Uses of Sociological Research*, London, Allen & Unwin.

Burgess, R.G. (1984), *In the Field. An Introduction to Field Research*, London, George Allen & Unwin (Publishers) Ltd..

Burgoyne, J. (1987), `Material happiness. Are the joys of family life largely reserved for the better off?', *New Society*, 80,1267:12-14, 10 April.

Burgoyne, J. & Clark, D. (1984), *Making a go of it: a study of step families in Sheffield*, London, Routledge & Kegan Paul.

Burrell, G. & Morgan, G. (1979), *Sociological paradigms and organisational analysis*, Aldershot, Gower.

Cabral, A.. (1973), *Return to the Source. Selected speeches by Amilcar Cabral edited by the African Information Service Monthly Review Press*, London, with A.I.S.

Cain, H. & Yuval-Davies, N. (1990), 'The 'Equal Opportunities Community' and the anti-racist struggle', *Critical Social Policy*, Issue 29 10,2:5-26.

Campbell, B. (1988), *Unofficial Secrets*, London, Virago.

Carby, H.V. (1982), 'Schooling in Babylon' in Centre for Contemporary Cultural Studies, *The Empire Strikes Back. Race and racism in 70s Britain*, London, Hutchinson in association with Centre for Contemporary Cultural Studies, University of Birmingham.

Caribbean Times, (1983), `ABSWAP is launched: Agents for change: Agents for liberation', 8 April 1983.

Caribbean Times, (1983), `To be Black or black?', letter to *The Caribbean Times*, 13 May p.8.

Caribbean Times, (1984), `The `Sun's' massive crime rate', 25 Feb.. p.8.

Carnall, C. & King, L. (1983), `Acknowledging racism, what it is and how it operates', *Harmony Newsletter*, 41:2-3 Spring.

Carroll, J. (1980), `Using Groups', *Adoption and Fostering*, 101,3:20-24.

Cashmore, E. (1988), *Dictionary of Race and Ethnic Relations*, Second Edition, London, Routledge.

Cate Shcaeffer, N. (1980), `Evaluating Race-of-Interviewer Effects in a National Survey', *Sociological Methods and Research*, 8,4:400-419, May.

Cavendish, R. (1982), *Women on the Line*, London, Routledge & Kegan Paul.

Chakrabarti, M. (1991), 'Anti-racist perspectives in social work' in A. Bowes & D. Sim (eds.) *Demands and Constraints: ethnic minorities and social services in Scotland*, Edinburgh, Scottish Council for Voluntary Organisations.

Chambers, H. (1989), `Vital need to treat each child independently `, *The Independent*, 28 Oct..

Channel Four (1985), *Black on Black*, 25 Feb..

Channel Four (1986), *The Anti-Racist Tendency. Diverse Reports*, 16 July.

Channel Four (1991), *The Black Bag*, 9 April.

Cheetham, J. (1972), *Social Work with Immigrants*, London: Routledge & Kegan Paul.

Cheetham, J. (1981a), `Open your eyes to strength', *Community Care*, 24 Dec..

Cheetham, J (1981b), *Social Work for Ethnic Minorities in Britain and the U.S.A.*, London, Department of Health and Social Security, Dec..

Cheetham, J. (ed.) (1982a), *Social Work and Ethnicity*, London, George Allen & Unwin, pp.83–97.

Cheetham, J. (1982b), `Positive discrimination in social work: negotiating the opposition', *New Community*, 10,1:27–37, summer.

Cheetham, J. (1987), `Colour Blindness', *New Society*, 26 June, pp.10–12.

Chestang, L. (1972), 'The dilemma of biracial adoption', *Social Work* 17,3:100–105.

Children First (1986), Account of launch by TOYNBEE, P., *The Guardian*, 23 June.

Chimezie, A. (1975), 'Transracial Adoption of Black Children', *Social Work*, 20,4:296–301, July.

Chimezie, A. (1976), 'Black identity and the Grow and Shapiro study on transracial adoption', *Journal of Afro-American Issues*, 4,1:139–152 Winter.

Chimezie, A. (1977), `Bold but irrelevant: Grow and Shapiro on transracial adoption', *Child Welfare*, 56,2:75–86.

Cicourel, A.V. (1964), *Method and Measurement in Sociology*, New York, Free Press.

Committee of Inquiry into the Education of Children from Ethnic Minority Groups (1981), *West Indian children our schools – Interim Report of the Committee of Inquiry into the Education of Children from Ethnic Minority Groups*, Cmmd. 8273, HMSO.

Community Care, (1989), `Transracial adoption: campaign slams blanket bans' 10 July, p.3.

Community Care, (1989), `Continuous agitation: Josie Durrant, former Assistant Director in Lambeth talks to Tim Lunn about the black experience of social services and the road ahead for equal opportunities' 13 July, pp.22–5.

Community Care, (1989), `Racism and adoption' 7 Aug., p.8.

Community Care, (1989), `Minister acts as race rages over foster baby', 31 Aug., p.4.

Community Care, (1989), `Crisis of identity' 7 Sept., p.5.

Community Care, (1989), `Tug of war over mixed race baby' 21 Sept, p.12.

Community Care, (1989), `Natural to place like with like' 28 Sept., p.10.

Community Care, (1989), `The costs of transracial adoption' 26 Oct..

Connelly, N. (1981), *Social Services Provision in Multi-Racial Areas*, London, Policy Studies Institute.

Connelly, N. (1989), *Race and Change in Social Services Departments*, London, Policy Studies Institute.

Cornwell, J. (1984), *Hard Earned Lives: Accounts of Health and Illness from East London*, London, Tavistock Publications.

Corrigan, P. & Leonard, P. (1978/1981), *Social Work Practice Under Capitalism*, Basingstoke, Macmillan Press Ltd..

C.R.E. (1981), Commission for Racial Equality, *Code of Practice for the Elimination of Racial Discrimination and the Promotion of Equal Opportunities in Employment*, London, C.R.E..

C.R.E. (1983), Commission for Racial Equality, *Children in Care. Submission to the House of Commons Social Services Select Committee Inquiry into Children in Care*, London, C.R.E., May.

C.R.E. (1990), Commission for Racial Equality, *Adopting a better policy: adoption and fostering of ethnic minority children*, London, C.R.E..

Daily Mail (1984), `Black, white – and happy: the foster mother and the super star who disprove the left's latest theory on race', 25 Feb..

Daily Star (1984), "If we really believe in equality, let's treat everyone as equals", 17 April.

Dale, D. (1987), *Denying Homes to Black Children: Britain's new race adoption policies*, London, The Social Affairs Unit.

Dando, I. & Minty, B. (1987), `What Makes Good Foster Parents?', *British Journal of Social Work*, 17,4:383–401, Aug..

David, M. (1986), `Morality and maternity: towards a better union than the moral right's family policy', *Critical Social Policy*, 16:40–56, Summer.

Davis, S., Morris, B., Thorn, J. (1984), `Task centred assessment for foster parents', *Adoption and Fostering*, 8,4:33–37.

Day, D. (1979), *The Adoption of Black Children: Counteracting Institutional Discrimination*, D.C.Heath, Lexington Books.

de H. Lobo, E. & National Children's Bureau (1978), *Children of Immigrants to Britain, Their Health and Social Problems*, London, Hodder & Stroughton.

Denney, D. (1983), `Some Dominant Perspectives in the Literature Relating to Multi-Racial Social Work', *British Journal of Social Work*, 13:149–174.

Dennison, A. (1987), `Men can play an active caring role', *Foster Care*, Mar., p.9.

Denzin, N.K. (1968), `On the ethics of disguised observation', *Social Problems*, 15,4:502–4.

Denzin, N.K. (1970), *The Research Act in Sociology*, London, Butterworth.

288

Department of the Environment (1983), *Local Authorities and Racial Disadvantage*, Report of a Joint Government/Local Authority Association Working Group, London, D.O.E..

Dex, S. (1983), `The second generation: West Indian female school leavers' in Phizacklea, A. (ed.), *One Way Ticket: Migration and female labour*, London, Routledge & Kegan Paul.

Divine, D. (1982), `Procedures on Fostering and Adoption – Who can do it?', *The Caribbean Times*, 22 Oct..

Divine, D. (1982), `Like or lump it', *The Caribbean Times*, 26 Nov..

Divine, D. (1982), `If you can, get involved', *The Caribbean Times*, 3 Dec..

Divine, D. (1982), 'The Black community must become more involved', *The Caribbean Times*, 10 Dec..

Divine, D. (1983), `Setting the scene', *The Caribbean Times*, 7 Jan.1982.

Divine, D. (1983), `The time has come', *The Caribbean Times*, 14 Jan..

Divine, D. (1983), `Shades of Black', *The Caribbean Times*, 11 Feb.1983.

Divine, D. (1983), `Coming out of the shadows', *The Caribbean Times*, 18 Feb..

Divine, D. (1983), `No problems', *The Caribbean Times*, 25 Feb..

Divine, D. (1983),'Defective, hypocritical and patronising research', *The Caribbean Times*, 4 Mar..

Divine, D. (1983), `Scandal of black children in care', *The Caribbean Times*, 11 Mar..

Divine, D. (1983), `Time for decision', *The Caribbean Times*, 18 Mar.1983.

Divine, D. (1983), `Black children in care – positive action needed', *The Caribbean Times*, 25 Mar..

Divine, D. (1983), `The black professional', *The Caribbean Times*, 1 April.

Divine, D. (1983), `A.B.S.W.A.P. is launched', *The Caribbean Times*, 8 April.

Divine, D. (1983), `Spinning the African web', *The Caribbean Times*, 20 May.

Divine, D. (1983), `Forging links with black American social workers', *The Caribbean Times*, 6 June.

Divine, D. (1983), `Putting the record straight', *The Caribbean Times*, 24 June.

Divine, D. (1983), `Beyond pathology', *The Caribbean Times*, 1 July.

Divine, D. (1983), `Strengths of black families', *The Caribbean Times*, 15 July.

Divine, D. (1983), `Melting pot or salad bowl?', *The Caribbean Times*, 29 July.

Divine, D. (1983), `Black families for black children', *The Caribbean Times*, 26 Aug..

Divine, D. (1983), `A.B.S.W.A.P.'s progress', *The Caribbean Times*, 2 Sept..

Divine, D. (1983), `We speak for ourselves', *The Caribbean Times*, 19 Sept. pp.3 & 8.

Divine, D. (1984), *Black children and Britain's welfare state – normalised repression*, talk given to City University Afro–Caribbean Society, London, 8 Mar..

Divine, D. (1988), `Social services must share know-how on ethnic needs', Report of speech by David Divine to the `Race and Social Services' Conference, London, May. *Community Care*, 26 May.

Dominelli, L. (1979), 'The Challenge to Social Work Education' *Social Work Today*, 10,25:27-29.

Dominelli, L. (1988), *Anti-Racist Social Work. A Challenge for White Practitioners and Educators*, London, British Association of Social Workers, Macmillan Education Ltd..

Dominelli, L. (1989), `An uncaring profession? An examination of racism in social work', *New Community*, 15,3:391-403.

Donovan, J. (1986), *We don't buy sickness, it just comes: health, illness and health care in the lives of black people in London*, Aldershot, Gower.

Douglas, J.D. (1971), *American Social Order: Social rules in a pluralistic society*, New York, Free Press.

Dowling, M. (1989), *Field observation in a social services team. Becoming a participant-observer - the process*, paper given at the British Sociological Association Annual Conference, Plymouth.

Dummett, M. & Dummett, A. (1982), `The Role of Government in Britain's Racial Crisis', in Husband, C. (ed.), *Race in Britain: continuity and change*, London, Hutchinson.

Earls *et al.* (1980a), `Behavioural problems in pre-school children of West Indian born parents: a re-examination of family and social factors', *Journal of Child Psychology and Psychiatry*, 21:107-117.

Earls *et al.* (1980b), `The prevalence of behavioural problems in three year old children of West Indian born parents', *Journal of Child Psychology and Psychiatry*, 20:96-121.

Ellis, K. (1981), `Can the Left Defend a Fantasized Family?', *In These Times*, 9 Dec. p.17.

Ely, P. & Denney, D. (1987), *Social Work in a Multi-Racial Society*, Aldershot, Gower.

Erikson, E.H. (1968), *Identity, Youth and Crisis*, New York, Norton, Faber.

Erikson, K.T. (1967), `A comment on disguised observation in sociology', *Social Problems*, 14,4:366-73.

Erikson, K.T. (1968), `On the ethics of disguised observation: a reply to Denzin', *Social Problems*, 14,4:505-6.

Etzioni, E. (1961), *A comparative analysis of complex organisations*, Glencoe, Illinois, Free Press.

Evers, H., Badger, F., Cameron, E. & Atkin, K. (1989), *Community Care Project Working Papers*, Birmingham: Department of Social Medicine, University of Birmingham.

Fenton, B. (1989), `Mixed-race child's parents may take case to Lords', *The Daily Telegraph*, 28 Aug..

290

Ferriman, A. (1989), `Racial policy puts future of `happy' child in jeopardy', *The Observer*, 3 Sept. p.4.

Fitzgerald, J. (1981) `Black parents for black children', *Adoption and Fostering*, 5,1:10–11.

Fitzherbert, K. (1967), *West Indian Children in London*, London, Bell.

Fitzherbert, K. (1984), ''Rallying cry' of racial limbo' *Social Work Today* 10 Jan.p.22

Fletcher, D. (1989), `White foster mother fights council over adopting black child', *The Daily Telegraph*, 4 Sept..

Fletchman–Smith, B. (1984), `Effects of Race on Adoption and Fostering', *International Journal of Social Psychiatry*, 30:121–128.

Flett, H. (1979), `Bureaucracy and Ethnicity – Notions of eligibility to public housing' in Wallman, S. (ed.), *Ethnicity at Work*, Basingstoke, Macmillan Press Ltd..

Foster Care, (1983), Letter to *Foster Care*, No.33, March.

Foster Care, (1985a), `Letters about transracial fostering and adoption' Jan., p.6.

Foster Care, (1985b), `Council policies on ethnic minority placements', Jan. p.10.

Foster Care, (1986a), `NFC calls for more realistic fostering allowances' Jan., p.5.

Foster Care, (1986b), `Foster parents deserve a better deal' Mar., p.4

Foster Care, (1986c), `Fashionable doctrine', Sept., p.4.

Foster Carter, O. (1986), `Insiders, Outsiders and Anomalies; A Review of Studies of Identity', *New Community*, 13,2:224–234.

Friedan, B. (1982), *The Second Stage*, London, Joseph.

Gabriel, J. (1989) 'Developing Anti–Racist Strategies' in Alock, P., Gamble, A., Gough, I., Lee, P., Walker, A. (eds.) *The Social Economy and the Democratic State: A new policy agenda for the 1990s*, London, Laurence and Wishart.

Gaffaney, P. (1989), `Minister acts as race row rages over foster baby', *Community Care*, 24 Aug. p.7.

Galtung, J. (1967), *Theory and Methods of Social Research*, London, Allen & Unwin.

Gayes, M. (1975/6), `Soul Kids', *Child Adoption*, 81,3:7–8; 82,4:19–20; 85:3,17–20.

George, V. (1970), *Foster Care: Theory and Practice*, London, Routledge & Kegan Paul.

Gibson, A. (1986), *The Unequal Struggle*, London, Centre for Caribbean Studies.

Gibson, A. (1979/80), *Social Services: A Bane to the West Indian Community*, London, West Indian Concern.

291

Gill, O. and Jackson. B., (1983), *Adoption & Race: Black, Asian and Mixed Race Children in White Families*, London, Batsford/British Agencies for Adoption and Fostering.

Gillis, J. (1986), `Weddings great and small', *New Society*, 18 July, pp.9–11.

Gilroy, P. (1987a), *There ain't no black in the Union Jack: the cultural politics of `race' and nation*, London, Hutchinson Education.

Gilroy, P. (1987b), *Problems in Anti–Racist Strategy*, London, Runnymede Trust.

Glaser, B.G. & Strauss, A.L. (1967), *The Discovery of Grounded Theory: strategies for qualitative research*, London, Weidenfeld & Nicolson.

Goffman, E. (1959), *The Presentation of Self in Everyday Life*, Garden City, New York, Doubleday & Co..

Gold, R.L. (1969), `Roles in Sociological Field Observation', *Social Forces*, 36,3:217–23.

Graham, H. (1983), `Do Her Answers Fit His Questions? Women and the Survey Method' in Gamarnikow, E. *et al.* (eds.), *The Public and the Private*, London, Heinemann, British Sociological Assoc., Chap.11 pp.132–146.

Grieco, M. (1989), *Organisational culture and organisational transformation: proximity, practices and laconic communication*, Paper presented to EGOS meeting on Organisational Transformation, Berlin.

Grow, L.J. & Shapiro, D. (1974), *Black children – white parents: a study of transracial adoption*, New York, Child Welfare League of America.

Grow, L.J. & Shapiro, D. (1975a), `Adoption of black children by white parents', Child Welfare, 54:57–59, Jan..

Grow, L.J. & Shapiro, D. (1975b), `Transracial adoption today: views of adoptive parents and social workers', New York, Child Welfare League of America.

Grow, L.J. & Shapiro, D. (1977), `Not so bold and not so irrelevant: a reply to Chimezie', *Child Welfare*, 56,2:86–91.

The Guardian (1983), `Mixed fortunes at home', Letters to *The Guardian*, 1 Feb.. in response to Anne Shearer's article of 29 Jan..

The Guardian (1983). `Step on the road to black couples adopting white children', 31 Jan..

The Guardian (1983), `Frauds alleged over race harmony grants', *The Guardian* 1 Feb.

The Guardian (1985), `How children became unequal partners', 24 Feb.

The Guardian (1986), `Our policy starts with the family. Report of the Conservative Women's Conference', 6 June.

The Guardian (1986), `They're all in the family', Editorial, 6 June.

The Guardian (1987), `Black candidates strive to diffuse labour row' 14 April.

The Guardian (1987), `Hattersley calls for end to Black Sections martyrdom', 1 May.

The Guardian (1987), 'Suspending Sharon', 1 May.
The Guardian (1987), `Short gives assurance on Black Sections', 5 May.
The Guardian (1987), `Concern at race curb on adoption', 11 May.
The Guardian (1987), `Public ceasefire over Black Sections' 3 June.
The Guardian (1988), `Don't rubbish anti–racism', 3 May.
Gurnah, A. (1983), `The politics of racial awareness training', *Critical Social Policy*, 11:6–20 Winter.
Hadfield, G. (1989a), `Suffer the little children. Youngsters are the losers as dodgmatists argue over same–race adoptions', *The Sunday Times*, 10 Sept..
Hadfield, G. (1989b), `Baby in a legal battle; `race not the only issue", *The Independent*, 22 Sept..
Hammersley, M. & Atkinson, P. (1983), *Ethnography: Principles in Practice*, London, Tavistock.
Hammond, C. (1990), `BAAF and the placement needs of children from minority ethnic groups', *Adoption and Fostering*, 14,1:52–3.
Harbridge, E. (1981), `Wanted: black families for black children', *Community Care*, 8 Oct. pp.21–22.
Hardy, J. *et al.* (1986), `Professional fostering: handicapped children' *Adoption and Fostering*, 10,2:19–21.
Harmony (1983), *Harmony Newsletter* 43 Autumn.
Harmony (1983), *Harmony Newsletter* 41 Spring.
Harris, V. (1987), `Changing Minds', *Social Services Insight*, 17 July, pp.18–19.
Hart, N. (1986), 'Lewisham's child care policy', *Adoption and Fostering* 10,1:26–29.
Henwood, M., Rimmer, L. & Wicks, M. (1987), *Inside the Family: changing role of men and women*, London, Family Policy Studies Centre, Occasional Paper, F.P.S.C., Oct..
Heywood, S. (1990), `Putting same race placement policy into practice', *Adoption and Fostering*, 14,2:9–10.
Hillman, J. (1986), `Was permanency ever more than a passing fad?', *Social Work Today*, 23 June.
Hilton, J. (1984), `Apartheid or multiculture?', *Foster Care*, Oct., pp.14–15.
Hodgkinson, L. (1985), `The black and white of fostering', *The Times*, 28 Aug..
Holman, R. (1968), `Immigrants and Child Care Policy', *Case Conference*, 15:7,255.
Holman, R. (1975), `Exclusive and Inclusive Concepts of Fostering', *British Journal of Social Work*, 5,1:69–84.
Holman, R. (1978), `A class analysis of adoption reveals a disturbing picture', *Community Care*, 26 Apr., p.13.
Holman, R. (1984), `Partners in care', *Social Work Today*, 12 Nov. p11.

Holmes, L. & Grieco, M. (1988), *Radical beginnings, conventional ends?: dilemmas and difficulties in the development of radical organisations*, Paper presented to Conference on the Managerial Labour Process, European Institute of Advanced Management Studies, Brussels, May.

Home Affairs Committee (1981), *Fifth Report 1980-81, 'Racial Disadvantage'*, House of Commons, 46-1, HMSO.

Honeyford, R. (1984), 'Education and race – an alternative view', *Salisbury Review*, winter.

Hood, C., Oppe, T.E., Pless, I.B., Apte, P. (1970), *Children of West Indian Immigrants. A study of one-year-olds in Paddington*, London, Institute of Race Relations.

House of Commons Social Services Committee (1983,84), *Children in Care*, London, H.M.S.O..

Howard, M. (1987), 'Politics and the Family', *Social Services Insight*, 5 June.

Howe, S. & Upshal, D. (1988), 'New Black Power Lines', *New Statesman and Society*, 15 July.

Hugman, R. (1987), 'The Private and the Public in Personal Models of Social Work: A Response to O'Connor and Dalgleish', *British Journal of Social Work*, 17:71-76.

Hugman, R. (1991), 'Organization and Professionalism: The Social Work Agenda in the 1990s', *British Journal of Social Work*, 21:199-216.

Humphries, J. (1977), 'The Working Class Family, Women's Liberation and Class Struggle: The Case of Nineteenth Century British History', *The Raiv of Radical Political Economics*, 9:25-41.

Hyman, H.H. *et al.* (1954), *Interviewing in Social Research*, Chicago, Univ. of Chicago.

Iganski, P. (1990), *Challenging Racism: Defining the Role of the White Researcher*, Paper presented at the British Sociological Association Conference, University of Surrey, April.

The Independent (1987), 'Labour suspends black activist', 30 April.

The Independent (1989), 'Racism in Liverpool', 19 Aug..

The Independent (1989), 'Child's move to black family upheld', Law Report, 1 Sept. p.14.

The Independent (1989), 'Adoption and the colour question', 28 Oct..

James, M. (1981), 'Finding the families', *Adoption and Fostering* 5,1:11-16.

Jayaweera, H. (1991), *Race, Ethnicity, Class and Gender: A Study of the orientations and identities of Afro-Caribbean women in Oxford*. D.Phil. Thesis, Univ. of Oxford.

Jenkins, R. (1963), 'The Fostering of Coloured Children', *Case Conference*, 10,5:129-134, October.

Jenkins, S. (1981), *The Ethnic Dilemma in Social Services*, New York, The Free Press; London, Collier Macmillan.

294

Jenkins, S. & Morrison, B. (1974), *The Identification of Ethnic Issues in Child Welfare*, Columbia University School of Social Work.

Jervis, M. (1986), `RAT's tales', *Social Services Insight*, 12 June, pp.12–15.

Jervis, M. (1990), `Balancing the damage', *Social Work Today*, 8 Feb. pp.16–17.

Jessel, D. (1985), `Heart of the Matter', BBC1 15 Sept..

Johnson, M. R. (1991), 'Race, social work and child care' in *Social Work and Social Welfare Yearbook 3*, Milton Keynes: Open University Press, Chapter 8 pp.95–107.

Jones *et al*. (1978), *Issues in Social Policy*, London, Routledge & Kegan Paul.

Jones, C. (1983), *State Social Work and the Working Class*, Basingstoke, Macmillan Press Ltd..

Jones, D. (1980), `Gossip: notes on women's oral culture', *Women's Studies International Quarterly*, 3,2/3:193–198.

Jones, E. (1981), *An examination of the structural bases of the social work response to male Afro–Caribbean youth in Britain*, M.A. Thesis, Univ. of Kent.

Jordan, R. (1985), `Children and Care: Was the real lesson of the Beckford case that social work under–vlues care?', *New Society*, 74,1198:460–61, 13 Dec..

Jordan, A. & Rodway, M.R. (1984), `Correlates of effective foster parenting', *Social Work Research and Abstracts*, 20,2:27–31, Summer.

Kadushin, L. (1972), `The Racial Factor in the Interview', *Social Work*, 17,3:82–87.

Kaniuk, J. (1991), 'Strategies in recruiting black adopters', *Adoption and Fostering* 15,1:38–39.

Katz, J. (1978), *White Awareness: Handbook for anti–racism training*, Norman, Univ. of Oklahoma Press.

Keddie, N. (ed.) (1973,1978), *Tinker, tailor... The myth of cultural deprivation*, Harmondsworth, Penguin.

Kelly, C., Sarbjit, C., Stober, J. (1990), `Black issues in child care – training for foster carers and adoptive parents', *Adoption and Fostering*, 13,3:29–33.

Kerridge, R. (1985), `Fostering Apartheid', *The Spectator*, 6 July pp.9–11.

Kinnon, U. (1984), `Ways of resolving areas of racial mis–understanding between worker and client', *Social Work Today*, 24 Jan. p.18.

Kirton, D. (1989), `Racism and Adoption', *Community Care*, 7 Sept. p.8.

Knights, D. & Wilmott, H. (1985), *Power and identity in theory and practice*, London, Routledge & Kegan Paul.

Kochman, T. (1981), *Black and White Styles of Conflict*, Chicago & c..

Kupfermann, J. (1983), `Love is more important than your parents' colour', *The Daily Mail*, 14 Feb..

Lacey, R. (1988), `Pressganging clients into accepting services', *Community Care*, 28 Jan. pp.30–31.

Ladner, J.A. (1977), *Mixed Families: Adopting Across Racial Boundaries*, Garden City, New York, Anchor Press/Doubleday.

Lal, B. (1983), `Perpectives on ethnicity: old wine in new bottles', *Ethnic and Racial Studies*, 6,2:154–173, 2 April.

Lalljee, M., Brown, L.B. & Ginsburg, G.P. (1984), `Attitudes, Disposition, Behaviour or Evaluation?', *British Journal of Social Psychology*, 23:233–244.

Lambert, L. & Streather, J. (1980), *Children in changing families: a study of adoption and illegitimacy*, Basingstoke, Macmillan Press.

Lambeth, London Borough of (1983), `Lambeth Black Children's Project', *Adoption and Fostering*, 7,1:6–7.

Lambeth, London Borough of, Social Services Directorate Working Group (1981), *Good Practice Guide for Working with Black Families and Black Children in Care*, L.B.L..

Laslett, B. & Rapoport, R. (1975), `Collaborative interviewing and interactive research', *Journal of Marriage and the Family*, 37:968–977.

Laurance, J. (1983a), `Should White Families Adopt Black Children?', *New Society*, 64,1076:499–501, 30 June.

Laurance, J. (1983b), 'No homes for black kids' claim untrue', *New Society*, 15 May.

Laurance, J. (1987), `White children placed in black foster homes', *The Observer*, 17 May.

Lawrence, E. (1982a), `Just plain common sense: the `roots' of racism' in Centre for Contemporary and Cultural Studies, *The Empire Strikes Back*, London, Hutchinson, pp.47–94.

Lawrence, E. (1982b), `In the abundance of water the fool is thirsty: sociology and black pathology' in Centre for Contemporary and Cultural Studies, *The Empire Strikes Back*, London, Hutchinson, pp.97–142.

Lee, G. (1987), `Implications of the Social Construction of Stigma. The Principle, Policy and Practice of Equal Opportunity' in Lee, L. & Loveridge, R. (eds.), *The Manufacture of Disadvantage*, Oxford, Oxford University Press.

Lepine, A. (1970), `Health and the immigrant child in care', *Child in Care*, 1:19 & 2:14.

Lewis, D. (1973), `Anthropology and Colonialism', *Current Anthropology*, 14,5:581–596. Liffman, M. (1978), *Power to the Poor*, London, George Allen & Unwin.

Lightfoot, L. (1989), `I love my white foster parents, but life would have been easier with a black family', *The Mail on Sunday*, 27 Aug. p.33.

296

Light Stanley, R. (1971), `The group method in foster home studies' in Tod, R. (ed.), *Social Work and Foster Care*, London, Longman Papers on Social Work.

Lindblom, C.E. (1965), *The Intelligence of Democracy*, New York, Free Press.

Lindsay–Smith, C. (1979), `Black Children Who Wait', *Adoption and Fostering*, 95,1:5–6.

Linton, R. (1949), `The Natural History of the Family' in Anshen, R.N. (ed.), *The Family: Its Function and Destiny*, New York, Harper & Row.

Lipsky, M. (1980), *Street–Level Bureaucracy – Dilemmas of the individual in public services*, New York, Russell Sage Fndn..

Liverpool, V. (1982), `The Dilemmas and contributions of Black Social Workers' in Cheetham, J. (ed.), *Social Work and Ethnicity*, London, George Allen & Unwin, Chap.18 pp.225–231.

Lowe, M. (1987), `Black children, black homes?', *Times Educational Supplement*, 3 July.

Lowe, M. (1989), `Partnership not rescue must shape the future' *Community Care*, 31 Aug.. pp.vii–viii.

Lowe, M. (1991), 'Little to lose, much to gain', *Community Care* 851:18–19 February.

Lukes, S. (1974), *Power: A Radical View*, Basingstoke, Macmillan.

Luthra, M. & Tyler, A. (1988), `Left in the dark on racism', *The Guardian*, 7 Sept..

Marable, M. (1984), *Race, Reform and Rebellion: The Second Reconstruction in Black America, 1945–1982*, Basingstoke, Macmillan.

Marable, M. (1985), *Black American Politics from the Washington Marches to Jesse Jackson*, London, Verso.

Maximé, J. (1986), `Some psychological models of black self–concept' in Ahmed, S., Cheetham, J. & Small, J. (eds.), *Social Work with Black Children and their Families*, London, Batsford in association with British Agencies for Adoption and Fostering.

Maximé, J. (1987), `Racial identity – and its value to black children', *Social Work Today*, 15 June p.6.

McKee, L. & O'Brien, M. (1983), `Interviewing Men: `Taking Gender Seriously" in Gamarnikow, E. *et al.* (eds.), *The Public and the Private*, London, British Sociological Association, Heinemann Educ. Books Ltd..

Melville, J. (1983),'The Inbetweeners', *The Guardian*, 15 Feb..

Merton, R. (1972), `Insiders and outsiders, a chapter in the sociology of knowledge', *American Journal of Sociology*, 78,1:9–47.

Miles, R. (1982), *Racism and Migrant Labour*, London, Routledge.

Mills, H. (1989), `Mother is given final chance to raise child', *The Independent*, 22 Sept..

Mitchell, J.C. (1983), `Case and situation analysis', *Sociological Review*, 31:187–211 May.

Modood, T. (1988a), `Who's defining who?', *New Society*, 4 Mar. pp.4–5.

Modood, T. (1988b), `'Black', racial equality and Asian identity', *New Community*, 14,3:397–403 Spring.

Modood, T. (1991), 'The Indian economic success: a challenge to some race relations assumptions', *Policy and Politics*, 19,3:177–190.

Morgan. D.H. (1979), `New Directions in Family Research and Theory', *Sociological Review, Monograph*, 28:3–18.

Morris, C. (1984). *The Permanency Principle in Child Care and Social Work*, Social Work Monograph 21, Norwich, Univ. of East Anglia & *Social Work Today*, July.

Morris, L. (1987), `The no–longer working class', *New Society*, 80,1266:16–18, 3 April.

Morris, P. (1985), `A common colour but not a common culture', *Community Care*, 26 Sept. p.9.

Morris, P. (1986), `Seeing red in black and white', *Community Care*, 24 July.

Mount, F. (1982), *The Subversive Family*, London, Cape.

Moynihan, D.P. (1965), *The Negro Family: The Case for National Action*, New York, Office of Planning and Research, U.S. Dept. of Labor.

Murdock, G.P. (1968), `The Universality of the Nuclear Family' in Bell, N.W. & Vogel, E.F. (eds.), *A Modern Introduction to the Family*, rev. ed. New York, Free Press.

Naipaul, S. (1982), `The Rise of the Rastaman', *The Observer*, 27 June, pp.25–6.

National Children's Bureau (1973), *Hightlight No. 3*, London, NCB.

National Children's Bureau (1978), *Patterns of Foster Care*, London, NCB, 20 Oct..

National Council for One Parent Families (1987), *Black one–parent families in Britain*, London: N.C.F.O.P., May.

Neale, T. (1987), `Why do we need black volunteers? Because they could be the link in anti–racism training', *Social Work Today*, 11 May, p.14.

Nissel, M. (1980), `The family and the welfare state', *New Society*, 7 Aug..

Nixon, J. (1983), `Social work in a multi–racial society', *Social Policy and Administration*, 17,2:142–156.

Ntshona, V.K. (1985), `Racial separation would reduce the quality of care says a black foster parent', *Foster Care*, Oct. p.9.

Oakley, A. (1974), *The Sociology of Housework*, London, Martin Robinson.

Oakley, A. (1976), *Housewife*, Harmondsworth, Penguin.

Oakley, A. (1979), *Becoming a Mother*, London, Martin Robinson.

Oakley, A. (1981), `Interviewing women: a contradiction in terms' in Roberts, H. (ed.), *Doing Feminist Research*, London, Routledge & Kegan Paul.

Oakley, A. (1987), `'The woman's place' What has been the effect of the feminist movement on today's families?', *New Society*, 6 Mar. pp.14–16.

The Observer (1989), `Black children `kept waiting for months' in the adoption queue', 10 Sept..

Ohri, A., Manning, B. & Curno, P. (1982), *Community Work and Racism*, London, Routledge & Kegan Paul.

Orlebar, J. (1983), `What it's like to be not so sweet sixteen...', *The Guardian*, 12 Jan..

Ouseley, H., Silverstone, D. & Prashar, U. (1982), *The System*, London, The Runneymede Trust and The South London Equal Rights Consultancy.

Owusu-Bempah, J. (1989), `Does colour matter?', *Community Care*, 26 Jan. pp.12–14.

Parents for Children (1976/7), *Parents for Children First Year's Report 1976/7*, London, P.F.C..

Park, P. & Rothbart, M. (1982), `Perception of Out-Group Homogeneity and Levels of Social Categorisation. Memory for the Subordinate Attributes of In-Group and Out-Group Members', *Journal of Personality and Social Psychology*, 42,1051–68.

Parker, R. (1988), `A child in trust: the issues for foster care' in Parker, R. et al. (eds.), *In Whose Trust? The Jasmine Beckford Inquiry and its lessons for foster care*, London, National Foster Care Association.

Parsons, Talcott (1949), `The Social Structure of the Family' in Anshen, R.N. (ed.), *The Family: Its Function and Destiny*, New York, Harper & Row.

Parton, N. (1986), `The Beckford Report: A Critical Appraisal', *British Journal of Social Work*, 16:511–530.

Paterson, S. (1966), `An Evening Child Welfare Clinic', *Medical Officer*, 11 Nov..

Patrick, J. (1973), *A Glasgow Gang Observed*, London, Eyre-Methuen.

Payne, S. (1983), Long Term Placement for the Black Child in Care, *Social Work Monograph 15*, Norwich, Univ. of East Anglia with *Social Work Today*.

Payne, M. (1979), *Power, Authority and Responsibility in Social Services*, Basingstoke, Macmillan.

Pearson, M. (1983), *Ethnic Minority Health Studies: Friend or Foe?*, Paper presented at Inst. of British Geographers Medical Geography Study Group Conference, Leeds.

Pearson, R. (1989), `Room at the top?', *Social Services Insight*, 28 Feb. pp.12–14.

Phoenix, A. (1990), 'Theories of gender and black families', in T. Lovell (ed.), *British Feminist Thought: A Reader*, London: Basil Blackwell, pp.119–133.

Pinder, R. (1980), *Individual Credibility and Institutional Constraint: The practical problems of dealing with difference*, Leeds, Univ. of Leeds, Centre for Social Work and Applied Social Studies.

Pinder, R. (1981a), `Ending Deprivation', *Community Care*, 27 Aug. p12.

Pinder, R. (1981b), *Dealing in Diversity: The Emergence of Culturally Competent Practice*, Leeds, Univ. of Leeds, Centre for Social Work and Applied Social Studies.

Pinder, R. (1983), `Respecting differences: the ethnic challenge to social work practice', *Social Work Today*, 14,22:10–15 8 Feb..

Pithouse, A. (1988), *Social Work: The Organisation of an Invisible Trade*, Avebury, reviewed in *Community Care*, 21 Apr.1988 p.43.

Platt, J. (1984), *The meanings of case–study method in the inter–war period*, Paper presented at the American Sociological Association Annual Meetings, San Antonio, Texas.

Platt, J. (1986), *What can cases do?*, Economic and Social Sciences Research Council Research Seminar, Coventry, Univ. of Warwick, 14 Mar..

Platt, J. (1988), `What can case studies do?', *Studies in Qualitative Methodology*, 1:1–23.

Pringle, K. (1991), 'A new clear family?', *Social Work Today*, p.20, 4 July.

Pryce, K. (1974), `Problems in minority fostering', *New Community*, 3:379–385.

Radio Four (1984), *Any Questions*, 17 Feb..

Radio Four (1984), *Any Answers*, 23 Feb..

Radio Four (1986), *Not All Black and White*, 23 Oct..

Radio Four (1989), *Phone Kate Aidie*, 5 Sept..

Radio Four (1991), *File on Four: Transracial Adoption, presented by Paul Barker*, 23 April.

Rapoport, R., Rapoport, R.N., Strelitz, Z. with Kew, S. (1977), *Fathers, Mothers and Others*, London, Routledge & Kegan Paul.

Raynor, L. (1970), *Adoption of Non–White Children: The Experience of a British Adoption Project*, London, George Allen & Unwin.

Rees, S. (1978), *Social Work Face to Face: clients' and social workers' perceptions of the content and outcomes of their meetings*, London, Edward Arnold.

Reese, S.D., Danielson, W.A., Shoemaker, P.J., Chang, T.K. & HSU, H.L. (1986), 'Ethnicity–of–Interviewer Effects Among Mexican–Americans and Anglos', *Public Opinion Quarterly* 50:563–572.

Reid, P. (1983a), `Black families dilemma', *The Caribbean Times*, 25 Feb. p.8

Reid, P. (1983b), `Black families under stress', *The Caribbean Times*, 25 Mar. p.8.

Reid, P. (1985), `Black families for black children: a self–evident case', *Foster Care*, July p.4.

300

Rhandhawa, M. (1985), `Prevention and rehabilitation with black families', *Adoption and Fostering*, 9:3,42–3.

Rhodes, P. (1984), `Race and Adoption', *Searchlight*, Sept. p.19.

Rhodes, P. (1989), `Fostering as employment: the mobility component' in Grieco, M., Pickup, L. & Whipp, R. (eds.), *Gender, Transport and Employment*, Oxford Studies in Transport, Aldershot, Gower.

Rich, A. (1980), *Lies, Secrets and Silences*, London, Virago.

Roberts, Y. (1988), `Anti–anti–racism. Uncomfortable lesson for the left', *New Statesman*, 6 May pp.14–15.

Robertson Elliot, F. (1986), *The Family: Change or Continuity?*, Basingstoke, Macmillan Education Ltd..

Robinson, J. (1991), 'Beyond the frontiers of fostring – the employment of a 'professional carer", *Adoption and Fostering* 15,1:47–9.

Rooney, B. (1981), `Active Mistakes – A Grass Roots Report', in Cheetham, J. et al. (eds.), *Social Work and Ethnicity*, London, National Institute for Social Work Training/Heinemann.

Rooney, B. (1982), `Black Social Workers in White Departments' in Cheetham, J. (ed.), *Social Work and Ethnicity*, London, George Allen & Unwin.

Roskill, C. (1979), `A different social work', *Social Work Today*, 10,2:17–20, 20 Feb..

Roth, J.A. (1962), `Comments on "secret observation"', *Social Problems*, 9,3:283–4.

Rowe, J. (1983), *Fostering in the eighties*, London: British Agencies for Adoption and Fostering.

Rowe, J. (1990), `Research, Race and Child Care Placements', *Adoption and Fostering*, 14,2:6–8.

Rowe, J. & Lambert, L. (1973), *Children Who Wait. A study of children needing substitute families*, London, British Agencies for Adoption and Fostering.

Roys, P. (1988), `Social Services' in Bhat, Carr–Hill & Ohri (eds.), *Britain's Black Population: a new perspective*, Second edition, The Radical Statistics Race Group, Aldershot, Gower.

Runneymede Trust (1976,1980), *Britain's Black Population*, London, Runneymede Trust.

Runyan, W.McKinley (1982), 'In defense of the case study method', *American Journal of Orthopsychiatry* 52:440–446.

Rutter, M. et al. (1974), `Children of West Indian immigrants – I Rates of behavioural deviance and of psychiatric disorder', *Journal of Child Psychology and Psychiatry*, 15,4:241–254.

Ryan, W. (1976), *Blaming the Victim*, New York, Vintage Books.

Samuels, A. (1979), 'Transracial adoption: adoption of the black child', *Family Law* 9,8:237–239.

Satow, A. & Homans, H (1981), `The Nuclear Family Rules OK?', *Journal of Community Nursing*, Dec. p.6-8.

Schroeder, H. & Lightfoot, D. (1983), `Finding Black Families', *Adoption and Fostering*, 7,1:18-21.

Schroeder, h., Lightfoot, D. & Rees, S. (1985), `Black applicants to Ealing recruitment campaign', *Adoption and Fostering*, 9,2:50-53.

Schuller, T. (1986), *A case study of case study problems*, Economic and Social Sciences Research Council Research Seminar, Coventry, Univ. of Warwick, 14 Mar..

Schuman H. & Converse, J. (1971), `The effects of black and white interviewers on black responses in 1968', *Public Opinion Quarterly*, 35:48-68.

Schutz, A. (1954), `Concept and thoery formation in the social sciences', *Journal of Philosphy*, 51,9:257-273.

Shaw, M. & Hipgrave, T. (1982), `Specialist fostering: a review of the current scene', *Adoption and Fostering*, 6,4:21-25.

Shaw, M. & Lebens, K. (1977), 'Foster parents talking', *Adoption and Fostering* 79:11-16.

Silverman, D. (1973), `Interview talk: bringing off a research instrument', *Sociology*, 7,1:32-48.

Silverman, D. (1985), *Qualitative Methodology and Sociology*, Aldershot, Gower.

Silverman, A. & Feigelman, W. (1977), 'Some factors affecting the adoption of minority children', *Social Casework* 554-561, November.

Simon, H.A. (1965), *Administrative Behaviour*, New York, Free Press.

Simon, R. (1978), `Black attitudes towards transracial adoption', *Phylon,* 39:135-142.

Simon, R. & Alstein, H. (1977), *Transracial Adoption*, New York, Wiley Interscience.

Simon, R. & Alstein, H. (1981), *Transracial Adoption: A Follow-up*, D.C.Heath, Lexington Books.

Simpkin, M. (1979), *Trapped Within Welfare*, London, Macmillan.

Sivanandan, A. (1982), *A Different Hunger – writings on black resistance*, London, Pluto Press.

Sivanandan, A. (1983), `Challenging Racism: Strategies for the `80s', *Race and Class*, 25,2:1-11.

Sivanandan, A. (1985), `RAT and the degredation of black struggle', *Race and Class*, 26,4:1-33 Spring.

Small, J. (1980), 'Black Families Unit (Interview)', *Adoption and Fostering* 4,3:41-42.

Small, J. (1981), `Wanted: Black Families for Black Children, *Community Care*, 8 Oct. pp.21-22.

Small, J. (1982), `New Black Families', *Fostering and Adoption*, 6,3:35.

Small, J.W. (1984a), `The Crisis in Adoption', *International Journal of Social Psychiatry*, 30,1/2:129-142 Spring.

Small, J. (1984b), `You have been brainwashed, John Small tells foster parents', *Foster Care*, Oct. p.11.

Small, J. (1986a), `Transracial placements: conflicts and contradictions' in Ahmed, S., Cheetham, J. & Small, J. (eds.), *Social Work with Black Children and Their Families*, London, Batsford, pp.81-99.

Small, J. (1986b), `Fostering Understanding', *Social Services Insight*, 1,33:16-23.

Smith, B. (1988), 'Something you do for love: the question of money and foster care', *Adoption and Fostering* 12,4:34-37.

Smith, D. (1976), *The Facts of Racial Disadvantage*, PEP Report. Harmondsworth, Penguin.

Smith, D. (1981), *Unemployment and Racial Minorities*, London, Policy Studies Institute.

Smith, D.E. (1979), `Sociology for women', in Sherman, J. & Peck, E. (eds.), *The Prison of Sex: Essays in the sociology of knowledge*, Univ. of Wisconsin Press.

Smith, R. (1984), `TV programme investigates London's `black babies battle", *Foster Care*, Oct. p.10.

Smith, R. (1985a), `Foster parents protest against Hackney's race policy', *Foster Care*, Jan. p.1.

Smith, R. (1985b), `Transracial Fostering: the debate continues', *Foster Care*, Oct. p.4.

Smith, G. & Cantley, C. (1985), *Assessing Health Care: A Study in Organisational Evaluation*, Milton Keynes, Open University Press.

Smith, B. & Noble-Spruell, C. (1986), `An Overview of Feminist Research Perspectives' in Marchant, H. & Wearing, B. (eds.), *Gender Reclaimed: Women in Social Work*, Marrickville, NSW, Australia, Hale & Iremonger Pty Ltd..

Social Work Today, (1987a), `RAT package scrapped', 16 Mar.p.2.

Social Work Today, (1987b), `Racism: the Birmingham strategy', Letter to *Social Work Today*, 11 May p.16.

Solesbury, W. (1976), `The Environmental Agenda', *Public Administration*, pp.379-397 Winter.

Solomon, B. (1976), *Black Empowerment: social work in oppressed communities*, New York, Columbia Univ. Press.

Solomos, J. (1988), `Institutional Racism: Policies of Marginalisation in Education and Training' in Cohen, P. & Bains, H.S. (eds.), *Multi-Racist Britain*, Basingstoke, Macmillan.

Solomos, J. (1989), *Race and Racism in Contemporary Britain*, Basingstoke: Macmillan Education Ltd..

Spender, D. (1980), *Man made Language*, London, Routledge & Kegan Paul.

Stacey, M. (1988), *Power, Responsibility and Accountability: a Critical Analysis of the British Medical Profession*, Paper presented to the Plenary Session, Medical Sociology Conference, York, Sept..

Staffony, P. (1986), `Fashionable doctrine', *Foster Care*, Sept. p.4.

Stewart, N. (1983), `Being black is not a burden but being British is a burden because we are also black in a white society', Black Youth Annual Penmanship Awards, *The Caribbean Times*, 4 Mar. p.12.

Stoecker, R. (1991), ' Evaluating and rethinking the case study', *Sociological Review* pp. 88–112.

Stone, M. (1981), *The Education of the Black Child in Britain. The Myth of Multiracial Education*, Glasgow, Fontana Paperbacks.

Stubbs, P. (1985), `The employment of black social workers: from `ethnic sensitivity' to anti-racism?', *Critical Social Policy*, 12:6–27.

Stubbs, P. (1987), `Professionalism and the Adoption of Black Children', *British Journal of Social Work*, 17,5:473–492.

Taylor, J.(1984), `The London Programme', London Weekend Television, 29 June.

Thethi, J., Skerritt, D., Morris, B. & Davis, S. (1988), `Preparation and teamwork: a multicultural approach to foster parent training' in Parker, R. (ed.), *In Whose Trust? The Jasmine Beckford Inquiry and its lessons for foster care*, London, National Foster Care, Association.

Theze, S. (1983), `Personal View', *Foster Care*, 33:12–13.

Thoburn, J., Murdock, A. & O'Brien, A. (1987), *Permanence in child care*, Oxford, Blackwell.

Thomas, L. (1984), `Black and proud of it', *Social Work Today*, 10 Dec. pp.16–17.

Thorne, B. (1982), `Feminist Rethinking of the Family', in Thorne, B. & Yalom, M. (eds.), *Rethinking the Family: Some Feminist Questions*, Longmans.

Thorogood, N. (1988), *Health and the Management of Daily Life Amongst Women of Afro–Caribbean Origin Living in Hackney*, Unpublished Ph.D. thesis, University of London.

Timmins, N. (1989), `Massive dose of persuasion', *The Independent*, 20 July.

Tizard, B. (1977), *Adoption: a second chance*, London, Open Books, Chap. 13 pp.180–186.

Tizard, B. & Phoenix, A. (1989), `Black identity and transracial adoption', *New Community*, 15,3:427–437 April.

Touraine, A. (1965), *Sociologie de l'action*, Paris, Seuil.

Toynbee, P. (1986) `Mix and Match' *The Guardian,* 23 June.

Troyna, B. & Williams, J. (1986), *Racism, Education and the State,* London, Croom Helm.

Turner, R. (1974), *Ethnomethodology,* Harmondsworth, Penguin.

Upshal, D. (1988), `Which way forward for black politics?', *New Society,* 4 Mar.pp.6–8.

Utting, W.B. (1990), *Issues of Race and Culture in the Family Placement of Children,* C1(90)2, London: Social Services Inspectorate, Department of Health.

Vernon, J. (1985), `Planning for children in care', *Adoption and Fostering,* 5:12–17.

Wainwright, H. (1978), `Women and the Division of Labour', in Abrams, P. (ed.), *Work, Urbanism and Inequality,* London, Weidenfeld & Nicholson.

Wallman, S. (ed.) (1979), *Ethnicity at Work,* Basingstoke, Macmillan Press.

Wandsworth, London Borough of (1986a), *Same race placement – a rationale,* Study Day on Recruiting Black Families in Adoption and Fostering, Work, 14 Feb., London, L.B. of Wandsworth Social Service Department, Adoption and Fostering Unit.

Wandsworth, London Borough of (1986d), *Golden rules for recruiting black families,* London, L.B. of Wandsworth Social Service Department, Adoption and Fostering Unit.

Wandsworth, London Borough of (1986e), *The Process of Assessment,* London, L.B. of Wandsworth Social Service Department, Adoption and Fostering Unit.

Wandsworth, London Borough of (1986f), *The Strengths of the Black Famly,* London, L.B. of Wandsworth Social Service Department, Adoption and Fostering Unit.

Wandsworth, London Borough of (1986g), *White workers' common misgivings or misconceptions about black families,* London, L.B. of Wandsworth Social Service Department, Adoption and Fostering Unit.

Weber, M. (1978), *Economy and Society,* Univ. of California Press.

Wilby, P. (1988), `Rags–bags against racism', *The Independent,* 19 May.

Yin, R.K. (1984), *Case Study Research: Design and Methods,* London, Sage Publications, Applied Social Research Methods Series, Vol. 5.

Young, K. & Connelly, N. (1981), *Policy and Practice in the Multi–Racial City,* London, Policies Studies Institute.

Zaretsky, E. (1982), 'The Place of the Family in the Origins of the Welfare State' in Thorne, B. & Yalom, M. (eds.), *Rethinking the Family,* New York, Longman.

Zimmerman, D. & Pollner, M. (1971), `On the everyday world as a phenomenon' in Douglas, J. (ed.), *Understanding Everyday Life,* London, Routledge.

Name index

Mitchell, J.C. 28
Modood, T. 9, 62, 261n
Morgan. D.H. 153n
Morgan, G. 92, 134
Morris, C. 24n, 111
Morris, L. 54, 74, 172
Morris, P. 54, 74
Morrison, B. 23, 23n
Mount, F. 153, 153f, 154, 155
Moynihan, D.P. 188n
Murdock, G.P. 154

Naipaul, S. 260n
National Children's Bureau 157, 188n
Neale, T. 60
Nissel, M. 154
Nixon, J. 27, 52, 61, 79, 79n, 82, 83, 88, 158, 160, 265
Noble–Spruell, C. 37
Ntshona, V.K. 55

Oakley, A. 40, 46, 153n, 154
O'Brien, M. 40
The Observer 272
Ohri, A. 7
Orlebar, J. 60
Ouseley, H. 26
Owusu–Bempah, J. 60n, 231n, 242, 272

Parents for Children 151n, 192n, 195, 195n
Park, P. 231n
Parker, R. 151, 159, 231n
Parsons, Talcott 153, 154
Parton, N. 24n, 132n
Paterson, S. 188n
Patrick, J. 31
Payne, S. 170, 170n, 183
Payne, M. 82, 83
Pearson, M. 173, 174

Pearson, R. 82, 82n, 84, 84n, 103, 105n, 271
Phoenix, A. 12, 13, 49, 62, 63, 266
Pinder, R. 83, 104, 133, 134, 136, 137, 150, 252
Pithouse, A. 105, 129
Platt, J. 28
Pollner, M. 46
Pringle, K. 265
Pryce, K. 2

Radio Four 19, 50n, 62n, 75, 124n, 271, 271n, 272, 274
Rapoport, R. 42, 153
Raynor, L. 11, 22
Rees, S. 24, 64, 196
Reese, S.D. 43
Reid, P. 14, 60, 124n
Rhandhawa, M. 64
Rhodes, P. 55, 58, 156, 156n, 157, 164, 172, 173, 195, 202
Rich, A. 199
Richards, M.P.M. 154
Roberts, Y. 60n, 107, 272
Robertson Elliot, F. 153, 154
Robinson, J. 265
Rollings, J. 6, 8
Rooney, B. 52, 64, 129, 160, 161, 211n,222n,231n,242 260 265,266
Roskill, C. 160
Roth, J.A. 33, 34
Rothbart, M. 231n
Rowe, J. 2n, 3, 21, 22, 61, 112
Roys, P. 8, 50, 59, 61, 133, 137, 138, 231n, 152, 157, 159, 161, 166
Runneymede Trust 157
Runyan, W.McKinley 27
Rutter, M. et al. 43, 188n
Ryan, W. 263

Sainsbury, E. 259

310

Samuels, A. 21
Satow, A. 153
Schroeder, H. 64, 89, 116, 131n, 138n, 185,
Schuller, T. 28
Schuman H. 44
Schutz, A. 31
Shapiro, D. 17, 50n
Shaw, M. 3, 172, 172n, 264
Silverman, D. 30, 31, 40, 40n, 46, 47, 48, 48n, 193
Silverman, A. 18
Simon, H.A. 129
Simon, R. 20, 81
Simpkin, M. 269
Sivanandan, A. 55, 60n, 108, 135, 174, 259n, 260, 260n, 262n, 272
Small, J. 2, 14, 15, 24, 39, 44, 55, 56, 57, 59, 60, 63, 64, 116, 122, 123, 124n, 166, 170
Smith, B. 3
Smith, Ba. 37, 40
Smith, D. 157
Smith, D.E. 40
Smith, R. 1, 50n, 55, 57n, 99, 124n
Smith, G. 83
Social Work Today 60n
Solesbury, W. 50
Solomon, B. 150
Solomos, J. 49, 50n, 66, 82, 99, 124n, 152, 157, 183, 187n, 258
Spender, D. 39, 199
Stacey, M. 153n, 185
Staffony, P. 124n
Stoecker, R. 27, 28, 37, 47
Stone, M. 32, 270
Strauss, A.L.
Streather, J. 153
Stubbs, P. 7, 24, 24n, 52, 57, 109, 123, 132, 133, 134, 138, 161, 176, 189, 211n, 222n, 227, 237, 241n, 242, 246, 251, 261, 265, 268

Taylor, J. 55, 58, 59, 74, 76
Thethi, J. 202, 203
Theze, S. 202
Thoburn, J. 24n, 112
Thomas, L. 227n, 258, 265
Thorne, B. 153n,
Thorogood, N. 48
Timmins, N. 185
Tizard, B. 11, 12, 13, 49, 62, 63
Toynbee, P. 105n, 271, 272
Troyna, B. 107
Turner, R. 31
Tyler, A. 81

Upshal, D. 49
Utting, W.B. 274

Vernon, J. 24n, 112

Wainwright, H. 154
Wallman, S. 150, 236, 240, 241
Wandsworth, London Borough Of 143, 188, 189, 251
Weber, M. 89
Welch, M. 64, 89, 128, 138n, 139, 152, 158, 159n, 170, 170n
Wilby, P. 107
Williams, J. 107, 138
Wilmott, H. 227, 228

Yin, R.K. 27
Young, L. 81
Young, K. 50, 79, 80, 81, 82, 83, 88, 93, 134, 136
Yuval-Davies, N. 262

Zaretsky, E. 154
Zimmerman, D. 46

311

Subject index

evidence, management of 61–3

recruitment of black foster parents 3, 24, 111, 124–9, 157–8, 255, 256, 257
  campaign for 140–50
  change in procedure of 135
  changes in procedure of 135
  criteria for 113–14, 116, 128, 162–4
  difficulties in 25, 63–4, 77, 120, 248
rejection 197–8, 258
researcher
  and action research 34–5
  and participant observation 30–2
  social role of 32–4
resistance to racial matching, institutional 59, 78, 81
role play, in assessment 206–7

same race placement *see* matching
self–assessment of applicants 204
single parent families 161–2, 163, 257
social control 7
  by social workers 159–60, 183, 267–8
social services department 8, 85
  black people's experiences of 135
  mistrust of 26, 138, 170, 180, 255
  responses of to multi–racial communities 10, 79
social work
  access to files of 224–6
  professionalism of 83, 267–8
social workers 6, 7, 8, 54, 105
  as agents of social control 159–60, 183, 267–8
  assessment of black families by 115, 125–7, 161–2, 174, 188–94, 199–200

attitudes of to racial matching 1, 3, 11, 51, 53, 64
care and control functions of 25
on change of policy 73–4, 75–6, 78, 87, 88–9, 102–3
and cultural pluralism 8, 158–9, 170–5
and ethnic minority group clients 79, 251
with foster parents as co-workers 221, 223, 224–30, 231–9, 252
intercultural skills of 115, 177–82, 185, 186
professionalism of *see* professionalism of social workers
as social engineers 2, 14
see also black social workers
Soul Kids Campaign 113
specialization 269
'stranger value' 45
structuralism 9
suitability of families 63–4, 120, 127–9, 161–3, 170, 254
surveys 39–40

training and assessment courses 201–19
transracial placements 23–4, 69, 71, 91–2, 267
  criticism of 11–18, 258
  ending of 121–2
  in USA 20–1

United States of America, placement policy in 19, 20–1, 53

validation of data 46–8
value conflicts 159–60

White Action Group 130–1

317